TEAM

TROUBLESHOOTER

HOW TO
Find and Fix Team Problems

ROBERT W. BARNER

DAVIES-BLACK PUBLISHING
PALO ALTO, CALIFORNIA

Published by Davies-Black Publishing, an imprint of Consulting Psychologists Press, Inc., 3803 East Bayshore Road, Palo Alto, CA 94303; 800-624-1765

Special discounts on bulk quantities of Davies-Black books are available to corporations, professional associations, and other organizations. For details, contact the Director of Book Sales at Davies-Black Publishing, 3803 East Bayshore Road, Palo Alto, CA 94303; 650-691-9123; fax 650-623-9271.

05 04 03 02 01   10 9 8 7 6 5 4 3 2 1
Printed in the United States of America

Library of Congress Cataloging-in-Publication Data
Barner, Robert.
    Team troubleshooter : how to find and fix team problems / Robert W. Barner—1st ed.
    Includes index.
        ISBN 0-89106-151-7
        1. Teams in the workplace. I. Title
    HD66.B366 2001
    658.4'02—dc21   00-064534

FIRST EDITION
First printing 2001

Contents

Team-Building Tools

Introduction

This book is about how you can take the first steps toward strengthening your team by quickly spotting and resolving problems that can significantly compromise team performance. I've written it for senior managers and those team leaders, members, or facilitators who are serious about learning how to address problems that are interfering with the effectiveness of their work teams.

There are already many books available on team building, and you're probably asking yourself what makes this one so special. The answer lies in what this book is not. It's not an abstract treatise on organizational development, it doesn't attempt to create a sophisticated psychological model of team dynamics, and it wasn't written by someone who has been locked in an ivory tower for the past ten years.

This work is based on my own twenty years of personal experience as both an outside consultant and a professional team facilitator who has survived and thrived as a team leader and manager within a number of different settings. I've directed teams concerned with cross-functional process or quality improvement and customer-supplier relationships; held the lead position in corporate reengineering teams (a truly thankless job if there ever was one); and managed intact teams working in areas ranging from executive development to human resources. That's not to say I don't still make mistakes from time to time, but the techniques and strategies I've laid out in this book have been invaluable in helping me to periodically stop, regroup, and quickly address team problems that might otherwise have derailed my teams.

Some Underlying Assumptions

Team Troubleshooter introduces a team improvement strategy based on five underlying assumptions. Understanding these assumptions will help you realize the full benefits of this book.

Individuals Can Affect Team Performance

I don't care whether you're a new team member, an experienced team leader, an outside facilitator, or someone who directs a traditional work group or who has been drafted to lead a cross-functional team—you can still play an important role in helping your team identify and address performance difficulties. This book will show you how. If you're concerned that you lack the influence or authority to make a productive impact on your team, don't be. Throughout *Team Troubleshooter,* you will be introduced to a variety of tools and techniques for identifying and addressing team-related problems. By taking the initiative and sharing these ideas with others in your team, you can help your work group perform at its best.

Teams Are Their Own Best Problem Solvers

If you think diagnosing team problems is a job best left to the "experts," think again. Team members and leaders are the ones who are most qualified to understand the types of job demands and challenges they are encountering, which may stand in the way of improved performance. What team members and leaders frequently lack is a tool kit that will help them align their separate views of team performance. This book provides such a tool kit.

As to the effectiveness of third-party facilitators, having been a team coach and facilitator for the past twenty years, I can tell you that facilitators vary widely in their training, interpersonal competence, and the level of trust they are able to inspire. You might get lucky and end up with a good one, but you could easily find yourself with someone who is only marginally adept. In addition, facilitators often have no more than a minimal amount of lead time to familiarize themselves with your team's operation. For this reason, if you do decide to employ a third-party facilitator, this tool kit may be helpful in giving you a head start on the team-building process.

Finally, keep in mind that people really only "own" business problems when they're directly involved in the solutions. This book will encourage team members to become accountable owners with a stake in improving their performance. By arming your team members with a diversified tool kit, you can encourage them to see themselves as active partners in the improvement process.

Up-Front Assessment Is Key to Team Problem Solving

I've seen a lot of well-intentioned team building quickly dissipate into small, ineffectual puffs of smoke and have witnessed other teams barely surviving the poorly constructed interventions suggested by their facilitators. Many of these negative outcomes could have been avoided if a little more effort had gone into accurately diagnosing the teams' performance problems. You can encourage full ownership in the team-building process by providing a mechanism by which team members (particularly those who have difficulty thinking on the fly) may carefully evaluate performance issues before they embark on the team-building session. This book will introduce you to a variety of tools that can help you build such team ownership.

Improve Performance with Direct Exploration of Performance Problems

Over the past twenty years, team-building consultants have discovered there's a lot of money to be made in creating and selling team exercises, which range from synthetic role-play scripts to the many "team survival" simulations that have recently flooded the market. Most of these tools are fun. Some may even be of value, especially when, as part of a public assessment center or training seminar, they enable individuals from different teams or organizations to assemble within the context of a team-building training program to learn more about their roles as individual team members.

On the other hand, synthetic simulations fall short of the mark when we're dealing with intact work teams whose members have developed a common history over time. We need to leverage the incredible value of this group experience and encourage team members to articulate the problems that prevent them from performing at their best. I believe facilitators who rely heavily on artificial exercises may do so because they're afraid to connect, head-on, with a team's actual experiences. The good news is that team interventions don't have to be intimidating. If you have a solid game plan (which I'll introduce in the first chapter), you can take the first steps toward putting a team back on track.

Problem-Solving Processes Apply to All Kinds of Teams

Up to this point, you may have been tempted to disregard my advice because you're not part of a traditional manager-directed team. Instead, you may be part of a self-directed work team, a cross-functional process-improvement team, or a customer-supplier team. It doesn't matter. You still have a job to do, which means you must deal with constraints and personalities (and sometimes prima donnas) and build successful relationships. Regardless of the industry or work function, all teams operate within standard parameters of team dynamics and performance constraints. Understand these factors and you will be on your way to improving your team's performance.

How to Get Started

Team Troubleshooter is a user-friendly owner's manual designed to help you step back and take a look at ways in which you can help resolve team performance problems. I've created a format that makes this book very different from other books on team building. Let's take a brief look at four alternative applications.

Personal Learning

If you're a team leader or member who is trying to figure out why your team is not performing as expected, I'd advise you to read the first section (Chapters 1–5), complete the Team Health Check in the Chapter 1 Tool Kit, score your results, and then consult the appropriate chapters listed in the Health Check. The Symptoms section in each chapter may provide a starting point for discussion with other members about your team's performance. In the process, you might find out more about your possible contributions to these problems and what you can do to resolve them.

Leadership Coaching

Presenting copies of this book to team leaders may encourage them to examine the factors behind the performance of their work groups. If you're a team facilitator, a leadership coach, or a person who manages team leaders, you can use *Team Troubleshooter* as a coaching and training tool. Ask selected team leaders to read Part One of this book, complete the Team Health Check, and read the appropriate chapters. Meet with them a few days later and exchange views on what they've read. This simple act is often the first step in encouraging team leaders to think through some of the key issues involved in their work groups' performance.

Team Problem Solving

If you're the leader or a member of a team that's currently experiencing serious performance problems, consider distributing copies of this text to your entire team. Ask each team member to read this Introduction and Part One and then complete the Team Health Check in Chapter 1. By averaging all the checklist scores, you will be able to quickly pinpoint your team's key performance issues. The scores can also help you determine which of the remaining chapters would be most helpful for your team. Before discussing team performance issues, members should read the selected chapters and be asked to share their views on which problem-solving interventions would be of most value to the team.

Team Development

You don't have to be sick to get better. Even if your team isn't experiencing serious problems, you can use *Team Troubleshooter* as a development tool. The Team Health Check can alert new teams to potential roadblocks in their attempts to tackle tough objectives, while experienced teams can use the checklist to identify challenges that may accompany changing business conditions. Examples of such situations might include a marketing team that is about to implement the company's first Internet venture, a manufacturing team confronted with corporate restructuring, or a human resources team that's been called upon to support an expansion into the international arena. The point is that, just as you don't have to wait until you have a heart attack to start an exercise program, you don't have to wait until your team is in dire distress to look for ways to strengthen its performance. The time to prepare is now.

How This Book Is Organized

This book is divided into two sections.

In **Part One,** Chapters 1–5 present the five-step model for guiding a team through the team improvement process.

Step 1: Identify the problem: Reach agreement with the other team members on the underlying causes of your team's problems.

Step 2: Explore your options: Consider different alternatives to improving your team's performance.

Step 3: Plan for action: Develop a plan for carrying out improvement activities.

Step 4: Gain commitment for your plan: Develop consensus with other team members on the need for change.

Step 5: Implement the plan and follow up: Put your problem-solving plan into effect, and then periodically step back and see if these actions are helping your team to address its most critical problems.

The premise behind this section is that being aware of problems is of limited usefulness without a solid methodology for attacking them. Even if you are a team member, not a leader or facilitator, you can still use this section to recommend a viable strategy for managing team improvement.

In **Part Two,** Chapters 6–17 introduce twelve of the most common pitfalls for teams. In this section, you will learn about the symptoms that identify these team performance problems and the underlying factors that most frequently contribute to them. Finally, you will learn what steps to take to help your team overcome these challenges. Each chapter contains a team-building tool kit with questionnaires, exercises, guidelines, and performance tools for exploring improvement strategies with your team.

To Wrap It Up

Transforming a team is no small endeavor. I know—I've been in this line of work for years. But I'm confident that the techniques and suggestions in this book will help you begin the process of strengthening your team's performance. The field of team building is expanding rapidly, and it grows stronger every time professionals engage in dialogue on key matters. If you want to exchange ideas on this subject or wish to comment on *Team Troubleshooter*, please feel free to drop me a line at ibscribe@aol.com. Good luck!

PART ONE

How to Identify and Solve Team Problems

Identify the Problem

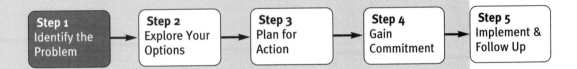

| Step 1
Identify the
Problem | → | Step 2
Explore Your
Options | → | Step 3
Plan for
Action | → | Step 4
Gain
Commitment | → | Step 5
Implement &
Follow Up |

At any one time, even the best teams are confronted with a confusing variety of problems and obstacles, ranging from communication meltdowns to the inability to recover from setbacks. Some of these problems may be confined to the team itself. Others, such as lack of customer focus, may represent organizational fault lines that have opened up between a team and surrounding work groups, external customers, or suppliers. The first step in helping a team improve its performance is to separate, out of this morass of problems, those that indicate underlying weaknesses, which, if left unchecked, can seriously impede a work group's success.

Many times, one of your primary challenges is being able to temporarily step away from your team in order to obtain an objective and unobstructed view of your principal problems. Consider an IT help-desk team whose relationships with its internal customers has been deteriorating. Perhaps the team has allowed its service standards to slip to the point that it can manage to respond only quickly, not effectively, to requests for assistance.

On the other hand, the problem may be the result of other factors, such as an inability to keep up with a rapidly growing employee population or communication problems between the team and its customer base. It's one thing to be able to spot the overt symptoms of team performance problems and quite another to determine the underlying causes of those problems. Alternatively, entanglement in a long-standing feud with another member of your team might color your judgment, leading you to believe that the entire team is rife with conflict, when, in fact, the opposite may be true.

The most effective way to address these challenges is to arm yourself with clear and unambiguous information about your team. Begin gathering this information by asking these three questions of yourself and the other team members:

1. What are the symptoms and underlying causes of team performance problems?

2. What is the trend line, or the projected trajectory of these problems?

3. How serious are the performance problems? If left uncorrected, what would be their impact on the team and the organization?

Let's run through these questions and see what they can tell us about the nature of team problems.

Symptoms and Underlying Causes

Chances are you've noticed symptoms or clues suggesting that your team has a performance problem. These symptoms might range from the subtle (such as a gradual but steady decline in work productivity) to the more obvious (such as team discussions that quickly turn into angry disputes). A reasonable first step in diagnosing a team performance problem is to inventory these symptoms and establish the underlying causes of your team's difficulties.

For example, if you observe that the members of your team put too much effort into low-priority objectives, or disagree on how to prioritize certain projects, this might suggest that they are having difficulty establishing a future direction (see Chapter 10). In the same way, a team that has been exhibiting symptoms such as demoralization, risk aversion, and finger-pointing might find that the underlying cause is its difficulty in dealing with a recent setback (see Chapter 14).

The Team Health Check, found in the Tool Kit at the end of this chapter, lists thirty-six symptoms of team performance problems and explains how they are related to twelve key causes of team dysfunction. By comparing individual scores on the Team Health Check, team members can quickly zero in on those performance problems that are relevant to their particular work group.

In Part Two of this book, each of the twelve underlying causes of team derailment is covered separately in its own chapter. The twelve causes are organized around four factors that interact to shape a team's performance. These factors are

1. Problems related to internal relationships (Chapters 6–8)

2. Problems related to team focus (Chapters 9–11)

3. Problems related to change and adaptability (Chapters 12–14)

4. Problems related to external relationships (Chapters 15–17)

Problems Related to Internal Relationships

This section discusses three team problems that relate to the ways in which team members interact with one another and with the team leader. I'm sure you've seen work groups that spend more time on internal conflict than on value-added work. When teams are dysfunctional—when members find themselves in continuous conflict or suffer repeated communication break-downs—their performance suffers. Quite frequently, a dysfunctional team may limp along for an extended period of time with its problems largely unnoticed by others, only to have these problems flare up when the team hits its first serious performance challenge. Business challenges and stresses, such as new reporting relationships or collapsed deadline schedules, test the robustness of team interrelationships. The three problems addressed in this book are

1. Intra-team (within team) conflicts (Chapter 6)

2. The communication challenges faced by virtual or distributed teams (Chapter 7)

3. Problematic member-leader relationships (Chapter 8)

Problems Related to Team Focus

This section discusses three problems associated with a team's ability to establish a clear direction and effectively organize itself to meet its business objectives. In my more than twenty years of working with teams, I've found that such performance issues are all too often neglected by team-building facilitators, who tend to attribute all performance problems to the failure of internal relationships. Although it's true that interpersonal dynamics are a key part of team functioning, it's also true that even a team with a great deal of strength in this area will find itself in serious jeopardy if it can't meet its performance objectives. This section introduces the following three team-building issues:

1. Lack of foresight (Chapter 9)

2. Lack of team direction (Chapter 10)

3. Lack of an effective team scorecard process (Chapter 11)

Foresight enables a team to anticipate new opportunities as well as problems. Teams with a good sense of direction have clear pictures of where they're headed and what their priorities should be. The scorecard process establishes clear criteria for evaluating effectiveness.

It's easy to understand how these three elements are related. For a team to achieve winning performance, it has to know its destination and what it can expect to encounter along its path. Add the ability to accurately measure performance, and you have a team that can punch through walls.

Problems Related to Change and Adaptability

This section addresses three problems that directly affect a team's ability to meet and overcome difficult work challenges. The three problems reviewed in this section are

1. Inability to adapt to change (Chapter 12)

2. Lack of innovation (Chapter 13)

3. Inability to deal with setbacks (Chapter 14)

In order to adapt to change, a team must be able to adjust quickly to new work demands and cope with the stresses associated with disruptive change. Through innovation, a team is able to move beyond the usual safe solutions to develop creative approaches to work challenges. Finally, a team that can deal effectively with setbacks will be able to get back on its feet after encountering a serious obstacle or reversal. Given the increasing velocity of change in our workplace, all three qualities are hallmark survival skills for any successful team.

Problems Related to External Relationships

This section discusses three problems that occur frequently when a team has difficulty relating to other work groups and key managers. Of the four factors that influence team performance, the management of external relationships tends to be overlooked most frequently by team leaders. This is unfortunate, given how important these relationships are to any team's success. Team members may interact effectively and be well aligned on goals, priorities, and performance standards, but these accomplishments are unimportant if other work groups and senior managers do not believe the team is making a genuine contribution to the organization. To explore this component of team effectiveness, teams must be able to view their performance from the outside. In other words, they must see their performance as their customers and stakeholders see it. This section covers the following three team performance issues:

1. Lack of senior-management sponsorship (Chapter 15)

2. Inter-group (team to team) conflicts (Chapter 16)

3. Poor customer relationships (Chapter 17)

   Without senior-management sponsorship, a team will have difficulty capturing support for its projects or objectives from its organization's senior-executive level. Inter-group conflicts are those that occur between a team and other work groups within an organization. The issue of customer relationships involves a team's responsiveness to the needs of its internal and external customers.

   Together, these three issues establish the organizational context for team performance; it can be wonderfully supportive and positive, or apathetic and negative. The difference can be extremely important during times of extensive organizational change, such as downsizing, restructuring, or critical turnover at the senior-staff level. In all of these situations, teams very quickly discover whether they have developed solid, constructive relationships with others in their organizations. These relationships bear directly on a team's level of support when implementing key business initiatives, its ability to capture staff and resources, and, in extreme cases, its survival.

What Is the Trend Line?

Just as with any other business problem, your team will find it helpful to plot the trend line for its performance problem. The first thing you'll learn is whether a problem is transitional, sustained, or episodic. A transitional problem is a temporary glitch created by short-term organizational or business constraints. Thus, team members who are entangled in conflict with one another (see Chapter 6) may realize that their problem is transitional, if, for example, it first became apparent about a month earlier, when they began putting in a lot of voluntary overtime to complete a major project. In this situation, the problem may clear up once the project is over. On the other hand, the team may be dealing with a significant, sustained trend, indicative of the fact that certain team members never really hit it off from day one. Finally, the problem could be episodic. By this I mean that it comes and goes on a predictable basis in response to certain work conditions such as budget reviews or tight deadlines.

Another trend-line factor is the projected trajectory of the problem. Team members must ask themselves if the performance problem appears to be increasing or decreasing over time. Or has it reached a plateau, where it remains basically at the same level? Although it takes only a few minutes for team members to chart the trend line for a performance problem, this activity can provide a lot of useful data. Given that your team may have multiple problems to tackle, and limited time and energy to devote to them, the trend line can help prioritize efforts among competing problems.

There are two ways to track trend lines. The first method is to track objective performance data over time. Examples would be

1. Percentage of late shipments

2. Number of customer complaints

3. Number of missed project milestones

4. Costs variances

5. Number of quasi–sick days reported by team members

In many cases, however, particularly when you're dealing with such factors as team relationships, this type of data simply isn't available. As an alternative, you might ask different team members to plot individual trend lines for a given problem and then compare their respective views.

Knowing the underlying causes and the trend line of a team performance problem improves your ability to determine its effect on both the team and the organization. You'll also be in a better position to predict the trajectory of the problem in the absence of any outside intervention.

Determine the Seriousness of the Problem

Assessing impact is important for several reasons. First, team members must be open to change and willing to experiment with new ways of working together before they can improve team performance. And since change can be a tedious and occasionally stressful experience, they need to know that the outcome will be worth the effort. Second, an awareness of the bottom-line impact of team performance problems can also help build a case for change when you're seeking support from team leaders or senior managers for recommended improvements. Finally, as with the construction of a trend line, listing areas of impact can help team members determine where they should invest their time and attention.

A good way to begin is to encourage the members of your team to discuss and list on a flipchart some of the negative effects of a specific performance problem. Chart 1 provides a basic checklist your team can use to identify the bottom-line impact of selected performance problems. Team members can also determine which of the thirty-six symptoms of team problems (see the Team Health Check in your Tool Kit) they have observed within their own group, as well as the relative severity of each symptom.

CHART 1

Bottom-Line Impact of Team Performance Problems

- Costs of redoing work

- Problems and costs associated with team turnover

- Errors and lower quality of work performance

- Work team distracted by preoccupation with team problems

- Reduced customer service and satisfaction

- Reduced service performance to other departments

- Slipped schedules and missed deadlines

- Loss of team credibility with the outside organization

- Increased overhead through ineffective management of team resources

Tool Kit

Tool #1

TEAM HEALTH CHECK

The Team Health Check lists thirty-six symptoms that are frequently associated with team dysfunction. Each set of symptoms pertains to a particular performance challenge. Ask your team members to rate the degree to which they've observed each of these symptoms within the team, then have one team member average the ratings for your entire team; Compare this information against your own scores. Use this feedback to identify those performance issues on which you and your team members are closely aligned as well as those on which you are divided.

Occasionally, you may find it useful to ask someone from outside your team to complete this checklist by noting the symptoms they've observed in your team. By taking this extra step, you can identify problems that are apparent to individuals outside your team. The combined information will be helpful in guiding your team as you select performance issues for team review.

EXERCISE 1 • TEAM HEALTH CHECK

Directions: Use this rating scale to indicate the extent to which the following symptoms have been observed in your team.

5: This is a recurring symptom, which we observe on an almost daily basis.
4: This is a frequent symptom, which we observe on a weekly basis.
3: This is a somewhat frequent symptom, which we occasionally observe within our team.
2: This is an infrequent symptom, which we seldom observe within our team.
1: This is an uncommon symptom, which we rarely, if ever, observe within our team.

	Rating
Chapter 6. The Team Divided: The Problem of Intra-Team Conflict	
1. We have difficulty resolving conflicts before they get out of control.	
2. The members of our team don't cooperate well on team efforts.	
3. Many of our team members are dividing up into warring cliques.	
Chapter 7. Transition Chaos: Managing the Virtual Team	
4. The members of our team have difficulty coordinating their separate work activities.	
5. We have to rely on others outside our team to keep us informed of our own activities.	
6. We have difficulty determining how far we can go in taking individual action.	
Chapter 8. The King Dethroned: Solving Member-Leader Conflict	
7. The members of our team circumvent our team leader to address issues or problems.	
8. Communications with our team leader are limited and tense, or hostile.	
9. Our team leader practices micromanagement.	

Tool Kit

Chapter 9. Painted into a Corner: Developing Better Foresight

10. We're frequently surprised by problems.

11. We tend to be reactive when it comes to problem solving.

12. We have difficulty interpreting the potential impact of large-scale changes.

Chapter 10. The Broken Compass: Finding a Sense of Direction

13. We have difficulty responding to questions that lie outside our individual work areas.

14. We must often stop and wait for direction from our team leader before we can proceed.

15. We experience a lot of conflicting priorities regarding projects and team responsibilities.

Chapter 11. The Missing Scorecard: Strengthening Accountability

16. We are forced to guesstimate our work quality and productivity.

17. We sometimes wonder if our good work is recognized by our organization.

18. We find it difficult to trace the underlying causes of team performance problems.

Chapter 12. The Brittle Team: Learning to Adapt to Change

19. Our team is anxious about the vague and unknown future.

20. We tend to respond to change in a slow and poorly coordinated manner.

21. The members of our team actively resist change.

Chapter 13. Stuck in a Rut: How to Foster Innovation

22. When tackling new problems, we rely too much on tried-and-true solutions.

23. Our team doesn't keep up with cutting-edge technology and work methods.

24. We fail to identify and exploit new opportunities.

Chapter 14. Reversals: Dealing with Setbacks

25. Many members of our team are unwilling to commit to tough performance goals.

26. We engage in retrospective thinking about setbacks that have already occurred.

27. We engage in a lot of finger-pointing to account for team problems.

Chapter 15. Cast Adrift: Securing Senior-Management Sponsorship

28. We tend to be the last to know about impending business or organizational changes.

29. Our team has difficulty getting approval for needed resources.

30. Our senior managers occasionally outsource our work.

Tool Kit

Chapter 16. The Raised Drawbridge: Resolving Inter-Group Conflict

31. We tend to take an adversarial approach to other work groups in our organization.	
32. Our communications with other work groups are restricted or hostile.	
33. Our conflicts with other groups often come to the attention of senior management.	

Chapter 17. Our Own Worst Enemy: Strengthening Customer Relationships

34. We've received repeated complaints about our service from internal and external customers.	
35. We are failing to track important changes in our customer base.	
36. Our customers repeatedly challenge our decisions.	

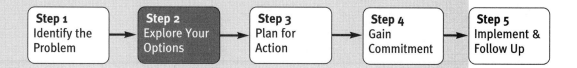

Explore Your Options

Step 1	Step 2	Step 3	Step 4	Step 5
Identify the Problem	Explore Your Options	Plan for Action	Gain Commitment	Implement & Follow Up

Once you have identified the problems that are adversely affecting your team's performance, your next step is to explore solutions for solving these problems. An effective problem-solving process is characterized by three features:

1. Balanced participation

2. Thorough analysis of alternative solutions

3. Innovative thinking

Work teams typically are made up of very different individuals. Some team members may have dominant personalities and will tend to force their opinions on others or discourage others from voicing their views. A few team members may feel they have little to contribute to the problem-solving process and will be reluctant to share their ideas with the rest of the team. Still others may need some encouragement before they feel comfortable about participating fully in the problem-solving process. These differences will most likely be apparent if your team is composed of people who represent different degrees of technical competence and reporting level. One of your goals should be to create a team experience that encourages full and balanced participation from all members. To do this, you will have to efficiently direct the flow of discussion while you elicit the full range of your team's opinions and ideas. Tool #4 in your Tool Kit at the end of this chapter, the Guide Sheet for Balancing Participation, will help you determine when and how to draw out or rein in team members during discussions.

The second goal for your team-building process should be to encourage your team to look below the surface, uncover those key factors that are responsible for the problem, and examine the organizational context. Ineffective teams engage in what I call "surface skimming"; that is, they never penetrate to the depths of a performance problem. Effective teams do their homework—they engage in a thorough analysis of any obstacle that could block their success. For example, if your team is tackling a lack of customer focus, members should think carefully about the implications for their organization, such as lost business, increased complaints, or (if the problem involves internal customers) disruptions in the flow of interdepartmental communications. Before devising solutions to this problem, they should also stop to consider the value of maintaining strong customer relationships within their organization. In short, an effective team-building process produces a detailed analysis of a team's performance problems and yields solutions that will meet the long-term needs, not only of your team, but also of the organization you serve.

In an effort to resolve performance problems quickly, some team members may offer the first solutions that come to mind or those they believe will be easiest to implement. Others may seek to appease the team leader and senior managers by suggesting what they feel are acceptable remedies. To avoid these responses, encourage your team to "think outside the box" and come up with the widest, most creative array of solutions. Quite frequently, team members must be willing to completely rethink their approaches to problems.

Three-Phase Problem-Solving Method

Effective team problem solving involves a three-phase process of exploration, analysis, and selection, as illustrated in Figure 1. Let's consider each of these three phases in detail.

Phase 1: Exploration

As Figure 1 suggests, the first phase of problem solving, exploration, entails encouraging your team to come up with the broadest range of creative solutions to the current problem. In this phase (represented by the expanding funnel in Figure 1), ask your team to suggest unique and innovative methods for resolving the problem. Ideally, team members will build upon and

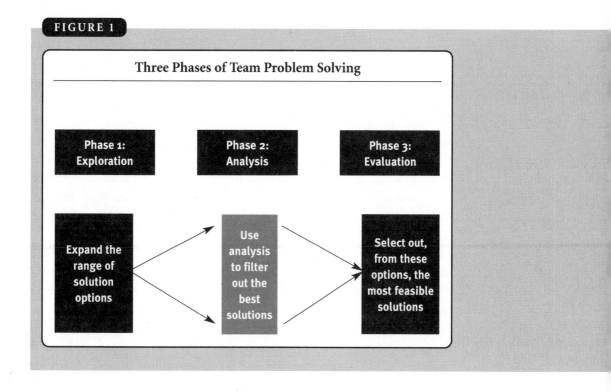

FIGURE 1

Three Phases of Team Problem Solving

Phase 1: Exploration — Phase 2: Analysis — Phase 3: Evaluation

Expand the range of solution options → Use analysis to filter out the best solutions → Select out, from these options, the most feasible solutions

develop one another's ideas, so that their final solution set represents a true synthesis of the thoughts of the entire team.

Strive for Balanced Participation

One of the most common pitfalls you're likely to encounter during this phase of problem solving is the concept of the team leader as hero. By this I mean that team members may rely too heavily on you, as the leader of the work group, to come up with all the creative solutions to their problem. This tendency will be particularly evident if you have a much stronger skill base or experience level than the rest of your team, or if some of the team members are intimidated by your leadership style. There are several steps you can take to discourage this behavior.

First, establish ground rules to foster group participation. Consider including guidelines such as "All ideas are equally valuable" or "Don't censor yourself—even if you aren't sure an idea may be useful, let us hear it anyway." Ground rules like these can stimulate the free sharing of ideas.

To maintain overall participation, you must avoid censoring others. It's easy for the team leader to inadvertently censor or dismiss the ideas of others.

Comments such as "Are you sure that idea would work?" tend to discourage participation. Another tactic that could be interpreted by team members as censorship is the rewording of their suggestions. For example, a team member may suggest creating a team vision statement to help remedy the team's lack of direction. If the team leader replies by saying, "I think what you mean is that we need clearer business objectives, isn't that correct?" and, without waiting for a response, records his or her version of this solution on the flipchart, the person who offered the suggestion may feel the team leader is trying to control the flow of ideas or force-feed solutions to the team. To avoid this situation, refrain from commenting on any idea until all suggestions have been made. In addition, if you're having trouble interpreting the ideas expressed by team members, ask them for clarification instead of rewording their suggestions.

Delay making suggestions of your own. In an effort to speed up the problem-solving process, some team leaders begin the discussion by offering a variety of solutions to the problem at hand. When this occurs, team members may be reluctant to express their own solutions, and the discussion is likely to switch from exploration to a comparative review of suggestions proposed by the team leader. Instead, consider soliciting solutions from the rest of your group before offering your own. If you're asked for your ideas early on in the discussion, reply that you'd like a few minutes to think through your responses before offering your ideas for review.

Generate a Wide Range of Innovative Solutions

A second factor that could prevent your team from fully exploring a problem is the tendency to present routine solutions, or those that are easily executed. Such solutions are safe—they are less likely to provoke conflict among team members—and are probably the same types of recommendations proposed earlier for similar problems. The difficulty is, of course, that such solutions don't necessarily represent your team's best thinking. Ideally, you want a wide range of solutions, including those that might be considered a little off-the-wall. During the second and third phases of the team-building process, you will have the opportunity to distill the initial list of suggestions by using selection criteria identified by your team. For now, however, encourage your team to generate as many innovative solutions as possible.

Inform your team that you are looking for multiple solutions. Teams often assume that their job is to immediately identify the single best solution to a problem. A simple way to get past this barrier is to tell your team that there are probably a number of ways to effectively resolve the problem and that you'd like to set a goal of identifying at least five different approaches to solving the problem.

Lighten the atmosphere by asking for the wackiest idea. No one wants to look stupid. Accordingly, when people are part of a group problem-solving meeting, they tend to be conservative in their thinking and express only safe solutions. To get your team past this obstacle, invite each person to come up with at least one wild or wacky solution to the problem. Encourage team members to take risks by offering your own zany solution. Don't worry about whether the solution is practical. The point is to shake up everyone's thinking so that the team will find it easier to build on creative ideas.

An alternative to seeking additional resources is to reframe, or redefine, the nature of your setback. The Tool Kit found at the end of this chapter outlines a simple method for reframing problems.

Follow the Three-Phase Model

Another roadblock you may encounter at this first stage of problem solving is the tendency of some team members to jump the gun and evaluate solutions as soon as they are proposed. If this reaction is not checked, your team will move too quickly into the evaluation process. In addition, some individuals may hesitate to voice their ideas, for fear that they will be under attack as soon as they express their opinions. There are several ways to counter this tendency.

Be sure to introduce the three-phase problem-solving model. If team members are aware that they are following a structured problem-solving process and evaluation of ideas is more effective during the final phase of this process, they will understand why they should wait for the appropriate stage of the discussion.

Set ground rules that discourage people from making premature judgments. One helpful ground rule is "Allow all ideas to be heard and posted before evaluating any one idea."

Depersonalize Ideas

If team members evaluate one another's ideas as soon as they're expressed, these evaluations may be taken as personal criticisms. Comments such as "Frankly, I just don't think Darrell's idea will work" tend to divide the team. You might add a ground rule that says "Evaluate ideas, not people. Refrain from making comments that could be viewed as personal criticisms." In addition, posting all ideas on the board for review makes them the common property of the team. When they finally are evaluated, team members are less likely to take criticisms personally.

Redirect members' comments. If one individual gets carried away and begins to evaluate a fellow team member's idea, you might interject a tactful comment such as "It sounds like you're moving into evaluation at this point. In line with our ground rule on postponing evaluation until the end, could we hold off on those comments until later in our discussion?"

Encourage Input from Outside Your Team

The team-building process should be confined to your own team, but there are times when input from others may be very useful. Consider asking for outside input when the problem area identified by your team directly affects the performance of other work groups. If, for example, the problem involves conflicts with other work groups (see Chapter 16) or lack of responsiveness to your customers (see Chapter 17), these groups should be solicited for ideas. In the same way, when the problem revolves around issues such as lack of senior-management sponsorship, consider asking your senior managers for input on your team's performance problem (see Chapter 15).

Quite often, teams are reluctant to expose their problems to those outside their work groups because they think it would be embarrassing or demeaning. Maneuver around this difficulty by framing the problem as an opportunity your team has identified for enhancing its performance. In other words, convert a performance problem into an improvement opportunity.

Before undertaking your team-building session, ask your customers and senior managers these four questions to gain a clearer perspective on their views of the team's performance problem.

1. How does this problem situation affect the performance of your work group (if you're addressing an internal customer) or our business unit (if you're addressing a senior manager)?

2. From your point of view, are there any factors (for example, poor communication, lack of resources, or information gaps) that may be contributing to this problem?

3. Do you have any suggestions on how we might improve in this performance area?

4. From your point of view, on what basis (for example, reduced downtime, declining error rate, or stronger service delivery) should our team evaluate the success of the improvements we put into place?

Additional suggestions for directing creative problem solving can be found in Chapter 13.

Phase 2: Analysis

The second phase of problem solving, analysis, is represented by the central image of the filter in Figure 1 (page 15). In this phase, members of your team determine the criteria (such as costs, time, and ease of implementation) they will use to evaluate potential solutions to their problem. The aim of this process is to decide on an objective and fair means of analyzing the relative merits of the different proposals that have been made by your team. You can initiate this phase of problem solving immediately after concluding Phase 1, or you can set aside time for this discussion in a separate meeting.

Consider Alternative Approaches

Many teams fail to fully utilize this phase of problem solving. They don't stop to consider alternative approaches to analyzing and reviewing a problem. One way to get your team to pause and reflect on its choice of problem-solving approaches is to begin with a simple introduction such as: "Before we try to evaluate and select a solution or solutions to our problem, it would probably be helpful to take some time to carefully review all of the potential solutions we have listed to make sure we really understand what's involved in implementing each one. We could collectively generate a split-sheet list of the pros and cons for each solution, or we could compile a list of questions we'd like to use to review each solution. There are probably several other possible approaches. What do you think we should do?"

Teams sometimes rush into selecting a solution without carefully evaluating all options. This is likely to be the case if they feel pressured to reach quick decisions, or if a team leader or dominant team member strongly favors a certain solution. One way to prevent this type of lopsided problem solving is to detach solutions from their owners. Advise your team to list all solutions on a flipchart so you can review them together before engaging in the analysis phase. Number each solution as it's listed, and instead of referring to "John's solution" or "Lisa's suggestion," refer to each one by its number. In addition, encourage team members to identify at least one benefit and one drawback for each solution before selecting or discarding it. Finally, refrain from offering your own analysis until the end of the discussion, after the other members of your team have had their say. Similarly, if one member of your team tends to sway the others, call on this person last, only after all other members have expressed their opinions.

Dealing with "Analysis Paralysis"

When faced with complex problems, some teams are so inundated with data that they begin to suffer a kind of "analysis paralysis" that can dramatically bog down the process. To remedy this situation, set a fixed time limit, such as ninety minutes, for team review. Tell team members that you would like to perform a check-in at the end of this time to see if they've made enough progress in their analysis to move on to evaluation. You may also ask your team the following questions:

- "Given everything we know about this problem, what are the one or two primary factors that should influence our decision?"

- "What facts do we absolutely have to know before we can move forward in decision making?"

- "Which aspects of this problem can we tackle with incomplete information?"

The Decision Matrix, which can be found in the Tool Kit at the end of this chapter, is another effective technique for this phase as well as the following evaluation phase of team problem solving. A decision matrix enables team members to reach agreement as to the relative importance of different selection criteria and to systematically match criteria to a variety of options.

Phase 3: Evaluation

The final phase of problem solving, evaluation, is represented by the contracting funnel in Figure 1. In this phase, your team evaluates the solutions they have generated. The best approach to completing this process is to encourage your team to discuss the relative merits of each solution before attempting to rate them.

Consider All Criteria

Most solutions must meet a number of criteria in order to be deemed effective. Sometimes, however, team members become so focused on one criterion—for instance, cost—that they fail to give equal weight to other criteria, such as time required for completion, ease of implementation, support of senior management, or the solution's impact on other work groups within the company. A team with a solid method for analyzing problems is capable of reviewing a number of solutions in terms of multiple criteria. This team has a better chance of selecting the most effective solution.

One method that can help your team is to list on a flipchart all of the criteria that are critical to making a decision and then review these criteria before evaluating any of the solutions. Thus, if your team was involved in

looking for ways to improve performance with one of your external customers, you might consider some of the following selection criteria:

- Any additional cost to the customer

- Temporary service disruptions resulting from a given solution

- Time required to implement the solution

- Your team's competence and experience with implementing the solution

- The degree to which a solution addresses the underlying reasons for the
  service problem

Having a list of criteria available as team members discuss different
alternatives will encourage them to ask the full range of questions regarding
the suitability of a given solution.

Achieving a Balanced Problem-Solving Approach

Sometimes, team members become attached to their own solutions. The multivoting technique is one way to encourage a more balanced approach, as it
requires team members to cast votes across different solutions. An overview
of this technique can be found in the Tool Kit at the end of Chapter 6.

As mentioned in Phase 2, the Decision Matrix in the Tool Kit at the end
of this chapter is helpful in both the analysis and the evaluation phases of
team problem solving. Two other useful tools, the Plus/Delta and Gallery
Techniques, are given in the Tool Kit section of Chapter 13. Once your team
has had an opportunity to discuss its solutions through the use of the Plus/
Delta or Gallery Technique, go back to the Decision Matrix for a final evaluation of the proposed solutions. By using the Decision Matrix, your team can
achieve a balanced review of all alternative solutions.

Tool Kit

REFRAMING TECHNIQUE

This technique involves redefining a problem by placing it within a completely different context. Quite often, our conception of a problem dictates the types of solutions we formulate to resolve it.

For example, a group of tomato farmers was concerned about the degree of damage sustained by their products during shipping. At first, the group defined its problem in the following terms: "How can we ship our tomatoes in a way that will reduce damage in transport?" This way of seeing the problem led the farmers to consider solutions such as alternate routes or different methods of packaging their tomatoes. It was only after the farmers had reframed the problem as "How can we make our tomatoes less susceptible to damage in transport?" that they came up with the innovative solution of selectively breeding the tomatoes to produce a thick-skinned variety that is less susceptible to damage.

The following steps can help you apply the reframing method to your own team problem:

1. Begin by writing a brief statement of your problem on a flipchart.

2. Next, challenge team members to come up with two or three ways of rethinking and rewording this statement. For example, if your team's problem is "How can we meet together more often to manage team projects?" suggest that another way of looking at the problem is "How can we each provide input on our project plans despite our different schedules and locations?"

3. Discuss the different lines of inquiry presented by the reframed statement. Perhaps instead of focusing on how to plan meetings that everyone can attend, the revised problem statement might lead to a completely different approach, such as purchasing GroupWare software so that your team can provide input on project plans from any location at any time.

4. Another version of this technique involves dividing your team up into two or three subteams. Assign each team to brainstorm potential solutions to a different definition of the problem. Later, bring the subteams together to compare their lists of solutions.

Tool Kit

DECISION MATRIX

This tool is one of the most commonly used methods for analyzing improvement ideas.

The first step in creating your matrix is to ask your team to help determine the criteria for evaluating their improvement ideas. The following are examples of frequently used criteria:

- **Effectiveness:** Will the idea actually have a positive impact on the team's work performance?

- **Cost:** How much will it cost to implement the idea?

- **Customer impact:** Will the idea help, not have a negative effect on, internal or external customers?

- **Feasibility:** Is the idea easy to implement?

- **Time:** Can the idea be implemented quickly?

- **Control:** Can the idea be put into action directly by the team?

After team members identify the criteria they wish to use, they should determine the relative importance of each one. A simple way of doing this is to assign values to each criterion based on a scale of 1–10 (with 10 meaning a criterion is absolutely essential and 1 that it's relatively unimportant). Provide team members with markers and ask them to score the criteria on the flipchart individually. Afterward, average each person's point values to arrive at the team's overall score.

Next, load the identified criteria into the vertical column of the Decision Matrix and insert the options you are reviewing in the top row. Chart 2 shows how a decision matrix might look for a team that's defined its performance problem as "lack of innovation." Note that the team has identified four solutions to this problem, which are arrayed on the top row of the matrix, and has scored the relative importance of the selected criteria in the ratings column. In the next section, I'll explain how to rate improvement ideas through the use of the matrix.

Now ask each team member to rate each solution on a 1–5 scale, in terms of its ability to meet your identified criteria. In the example shown in Chart 3, the five members of our hypothetical team have rated their four solutions against the criterion of "effectiveness." Below their individual scores, you can see the averaged scores for these solutions (4.8, 3.2, 2.2, 3.0).

Remember that the team also rated the relative importance of each criterion, and "effectiveness" received the highest possible rating, or 10. By multiplying this rating by each average score, we arrive at the team's final

Tool Kit

CHART 2

Decision Matrix for Lack of Innovation						
Criteria	**Criteria Ratings**	**Solution Options**				
		Perform external benchmark studies	*Attend technical conference as a team*	*Submit team improvement project to annual corporate continual improvement contest*	*Form learning consortium with other local companies*	
Effectiveness	10					
Cost	6					
Customer impact	8					
Feasibility	9					
Time	4					
Control	8					
Total						

scores for the four solutions (shown in bold) in relation to the criterion of "effectiveness": 48, 32, 22, and 30. Continue this process for each criterion to determine total scores for every cell in the matrix, and then add the scores within each column for the final total score for each solution.

The solution with the highest total score would normally be the team's selected solution. If, however, several solutions receive similar scores, this would suggest that the team should engage in further discussion before ending its evaluation. In addition, your team may decide to pursue more than one solution simultaneously, which makes problem evaluation a lot simpler.

Tool Kit

CHART 3

Partially Completed Decision Matrix for Lack of Innovation					
Criteria	**Criteria Ratings**	**Solution Options**			
		Perform external benchmark studies	*Attend technical conference as a team*	*Submit team improvement project to annual corporate continual improvement contest*	*Form learning consortium with other local companies*
Effectiveness	10	5, 5, 4, 5, 5 = 4.8/**48**	4, 2, 2, 5, 3 = 3.2/**32**	4, 1, 1, 2, 3 = 2.2/**22**	3, 3, 3, 3, 3 = 3/**30**
Cost	6				
Customer impact	8				
Feasibility	9				
Time	4				
Control	8				
Total					

Tool Kit

Tool #4

GUIDE SHEET FOR BALANCING PARTICIPATION

One of your responsibilities as team leader is to make sure all team members have the chance to express their opinions during team meetings. You may find that some team members voice their ideas more readily and forcefully than the others, who may feel intimidated and reluctant to share their ideas. Use the guide sheet in Chart 4 to determine when and how to balance participation during team discussions. Solutions derived from a variety of suggestions often prove to be the most successful in addressing team problems.

Tool Kit

CHART 4

Guide Sheet for Balancing Team Participation

When to Draw Out Team Members

- When they appear intimidated or awed by the suggestions and comments of other, more experienced or knowledgeable members
- When they seem to be censoring themselves or stop speaking before completing a thought
- When they are struggling to formulate ideas quickly
- When they can't break past the commentary of dominant team members
- When they've been silent for an extended period of time

How to Draw Out Team Members

- Call on them by name and ask them to share their ideas.
- Break your team into subgroups assigned to different issues. The smaller groups provide a less intimidating setting for sharing ideas.
- Attend to nonverbal clues. "Jeff, I can tell from the way you're shaking your head that you have some concerns with that idea. Tell me about it."
- Engage your team in silent idea generation; ask members to write their ideas anonymously on index cards for team review.
- If certain team members have difficulty "thinking on their feet," e-mail your team members before the meeting and ask for their input. During the meeting, credit them for their ideas.
- Draw out quiet team members before the meeting or during breaks. Provide an opening for those members during the meeting by saying, for example, "During the break, Sara brought up a great idea for tackling our cost problem. Sara, would

When to Rein In Team Members

you mind sharing that idea with the team?"
- When they dominate the discussion
- When they appear to be intimidating others or pressuring them into favoring their points of view
- When they aren't thinking their thoughts through before speaking

How to Rein In Team Members

- When they fail to pick up on subtle clues that others wish to be heard
- Conduct a structured discussion in which each person is asked to present only one idea for review. Continue until all ideas have been exhausted.
- At the beginning of the meeting, post ground rules encouraging free discussion. When a member violates those rules, pause and remind the entire team of the posted guidelines.
- Use a prompting phrase to alert team members that they need to step back and listen, such as "Bill, could you hold that thought for a second? Mary's been trying to get something on the table."
- Use nonverbal signals, such as a time-out sign, to suggest that dominant team members give others a chance to speak.
- If these suggestions aren't working, take a 5-minute break. Call the dominant team member off to the side and offer helpful coaching, such as "I can see you're putting a number of good ideas on the table. My concern is that a lot of other people are passively listening and not bringing up their own ideas. When we go back into the meeting, I'd like you to help me

3

Plan for Action

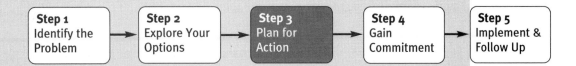

| **Step 1** Identify the Problem | **Step 2** Explore Your Options | **Step 3** Plan for Action | **Step 4** Gain Commitment | **Step 5** Implement & Follow Up |

After working with your team to identify a tentative solution, you must construct a viable action plan together. In my experience, poor action planning is one of the main reasons team improvement efforts fail to produce desired results. Typically, at the end of a team problem-solving session, the meeting room is plastered with flipcharts containing generalized descriptions of solutions to various team performance problems. Toward the end of the day, with little energy or time remaining, the participants plant their victory flag and congratulate themselves on a job well done. If someone expresses concern about the lack of clear action planning, the rest of the team quickly assures this person that the action process is self-explanatory and the subject requires no additional discussion.

A few weeks later, when the hoped-for improvements have not materialized, team members find themselves in a quandary. Did they fail to progress because they incorrectly defined their performance problem, did not identify valid solutions, or implemented their action plan poorly? Or is the situation the result of factors beyond their control?

A concise, unambiguous action plan that is fully supported by your team will help you avoid such a disappointing outcome. A good action plan should cover the following topics:

- What's doable? How much improvement activity can we manage over the next few weeks?

- What's fair? How can we ensure that everyone on our team is an equal partner in our improvement project?

- Where do we need help? For what areas of the project will we need the help of other work groups or managers? How will we go about securing it?

- What could go wrong? In attempting to accomplish our plan, what obstacles are we likely to face and how can we circumvent them?

Constructing a Team Improvement Plan

There are five steps for constructing a team improvement plan:

1. Identify required actions

2. Agree on desired outcomes

3. Ask for or assign accountability for specific areas

4. Construct an action-planning chart

5. Perform troubleshooting

The initial products of team improvement discussions are not improvement actions, but good intentions. That is, team members talk in general about the types of improvements they want to make while neglecting to pinpoint the precise actions that will help them achieve those results. Your challenge is to convert these good intentions into a list of required actions. Chart 5 shows the progression from identifying problems and formulating intentions to taking specific actions for four team improvement problems.

Team members must reach agreement on the results they expect from each action. If you feel that a meeting with an internal customer group will reduce service complaints by 20 percent over the next six weeks, then say so.

CHART 5

Intentions Versus Actions		
Team Improvement Area	**Intention**	**Action**
We seem to lack foresight. Team members are too often taken by surprise with performance problems, such as errors or project delays	We'll pay more attention to our planning.	During the next six weeks, each project leader will create a troubleshooting checklist detailing potential obstacles and indicating appropriate preventive actions.
Communication breakdowns are occurring within the team.	We'll schedule more meetings.	During the next three weeks, Theresa will schedule two videoconferences. The meetings will take place after 1 P.M. Eastern time to allow for the time difference on the West Coast.
We're experiencing a lack of direction. There is some confusion within our team regarding our objectives and direction over the next few years.	During the next few weeks, we'll discuss each team member's view of our team vision.	By the 15th of this month, our team will meet to draft a vision statement. Prior to this meeting, each team member will compile a list of projected changes in our customer base, service output, and organizational charter for the next two years.
We're receiving an increasing number of complaints from our internal customers.	We'll ask our internal customers for feedback on our performance.	On the 23rd of this month, Jim and Lisa will conduct a focus group with representatives from our engineering department to identify service areas in which our performance is less than satisfactory.

If you expect a change in your team communication process to completely eliminate reworking and errors caused by poor communication, be explicit about the desired outcome. Clear definitions of anticipated success criteria will help your team reach alignment on its improvement process. Without this alignment, it's quite possible that your team could successfully implement its improvement plan yet disagree completely on whether the plan was a success.

It's especially important to articulate those "soft outcomes" that are hard to express verbally. If, for example, you hope that the members of your team will become more "mutually supportive" as a result of the team-building experience, what exactly do you mean by this? Do you want team members to be more willing to pitch in and help one another during peak work periods, or are you hoping that more experienced team members will evidence a greater willingness to coach and mentor some of the newer members of your team?

Quite often, several team members will volunteer to work together to complete a given task. Whenever this occurs, select one team member to take the lead in coordinating these efforts. Even when you're depending on others outside your team to complete certain elements of the action plan, a team member should be assigned to initiate and follow up on their actions.

An action-planning chart provides your team with a clear breakdown of accountabilities. For a sample chart, refer to the Tool Kit at the end of this chapter.

One of the most effective ways to encourage full team accountability for performance improvement is for team members to collectively troubleshoot the plan. This means anticipating, *before* they commit to action, the types of roadblocks they are likely to encounter and the steps they can take to eliminate or overcome these problems. During the troubleshooting process, your team should address questions such as the following:

- What could go wrong with our plan?

- What trigger events might alert us to the onset of these problems?

- What steps can we take now to prevent this problem?

- What steps do we plan to take to correct this problem, should it occur?

- Outside our team, on whom can we depend for support?

A troubleshooting discussion encourages team accountability by increasing individual empowerment. Team members are much more likely to take the initiative in responding to crises if they agree in advance on how to handle them. One final aspect of troubleshooting involves auditing the team action plan for balance and fairness. If a quick look at the plan reveals that one team member has been burdened with almost half the action items, other team members aren't carrying their weight, and some actions should be reassigned.

ACTION-PLANNING CHART

One way to ensure that your proposed solutions are actually translated into action is through the use of the Team Action-Planning Chart in Exercise 2. Note that the chart identifies actions that need to be taken, who will be responsible for completing them, and the initiation and completion dates for each action. The final section of the exercise requires agreement on the dates when team members who are responsible for specific actions report back to the group on their progress.

Here are a few suggestions for completing the chart:

1. Make sure that everyone on your team has input into the construction of the chart.

2. Try not to tackle too many problems at once. Focus each action-planning chart around a single problem and solution set.

3. Examine the chart to confirm that team members have taken on their fair share of work.

4. Make certain that one team member is assigned as lead coordinator or director for every action.

5. Consult your appointment calendars when you're completing the chart. Check for potential conflicts—for example, deadline dates that fall on weekends, holidays, or days when team members simply won't be available.

6. Scan your appointment books to confirm that team members who have agreed to complete action items will actually be on-site on those days.

7. Save the chart electronically for e-mail distribution to your team and to any outsiders who will be involved in implementing the final action plan. That way, you can easily update the chart as needed.

Tool Kit

EXERCISE 2 • TEAM ACTION-PLANNING CHART

Action to be taken	Team member(s) responsible for action	Date this action will begin	Date this action will be completed	Date for team review

Gain Commitment for Your Plan

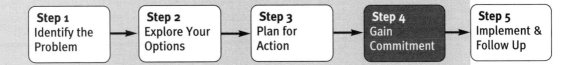

| **Step 1** Identify the Problem | → | **Step 2** Explore Your Options | → | **Step 3** Plan for Action | → | **Step 4** Gain Commitment | → | **Step 5** Implement & Follow Up |

Let's assume that you've done your investigative homework. You've compared notes with the other members of your team, and, as a group, you've concluded that you all need to focus your improvement efforts on a certain area. As a team, you've explored the problem in detail and have selected a set of actions for strengthening team performance. Finally, you've put together an action plan for implementing your solution.

Now what? Once a team has chosen a course of action, members tend to want to rush out and immediately implement the proposals. In my experience, this is a big mistake. You first need to step back and confirm each team member's willingness to move toward improving the situation. There's a big difference between acknowledging a problem and being willing to do something about it.

What Do We Mean by Commitment?

When a team is truly committed to improving performance, team members are aligned on five points:

1. They believe that the performance problem they have identified is urgent and critical in nature and requires immediate attention.

2. They believe the problem is solvable; that is, they feel both capable and empowered to correct the problem.

3. Team members agree on the size and scope of the problem. They may think it will be easy to solve, demands extensive efforts, or requires a more moderate degree of work of their part.

4. Team members view themselves as equally accountable for the success of the team improvement effort. They do not attempt to push the problem off onto their team leader or facilitator.

5. Team members agree that the selected improvement actions represent the most effective and feasible course of action.

The Team Commitment Audit found in your Tool Kit can help you determine where your team stands in terms of these five components of team commitment.

How to Capture and Confirm Commitment

There are three steps to capturing and confirming team commitment.

Acknowledge Concerns and Reservations

As they evolve, teams quickly establish fixed routines, norms, and ways of interacting. These behavior patterns may not be useful—they may even be self-destructive—but at least they're familiar. Whenever you ask people to change, you're asking them to step out of the comfort zone defined by their current behavior and try something that may be new and unsettling. Before team members can offer their commitment, they must first acknowledge that they've reached a critical pain threshold; that is, they must believe that the discomfort of trying out new behaviors is outweighed by the distress created by the current situation.

It's understandable that the members of your team may feel some anxiety about tackling team performance problems. Some people may believe they don't have the time to take on additional projects, or they may think the problem under review is too large or complicated to tackle. To others, the problem may appear too sensitive to be resolved through team discussion. Still others may have placed the responsibility for improving their situation solely on the shoulders of the team leader or facilitator. Capturing team commitment means getting team members to acknowledge that they're all responsible for making their team a success. They must understand that team leaders and facilitators may provide necessary guidance and direction but can't carry the full burden of change. Team success depends on the best efforts of every individual member.

Some team members may hesitate to openly express concerns and reservations about proposed team improvements, but it's important to allow them to do so. One effective approach is to acknowledge from the start that there are certain reasons why it may be difficult to attack the problem. You might begin with an introduction similar to the following: "Before we continue, I think it's important for us to openly discuss any concerns or reservations we might have about our ability to move forward on this problem. I'll be the first to admit that we've selected a difficult problem for review—one that could require a lot of extra time and effort. What I'd like to do is go around the table and listen to any concerns you might have. As you talk, I'll post your comments on this flipchart for review. If you don't have anything to add for the moment, just say 'pass,' and we'll skip you for now but check back with you at the end. As a ground rule, I'm going to ask you not to comment on anyone's concerns until we have everything listed on the board.

Perform an Audit

It's also important to calibrate the team's level of commitment because members often respond differently to the need for change. Some people are eager to leap forward and tackle new challenges; they're prepared to fully invest themselves in strengthening the work group. Others doubt that anything they do will significantly affect their team's performance. Unfortunately, those with the most serious reservations don't always state their views openly. Instead, they often express their concerns indirectly (through cynical comments or halfhearted cooperation) after their team has embarked on a course of action. When you calibrate commitment, you're determining the full range of support within your team.

One simple way to do this is to ask each team member to give you a number from 1 to 10, with a 10 representing a 100 percent level of commitment to tackling the problem and a 1 indicating a minimal level of commitment. After posting these numbers on the flipchart for review, invite members who expressed low levels of commitment to share their concerns. Next, ask them the following question: "What actions could we take that would enable you to raise your level of commitment?" Very often, their answers will involve very small actions on the part of the team that can dramatically ease their discomfort. These actions might include:

- Agreeing to pilot a solution on a small scale before undertaking a big change

- Assigning the hesitant team member to the subteam that will be monitoring the results of the improvement effort

- Conducting frequent check-ins with the entire team to assess progress on the improvement effort

- Making small refinements to the proposed improvement plan

Ask for Public Affirmation of Commitment

Once your work group has agreed on ways to address team members' concerns, go back and once again ask members to voice their levels of commitment to the project. Over the past twenty years, a great deal of research has shown that people who publicly affirm their commitment are far less likely to renege. For this reason, one of the strongest moves a team leader can make is encouraging team members to publicly affirm their commitment to the team as a whole.

Sometimes, a team starts out being very enthusiastic about tackling a performance problem, but the excitement quickly fades with the first serious roadblock. The simple act of voicing their commitment to change is often enough to keep team members from backsliding when they run into difficulties.

If you think team members may feel intimidated about openly voicing their concerns, consider making use of the Team Commitment Audit form in the Tool Kit.

TEAM COMMITMENT AUDIT

Tool #6

The Team Commitment Audit in Chart 6 allows team members to provide anonymous feedback on their commitment to the solution they have jointly identified. Note that the audit asks team members to rate their commitment in five areas:

- **Criticality:** How urgent is this problem?
- **Solvability:** How much of this problem can we solve ourselves?
- **Scope:** How difficult will it be to solve this problem?
- **Accountability:** How responsible do I feel personally for solving the problem?
- **Solution feasibility:** Will the proposed solution effectively solve our team's problem?

To complete the Team Commitment Audit, take the following steps:

1. Ask each member of your team to complete the audit by circling the appropriate rating statement for each of the five areas.

2. Have a team member collect these forms. Shuffle them, and, beginning with the top-most form, call out the score for each area. For example, under "Solvability," if the team member has circled the statement "We are able to make minor improvements to this problem," then that area would receive a score of 3.

3. Using hatch marks, record all the scores on the Team Commitment Audit Scoring Form shown in Exercise 3.

4. You may also wish to calculate your team's averaged scores for each area.

5. These scores can reveal your team's true level of commitment to the proposed solution. In addition, the audit can help you identify which areas are perceived differently by team members. With this information, you are in a much better position to anticipate and address problems of commitment that might otherwise diminish the effectiveness of your problem-solving process.

Tool Kit

CHART 6

Team Commitment Audit

Scoring Range	1	2	3	4	5
Criticality	This problem is not urgent. We can easily wait several weeks before acting on it.	This problem requires a minor degree of attention over the new few weeks.	This problem requires a moderate degree of attention over the next few weeks.	This problem is important and requires us to quickly move on it.	This problem is critical and requires our immediate attention.
Solvability	This problem is completely beyond our ability to solve.	The only action we can take is to recommend improvements to management.	We are able to make minor improvements to this problem.	We are able to make substantial improvements to this problem.	We should be able to largely solve this problem ourselves.
Scope	This problem is "low-hanging fruit"—it's easy to solve.	This problem will require some minor effort by our team over a few weeks.	This problem will require a moderate degree of effort by our team over a few weeks.	This problem will require significant amounts of effort by our team over the next few months.	This problem will require an extensive amount of effort by our team over the next several months.
Accountability	I don't view myself as being accountable for solving this problem.	I view myself as having some minor responsibility for solving this problem.	I view myself as being somewhat accountable for solving this problem.	I view myself as being moderately accountable for solving this problem.	I view myself as being fully accountable, with the other members of my team, for solving this problem.
Solution Feasibility	The solution selected by our team will not work.	The solution selected by our team will have a minor positive impact on the problem.	The solution selected by our team will have a moderate positive impact on the problem.	The solution selected by our team will have a significant positivie impact on the problem.	The solution selected by our team will greatly improve the problem.

EXERCISE 3 • TEAM COMMITMENT AUDIT SCORING FORM

Commitment Areas	1	2	3	4	5
Criticality					
Solvability					
Scope					
Accountability					
Solution Feasibility					

Implement the Plan and Follow Up

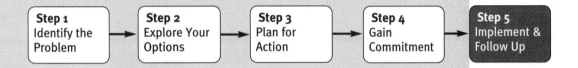

Step 1 Identify the Problem	Step 2 Explore Your Options	Step 3 Plan for Action	Step 4 Gain Commitment	Step 5 Implement & Follow Up

You are now ready to implement and track the results of the solution your team has developed with the action-planning process. As team leader, there are several steps you can take to help make the implementation phase a success.

Strategies for Successful Plan Implementation

First, your team should agree on a tracking process. Determine which team member will be responsible for tracking the team's progress on key actions. It's important to remember that the team leader or facilitator is not supposed to assume full responsibility for policing the actions of the team. This responsibility should be rotated among different team members.

With the process of implementation under way, be alert for signs of slippage. During the initial action-planning session, team members are usually excited about the idea of improving their performance. They may readily commit themselves to the performance solution. Over succeeding weeks, however, as work schedules become crowded, team members naturally tend to fall behind on the completion of key project steps. That proposed customer survey is never designed, for example, or the benchmark review of other companies somehow fails to appear. To counter this type of procrastination, watch for signs of slippage in tasks and project schedules during the first few weeks of the implementation phase. If you find that certain team members are falling behind on their commitments, ask them what steps they plan to take to catch up so they can meet the requirements of their action plan.

It's also a good idea to provide information on shortfalls and project defaults (when team members fail to complete key tasks on time) to your team. Schedule regular reviews during team meetings to ascertain the progress your team has made on the action plan. You might also use these sessions to brainstorm suggestions for overcoming any hurdles your team has encountered while attempting to implement the solution. Topics may include some of the following:

- Difficulty obtaining support from outside groups or managers

- Not enough time to complete implementation steps

- Certain aspects of implementation are more complicated than initially assumed

During implementation, perform both a process check and a results check. A results check focuses on whether your team is making progress on stated goals. A process check addresses how team members feel about the approach they are taking and might note concerns such as the following:

- Some team members have begun to feel left out of the problem-solving process

- One individual has made a personal decision to depart significantly from the team's plan of action—without informing other members of the team

- Implementing your team's solution is causing problems for other work groups within the organization

- Some team members require supplemental coaching or direction on how to complete certain action steps

Finally, remember that no action plan is completely foolproof. You should be prepared to make some midcourse corrections, such as readjusting project accountabilities within your team, revising your initial time schedule, or exploring additional problem-solving techniques. You may also have to meet with your team to revise parts of the solution that have proved less practicable. The list of team-building tools at the front of this book will help you find the appropriate techniques.

Importance of Follow-Up

Once your team has undertaken its problem-solving project, the next step is a follow-up discussion for evaluating results. Almost all teams engage in follow-up activities of some kind, but these activities are frequently sporadic and poorly constructed. In this section, I'm going to suggest a few guidelines to make the follow-up process more effective.

Let me begin by suggesting that a well-constructed follow-up discussion should accomplish four objectives.

First and foremost, the discussion should enable you to see if your team's intervention has improved the original problem situation. If your team identified a problem involving a steep increase in complaints from internal customers, have complaints decreased? If your team was working on a problem with conflicts among team members, are these conflicts on the decline?

The follow-up discussion also provides an opportunity to gauge your team's comfort level with the improvement process. Do team members feel their coworkers have honored their commitments regarding action items? Do they believe that the team has made substantial progress toward improving the situation? Are they pleased with the progress they've made so far?

Any team improvement project offers team members the chance to learn more about their own interactions. The follow-up discussion should include a review of lessons captured from this experience that can be applied to future performance challenges. These lessons may include how to function more effectively with other work groups, how to track and accurately assess the underlying causes of performance problems, or best practices that can be imported from other work groups or organizations and successfully applied to your team.

Finally, the follow-up process is an opportunity to reinforce the value of making and keeping team commitments. Many teams form action plans and never again take them out for review. By actually conducting a follow-up session and asking team members whether they've kept their commitments, you make a strong statement about the importance of team accountability. This message comes across even louder if you are prepared to model commitment for your team.

Conducting the Follow-up Session

An effective follow-up session requires giving careful thought to four major elements: planning the meeting, checking the team's progress against the initial action plan, assessing the adequacy of the present plan, and evaluating the team improvement process itself.

Plan the Setup for Your Meeting

Schedule the meeting at an appropriate stage in the process. Ideally, you should allow your team enough time to make significant progress with the problem. On the other hand, if you wait too long, it will be difficult to reinforce and assess the actions of team members at the meeting. As a general rule, I recommend meeting for the follow-up session six to eight weeks after the team problem-solving session.

Set a positive tone for the meeting. Some team members may be afraid that the follow-up session will take a critical tone, especially if your team has been struggling to progress with its improvement plan. To allay these concerns, I recommend setting a firmly positive tone for the meeting. When you announce the meeting date, commend your team for tackling a tough performance problem and emphasize your excitement about being able to meet with them and obtain their feedback on the improvement process.

Occasionally, it's a smart move to meet individually with a few team members before the follow-up session to get an informal read on your team's mood and identify any issues that might surface during the session, such as

- The degree to which you, as a team leader, have been accessible to and supportive of your team during the team-building process

- Obstacles, such as lack of time or resources and lack of support from adjacent work groups, that may have decreased your team's ability to make substantial progress on improvement activities

- Concerns about not following up on commitments

- Additional information uncovered since your team problem-solving session that might indicate additional improvement areas

Conduct a Progress Check

Go back to your team's action plan (see Chapter 3) and determine whether all the prescribed problem-solving activities have been completed. If some still remain to be done, don't focus on why but instead ask your team to project ahead and discuss ideas for overcoming roadblocks and developing a time frame for completion. Then go back to the success criteria you established as part of your action plan and ask team members to evaluate the success of their game plan according to each of these criteria. All in all, how successful has the team been in addressing the identified performance problem? What has or hasn't worked?

Determine Whether Further Action Is Needed

This step might involve expending additional effort on the current plan (if some team members have been negligent about meeting their commitments), expanding the time frame for completing improvement actions, or revising the existing plan to accommodate new information your team has uncovered while working to resolve the problem. This is also the time to find out whether team members have identified more team problems, which should be reviewed and targeted for attention.

Conduct a Process Check

Finally, ask the members of your team how they feel about the process they've just experienced. Find out what they would do differently if they were going to engage in more team problem-solving projects over the next few months. One way to conduct this type of evaluation is by using the Process Check Sheet in your Tool Kit. This is also the time to invite your team to share with you the lessons they've learned by participating in the improvement experience. You may find that completing the Lessons Learned Questionnaire (see Tool #29 in the Chapter 11 Tool Kit) will encourage team members to think through the improvement process as a learning experience before they participate in this session.

How to Identify Success

Teams sometimes make the mistake of relying on their own judgment to determine whether their improvement strategies have been successful. This very limited field of vision doesn't take into account input from your customers, senior managers, and those work groups that are directly affected by any changes you've made to your work processes. All of these groups may see the success of your improvement strategies in entirely different ways.

Case in Point: The HR Recruiting Team

I know of one HR recruiting team that decided to improve its responsiveness to internal customers by creating more rigorous and elaborate work processes. Over the course of their improvement efforts, team members proudly posted on the walls laminated flowcharts illustrating their revised work processes and created manuals for the additional documentation they had developed to track their recruiting efforts.

Unknown to the team, however, its internal customers perceived these changes as a hindrance rather than an improvement. Some departments complained that before they could post and recruit for new positions, they had to complete a number of documents, many of which requested very similar types of information. The recruiting team's flowcharts described revised work processes that enhanced its own operating efficiency but were significantly more time-consuming and bothersome for the rest of the organization. The recruiting team only began to understand and correct these problems after inviting internal customers to give input on the success of their improvement process.

What to Do if Your Team Is Not Successful

Don't allow team members to discount their efforts. Quite often, teams concentrate on the part of their improvement effort that didn't work and overlook any small successes they might have had.

To overcome this tendency, start out your discussion by asking your team to take a look at those aspects of their improvement efforts that *have* been successful. For example, assume that your team was trying to decrease the number and intensity of altercations between team members. You may have found that although your team did experience a few disagreements in the time period following your team-building intervention, the nature of the conflict has changed substantially. Perhaps these incidents are more constructive in focus or appear to be less volatile. It may also be that they're resolved more quickly. In what areas has your team seen substantial improvements?

During the follow-up session, you may find that some team members have failed to meet their commitments to complete certain action items. As you begin the discussion, these individuals will probably be on the defensive. Expect them to enter the meeting armed with excuses for why they haven't been able to take action. These reasons may range from lack of time to lack of support from other departments. It's usually unproductive to go back and try to force individuals to justify their actions (or their inability to take action). A more useful approach is to ask team members to itemize what they have and have not accomplished and then ask the following question: "What actions could you take during the next few days to help us get the results we're looking for?"

Tool Kit

PROCESS CHECK SHEET

Tool
#7

Sometimes, a team's performance-improvement efforts aren't completely successful. When this happens, it's important to approach this situation as another opportunity to understand and solve a problem. Chart 7 shows the five principal reasons for unsuccessful team improvement efforts, provides examples for each one, and outlines suggested actions to address them. Try to apply this analysis to your team the next time you encounter less than satisfactory results with your team problem-solving efforts.

CHART 7

Process Check Sheet		
Reason for Failure	**What to Do About It**	**Example**
You've identified the wrong problem.	• Go back to the drawing board and reevaluate your problem. • Be very cautious about having a single member of your team interpret your team's problems, or having your team interpret the concerns of other work groups. • Ask yourself what symptoms your team has ignored or overstated. • Ask others outside your team for input on how they're being affected by your team's performance problems. • Read Chapters 6–17 very carefully for potential interactions of different team problems.	A corporate recruiting team knew it was having difficulties meeting the needs of internal customers but defined the problem as excessive cost-per-hire. After taking several actions to reduce recruiting costs and then discussing these corrective actions with customers, the team discovered customers were far less concerned about cost-per-hire than they were about the time it took to fill a position.

Tool Kit

Process Check Sheet *continued*		
Reason for Failure	**What to Do About It**	**Example**
You've identified the correct problem but the wrong underlying cause for the problem.	• Solicit additional input on your team's performance directly from individuals and work groups outside your team. • Try to obtain hard data to help substantiate the true cause of your team's performance problem. • Ask yourself when the problem was first noticed and try to determine its trend line. • Consider what changes might have been taking place within your team at the time. • Explore what current factors may be contributing to the problem.	A cross-functional quality improvement team was set up to resolve recent complaints from a corporate customer. The team put together a detailed improvement plan, only to have it shot down by the customer's quality assurance manager. Later, the team discovered that this manager had long resented what he viewed as the "arrogant" behavior of one of the team members. Armed with this information, the team formulated a new action plan and resolved the underlying issues with the angry manager.
You've identified the correct problem and underlying cause but implemented the wrong improvement solution.	• Seek the advice of others within or outside your company who have successfully tackled this problem. What solutions did they implement? • Ask yourself if your team covered the broadest range of solutions, or if they settled for the most convenient or routine solution. • Consider performing a best-practices review to see how other companies have resolved similar problems. • Try to determine whether your team chose an ineffective or unfeasible solution.	An HR team conducted an organizational effectiveness survey that showed widespread dissatisfaction among company associates regarding the lack of career opportunities. The team attacked this problem by putting months of effort into designing a career development program. When the program was presented, it met with a high degree of cynicism from many employees, who felt that while the program provided excellent skills training, its lack of a job posting process and formal career paths made it difficult for them to take advantage of career opportunities.

Tool Kit

You've put the right improvement action in place but failed to effectively implement it.	• Question whether your team has allowed adequate time to review the solution. Many team problems can't be fixed overnight. • Ask if additional resources would make a difference in the success of the implementation plan. • Consider whether this is the best time to implement the plan. Would it be better to wait until conditions change? • Finally, ask yourself if you have the full support of your organizational stakeholders? Does everyone really want this solution to work?	In attempting to attack the problem of "lack of innovation," a marketing team performed a few limited best-practices studies within its own field to see how other, related companies were encouraging innovative performance. In retrospect, the team realized that it hadn't gone far enough in its review. The second time around, the team revised its study to go outside its industry and include input from some of the most creative companies in the United States.
Your team has encountered factors completely beyond its control that have reduced the effectiveness of the original improvement plan.	• Leverage all possible support from senior management to eliminate these barriers. • Consider putting a hold on your implementation plan until the situation stabilizes. • Ask if there is a way to bolster your plan. • Make every effort to anticipate future roadblocks (see Chapter 9).	A support team developed a reasonable action plan for establishing clearer direction over the next one to three years. Halfway through its efforts, a department-wide reorganization forced the team to rethink many of its original operating assumptions.

PART TWO

The Team Tool Kit

- Improving Internal Relationships
- Strengthening Team Focus
- Dealing with the Challenges of Change
- Mending External Relationships

Improving Internal Relationships

The Team Divided

The Problem of Intra-Team Conflict

Quite often, team leaders and members make the mistake of focusing so much on the day-to-day tasks of meeting objectives, negotiating with other work groups, and solving technical problems that team relationships are left out of the equation. It would certainly be a lot easier if we could treat a team as if it were nothing more than some sort of logical, predictable machine. Then we could simply program the team with its objectives, place it on automatic, and wait for it to achieve its stated goals.

Unfortunately, that's not the way things work. Teams are composed of people, and as we know, people are sometimes unpredictable, uncooperative, and contradictory. In addition, all teams face pressures that make it difficult for their members to work together in harmony. A team can find itself under pressure to meet stringent deadlines or conform to exacting productivity or quality standards. Members may find themselves suffering from burnout caused by long hours or severe working conditions while faced with the need to continually negotiate the best approach to meeting goals and managing team resources. Sometimes, team members may disagree on how to pursue objectives or manage the team's customers or suppliers. When we consider the larger picture, teams can also find themselves caught up in the stress and uncertainty of the kinds of broader organizational changes—mergers, restructuring, redefining of corporate charters—that can rock work groups to their foundations. Faced with these pressures, even members of the most exceptional teams will occasionally find themselves involved in conflict.

The question to consider is not whether the members of your team sometimes find themselves enmeshed in conflict; at times, all teams experience internal conflicts. The true question is, are these conflicts so pervasive and damaging that they could pose a serious obstacle to your team's long-term success?

Role of the Team Leader

It may be that you are reluctant to ask for your team's help in resolving conflicts because you feel that, as the team leader, the burden for conflict resolution rests entirely on your shoulders. This is not only inaccurate; it can also be detrimental to both you and your group in a number of ways.

Basically, team leaders who appoint themselves sole arbitrators and harmonizers for their teams are headed for disaster. Assuming such a role makes drastic demands on your limited amounts of available time and energy. It places you in a patronizing, parental position that encourages your team members to abdicate personal responsibility for preventing and solving conflicts with their coworkers. In addition, by attempting to take care of everything for team members, you deny them the chance to develop skills that will be of use in managing a variety of conflicts, such as those involving other work groups, customers, or suppliers. Inevitably, intervention-type rescues for team members backfire. No matter how impartial you try to be, some team members will probably view your actions as unfair and arbitrary.

Alternatively, you may be hoping to rely completely on a professional third-party facilitator for assistance. Although facilitators may be able to teach important relationship skills and guide team members through conflicts, they can't help you manage your team's day-to-day operations. Instead, a team must learn to detect and avoid potential conflicts and successfully manage those that can't be prevented.

The Symptoms

Teams that are caught up in destructive internal conflicts exhibit a number of consistent symptoms, some of which represent ineffective responses to the situation.

Rapid Escalation of Minor Conflicts

Small conflicts tend to escalate quickly until they're out of control. This is one of the most common symptoms of a team that is trapped in conflict. If relatively small one-on-one disagreements swiftly expand to engulf other team members, the team leader, or (even worse) senior managers, your team has a serious problem that demands prompt attention.

Self-Imposed Isolation

Some team members may choose isolation in order to remove themselves from conflict situations. While this may prevent arguments, it also slows down work efforts and creates information bottlenecks. Team members who seal themselves off in their offices or cubicles and simply stop communicating with the other members of their team are just digging in for a long siege.

Isolation often leads to territorial behavior among team members. Signs include establishing firm boundary lines around work areas, PCs, responsibilities, and even support personnel. When team members attack coworkers for infringing on their turf, the parties involved are in conflict.

Breakdowns in Communications and Personal Relationships

Naturally, isolated team members can't inform one another of significant events, changing circumstances, or problems. In the same way, information you share with certain team members is not passed along to other coworkers. This lack of communication, or communication that is terse and guarded, interferes with the smooth flow of work processes.

In addition to being reluctant to maintain physical and verbal contact within the team, team members may also hesitate to offer help to coworkers. When people who formerly worked well together begin to look out only for themselves, it's a sure sign that your team has been caught up in an ongoing cycle of conflict.

Use of Intimidation

Instead of refusing to engage one another, some team members may try to force coworkers to give in to their demands by using arguments, veiled threats, or other forms of intimidation. They may also attempt to verbally dominate other members during team meetings. These tactics might create the appearance of agreement within a specific situation, but team members who feel they are being bullied may fight back later in less obvious ways such as manipulation and withdrawal of support.

Formation of Cliques

Team members may also attempt to control conflict by seeking allies among other members. Sometimes this also involves soliciting support from individuals who hold strategic positions in other work groups or pressuring their own team leader to take sides on an issue. When certain members consistently oppose other members, regardless of the issue under discussion, their behavior relates not only to the matter at hand but also to long-standing grievances between the factions.

Team members may seek help in outmaneuvering or overpowering their opponents or may try to isolate them from the rest of the team. This behavior leads to the formation of mutually hostile cliques. Cliques ostracize other team members and target them for retribution, which may involve excluding them from meetings or e-mail distribution lists or pointedly ignoring them in social situations.

Manipulative Behavior

You could think of manipulation in the workplace as several team members trying to outmaneuver one another on the organizational chessboard. Some of the most common tactics are false rumors, denial of support, inciting coworkers to actions that interfere with the work of targeted team members, and blatant character assassination. Over time, this process could very well lead to an escalating game of one-upmanship involving all parties.

Another form of manipulation is the well-known corporate game of trying to make a coworker look bad in the eyes of the team leader and senior managers. For example, a team member might wait for an opportunity to expose a coworker's mistakes in public instead of discussing the matter in private, or, at the first sign of a performance problem, team members may immediately implicate other individuals as the source of these problems.

Unproductive Criticisms

Criticisms expressed in a hostile and inflammatory manner are symptomatic of a team in conflict. Team members caught up in this kind of negative situation tend to engage in personal attacks that are meant only to hurt other people.

Case in Point: The Customer Service Team

The customer couldn't believe what she was seeing. When she first stopped by the store's customer service department to pick up a credit card application, she expected the process to take about five minutes, and here it was, twenty minutes later! The problem started when she sat down with one of the service representatives to discuss the application process. Within two minutes, another employee came over and began arguing with the first employee about the correct way to complete the application. The next thing the customer knew, the two employees were engaged in what appeared to be an all-out war, and she was caught in the cross fire.

Obviously, she thought, they didn't want her business if they were willing to waste her time on their personal arguments! Well, there were other stores that would appreciate her business and could certainly handle something as simple as a credit card application! With this in mind, she gathered up her packages and left the store.

As he observed the events from across the room, Jason Harrison thought carefully about what he should do next. Although, given his distance from the situation, he couldn't overhear the conversation between Vera and Tom, he could see that they were becoming increasingly agitated. He also observed that they'd become so caught up in their argument that neither one noticed when the customer got up to leave. What had begun as minor bickering a few weeks ago had continued to grow until the conflict was now obvious to others on the team—and, evidently, to customers as well. It was time to do something about it, and quickly.

The Underlying Causes

Conflicts such as the one in our Case in Point develop for a variety of reasons. You may recognize some or all of the following conditions in your work group or in other teams within your organization.

Lack of Consensus-Building Skills

From time to time, every team needs to resolve some tough work issues. If team members don't have the skills to obtain consensus, these situations quickly become conflicts. Teams don't necessarily have to reach complete agreement on all issues, but the very act of striving for consensus makes team members feel that their needs and concerns have been given a fair hearing. When team members lack a forum for airing their concerns or seeking resolution on issues, or if they don't know how to manage the process of consensus building, they may feel that their only options are force and intimidation.

Another factor to consider is that consensus-building sessions provide team members with a balanced and more impartial audience for feedback and evaluation. When team members receive similar responses from several coworkers, they're less likely to feel that the feedback is biased and personal in nature.

Disagreements on Agendas and Priorities

Team members will not always have the same agendas and priorities. These differences naturally create a certain amount of tension within the team. If team members feel they're locked in a win-lose situation, they may become defensive and stop looking for ways to achieve mutual victories with their coworkers. Instead, they may turn their attention to winning at any cost.

Power Imbalances Within the Team

Another common cause of team conflict is unequal distribution of power among team members. All people want to be treated in a fair and respectful way, regardless of seniority, rank, or technical proficiency.

At the same time, keep in mind that anyone who has survived in a large organization for any length of time has probably become adept at the art of guerrilla warfare. As the old saying goes, "paybacks are hell." If certain team members feel they have been forced to cave in to the demands of dominant or senior-level coworkers, they may react in a covert fashion by withholding information, engaging in vicious rumormongering or gossip, or gathering allies for a retaliatory strike against those whom they view as their opponents.

Differences in Communication Style

We all have very different communication styles. Mine tends to be fairly task focused and directive: I think on my feet, like to thoroughly understand issues before I discuss them with others, get to the point very quickly, avoid small talk, and remain focused on my tasks at work. Yet I work with a variety of professionals who represent every conceivable communication style. For example, one of my associates has a communication style that is characterized by the following features:

- She's more likely to warm up to a topic slowly with a lot of small talk.

- She tends to shift quickly among many topics.

- Instead of analyzing and itemizing key points before participating in a discussion, she prefers to walk in with a blank notepad and work through her ideas as she presents them.

You can see that having such different communication styles could make communication between the two of us very difficult. Fortunately, recognizing our differences makes it a lot easier to work together effectively. If team members don't understand how communication styles affect their relationships with their coworkers, they are less likely to make allowances for their differences and more prone to experience those differences as irritations.

Inability to Detect the Onset of Conflict

Team conflicts seldom appear without warning. It's easy for the astute observer to spot the nonverbal clues of imminent conflict—tenseness in the voice and face, growing physical agitation, sudden flare-ups in team meetings, covert meetings behind closed doors, formation of cliques that exclude other team members who may not have the interpersonal skills to perceive that coworkers are irritated or frustrated by their behavior. If these warning signs remain unnoticed and unaddressed, the result can be a major altercation.

Lack of Conflict-Managing Skills

Many people reach adulthood armed with a few simple communication tools, such as verbal domination, intimidation, or sarcasm, but are not equipped to tactfully resolve conflicts. These basic (though maladaptive) tools, along with a high degree of technical proficiency, may enable a person to perform well in the first few years on the job. Eventually, however, this individual may settle into a work environment characterized by increasingly complex and subtle issues, alongside team members who are more than able to hold their own in a conflict. At this point, the absence of relationship skills becomes evident to the organization at large. If left uncorrected, these deficiencies may result in career derailment (plateauing or termination) for these individuals.

Ambiguous Roles and Responsibilities

A common source of irritation for team members is uncertainty about their respective roles in managing customers or suppliers, providing project direction, or representing their team to key stakeholders. Without some clarity on these issues, team members are prone to erecting protective barriers around their job responsibilities or engaging in petty bickering over accountabilities. Problems in this area also quickly become visible to people outside the team and, if left unaddressed, can damage the team's reputation with other departments and work groups.

The Treatment

Every team encounters issues that are potential sources of conflict. When conflict does occur, act promptly to control the situation. Some of the following methods may be useful to you.

Develop and Model Guidelines

First, develop team guidelines for managing conflicts. During one of your staff meetings, suggest to your team that one way to prevent conflicts is to develop and agree to follow guidelines for preventing and resolving conflicts. Some of the most useful general guidelines include:

- No personal attacks. Stick with the facts about how another team member's behavior is affecting you and the rest of the team. For example, a statement such as "You're irresponsible and only think about your own priorities" is a personal attack. Express the same idea by saying, "During the past month, you made commitments to attend two project meetings and then backed out at the last minute because it was inconvenient for you. We really had to scramble to find someone to take your place, and that's just not fair to me or the rest of the team."

- Avoid heated outbursts. If you feel you're starting to lose control of your emotions, ask for a five-minute cool-down period before continuing the discussion.

- Confront the other parties directly instead of discussing them with others.

- Never assume hostile intent. Team conflicts are most often caused by such factors as communication breakdowns, unclear roles, and conflicting agendas, not by a desire to do harm to others. If you don't understand the reasons for another person's behavior, ask about it and reevaluate your assumptions.

After the team has formulated its guidelines, model them for the rest of the team. It's important for team members to see that you take these guidelines seriously or they might not be willing to adhere to them either. Periodically ask team members for feedback on your approach to dealing with conflicts. At the same time, let them know you're trying to improve personally in that area.

Identify Areas of Possible Conflict

It's also wise to map out the locations of what I call "organizational quicksand." Systematically scan through your team's list of objectives and upcoming projects for issues that may cause problems. Examples include deciding which team members will be assigned to choice projects and who will take the lead on those projects, and how to allocate scarce resources among competing projects. After listing areas of potential conflict, invite your team to discuss ways of addressing them. Experience has shown that the more time you spend discussing an emerging conflict, the less emotional an issue it will be. It seems to be easier for most people to think dispassionately about solutions to a potential problem than to regain their objectivity once they are deeply submerged in it.

Act Immediately to Control Conflict

When conflicts arise, make an effort to contain them. As I've already cautioned, team conflicts have a way of quickly spreading beyond control. Some of the following actions may be helpful to you:

- Remind team members about the guidelines they developed for managing conflicts.

- When you hear of a conflict between team members, meet with them individually and perform a brief check-in to determine if they're trying to address the issue. Ask them to take responsibility for the situation and get back to you as soon as they've resolved it.

- If you see team members arguing in a team meeting or a public forum, tell them their conduct is hurting the team and suggest they continue their discussion in private.

- Caution team members against inflammatory e-mail (flaming) or voice mail. Suggest allowing twenty-four hours to think through a message before sending or leaving it.

- Meet briefly with team members who are trying to pull coworkers, or individuals outside your team, into their conflict. Explain firmly that they have a lot of freedom in deciding how to resolve their disagreement, but when they begin to affect the team's reputation, it becomes *your* problem, and one that you won't tolerate. Warn them about behaving in ways that could permanently damage their team.

Third-Party Intervention

Despite everyone's best efforts, team members may have a difficult time working through a conflict on their own. When this happens, it's often advisable to suggest that they ask a neutral team member to facilitate their discussion. All parties involved must understand that the role of this informal facilitator is not to take sides, pass judgment, or impose solutions. Rather, this person acts to ensure that all viewpoints are on the table and that team members follow the conflict-management guidelines adopted by your team.

The facilitator may begin by asking both sides to describe the matter at hand. After listening carefully to them, he or she should restate the issue in an objective way. Frequently, this approach counters the tug-of-war aspect that makes the conflict a win-lose competition. In addition, by restating the issue objectively, the neutral third party removes any biting or sarcastic remarks that may have been attached to the conflict. Finally, hearing the facilitator's description of the problem gives those who are personally involved some emotional distance and allows them to concentrate on the facts that underlie the issue.

Coaching for Conflict-Prone Individuals

If you find that some team members have a hard time working with others, consider sending them to an outside seminar or workshop that specializes in interpersonal relationship skills. There are a variety of such seminars available.

As a first step, you might try contacting the American Management Association (212-586-8100). Team members who can't seem to understand how their behavior affects their coworkers might benefit from one of the many excellent programs conducted by the Center for Creative Leadership in Greensboro, North Carolina (336-288-7210). The center offers several public workshops that utilize communication simulations, training, and feedback from other program participants. They also offer 360-degree surveys, which provide consolidated, anonymous feedback on participants' behavior from coworkers, managers, and direct reports.

Avoid the "Kitchen Sink" Syndrome

I use the term "kitchen sinking" to describe the common practice of beginning with one point of disagreement and then throwing in a variety of unrelated topics. In other words, people toss everything into the discussion except the kitchen sink, and the next thing you know, the argument has grown to cover additional and possibly unrelated topics and is suddenly even further from resolution.

Team-related arguments are subject to the same laws of exponential expansion. To keep conflicts from widening in scope, it's important to intervene promptly during the first few minutes of a discussion by saying something like, "Before we go further, let's see if we can at least agree on how to define the issue we're facing. The way I see it . . . ," and then offer a brief, objective description of the issue at hand. As soon as one party throws an unrelated issue onto the table, note the shift in agenda and ask if digressing onto a second topic is desirable at this time.

Pursue Alignment on an Incremental Basis

If you're trying to resolve several issues at once, suggest tackling them in ascending order of difficulty, from the most minor to the most complicated. Start with situations that you feel can be easily resolved and gather positive momentum as you continue your discussion. By the time you get to the hardest ones, you'll already have found a few areas of agreement and the tension level should be somewhat lower.

Place Conflicts Within the Context of Agreement

When people disagree, they naturally tend to focus on the conflict. Counter this reaction by reminding team members of all the agreements they've been able to reach up to this point. For example, you might say something like, "I think it's important to stop and place this disagreement in perspective. We all know we've been experiencing an increase in customer service problems, and we all agree we need to correct this problem. In addition, over the last hour, I've heard a lot of agreement on our need for a customer survey that includes representation from our four key market areas. We also agree that we need to create this survey in time for our next customer service forum. It seems the only issue left to resolve is whether this survey should be designed internally or farmed out to a consulting service. Is that about it?" This kind of statement reminds team members of their overall progress toward resolving key issues.

In a related approach, encourage opposing parties to separate acceptable aspects of a solution from those they consider unacceptable. Tool #10, the

"Baby and Bathwater" Technique, details one method of implementing this procedure.

Another related approach is keyed to the onset of a discussion, when you're encouraging team members to discuss their respective views. You may want to help conflicting parties articulate the underlying needs and concerns that fuel the strong positions they're defending.

Recognize Agreement As It Occurs

Each time your team reaches agreement on a point, summarize it verbally. Then, if team members concur with your summary, record the statement on a flipchart. This suggestion may sound trite, but in fact it's easy for team members to forget those points on which they've already reached agreement when they're caught up in the heat of discussion. In addition, I've witnessed many conflict-resolution sessions in which apparent agreements don't hold up once they're set down in writing.

Temporarily Table Issues That Provoke Strong Disagreement

See if you can temporarily postpone sensitive issues for later review. Write them down on a flipchart, and then go back to them at a later time. This allows you to gather positive momentum from areas of agreement while you consider the best way to approach the problem. At the same time, team members with strong feelings about the conflict will have a chance to cool down and evaluate their views.

Consider the following example. A few years ago, I was facilitating a process improvement team when it hit a brick wall at one of its meetings. More specifically, team members were firmly divided into two camps over the best way to design a customer-complaint management system for the company. Instead of forcing the team toward agreement, I asked participants to divide into their two respective subgroups and then asked each subgroup to use a portion of the flipchart to write down their particular version of the process section on which they disagreed. Participants were not allowed to continue the discussion until all other elements of the process flow had been mapped. We then posted the two versions for joint review. By the time we were ready to move back to our sticking point, the team could see clearly which of the two versions would most effectively meet their needs.

Perform Periodic Check-Ins

If you're facilitating the resolution of a conflict between two or more team members, stop the action occasionally and ask three questions:

- "How do you think we're doing?"

- "Are we making progress on this issue?"

- "Do you feel your views are being heard?"

This type of check-in provides a temporary time-out for individuals who feel they are locked in conflict. One method for performing a check-in is to "freeze" the action and ask team members to provide anonymous feedback on how effectively they feel they are working together on an issue. The Nominal Group Technique in your Tool Kit (page 71) offers one such check-in method.

Related Problems

The following chapters contain more specific details about problems related to team conflict.

Chapter 7 (Transition Chaos: Managing the Virtual Team)—Team conflicts are intrinsically connected to communication breakdowns within the team. There's a circular cause-and-effect relationship at work, as communication problems often result in team conflicts, which, once formed, result in a variety of situations (such as the unwillingness to freely share information) that further disrupt a team's communication channels.

Chapter 8 (The King Dethroned: Solving Member-Leader Conflict)—A team's leader can play a pivotal role in the creation and escalation of conflict. Even when team conflicts are not directly caused or exacerbated by team leaders, those who have not formed strong relationships with their teams are unable to take on the critical roles of harmonizer and team facilitator.

Chapter 16 (The Raised Drawbridge: Resolving Inter-Group Conflict)—Team members may respond to conflict by trying to enlist the aid of allies within or outside their own work group. They may also use enlistment sessions as forums for criticizing their coworkers' performance, which serves only to tear down their team's reputation and sets the stage for conflicts with other work groups. In addition, individuals who lack the skills to resolve inter-team conflicts are not likely to succeed in managing conflicts with other groups.

Chapter 17 (Our Own Worst Enemy: Strengthening Customer Relationships)—Team conflicts are frequently manifested as communication breakdowns and service interruptions, which will lead to a sharp decline in customer satisfaction.

Tool Kit

Tool #8

THOMAS-KILMANN CONFLICT MODE INSTRUMENT

Identifying your conflict style and how it can work for or against you is an important part of your ability to resolve conflict. You can achieve a better understanding of your style with the *Thomas-Kilmann Conflict Mode Instrument*, a conflict evaluation instrument developed by two management consultants, Dr. Kenneth W. Thomas and Dr. Ralph H. Kilmann.

The instrument is based on the theory that people tend to develop habitual ways of responding to interpersonal conflicts, which they then incorporate into their overall communication styles. It presents thirty paired statements and asks respondents to choose the statement within each pair that more closely describes their typical conflict-resolution style.

A scoring matrix helps respondents determine which of these major conflict-resolution skills they tend to apply:

- **Competing:** Tends to aggressively exercise power at the expense of others.

- **Accommodating:** Tends to neglect own concerns to accommodate the needs of others.

- **Avoiding:** Tends to respond to conflict with withdrawal, avoidance, or sidestepping of issues.

- **Collaborating:** Tends to work with others to find the best possible solution for both parties.

- **Compromising:** Tends to find an expedient solution that partially meets the needs of both parties.

Consulting Psychologists Press, the company that publishes this survey, also sells a *Facilitator's Guide* that is especially adapted for the survey and can be used to address such issues as the implications of over- or underuse of a particular conflict-resolution skill. You may contact them at www.cpp-db.com or at 800-624-1765.

NOMINAL GROUP TECHNIQUE

With this technique, team members anonymously write their ideas for resolving a problem on index cards. This technique is particularly useful in the following situations:

- Team members may need time to sort through their thoughts. When people write down concerns or ideas, they tend to be less emotional and are able to carefully assess the issues at hand.

- Some team members may feel uneasy about openly expressing their ideas in front of other, more dominant, team members.

- Opposing parties may be reluctant to reveal their underlying concerns to you as the team leader and conflict facilitator.

Follow these steps to complete the procedure:

1. Provide team members with index cards for their responses.

2. When you've collected the cards, give your team a ten-minute break while you summarize their ideas on a flipchart.

3. When they return, take everyone through a systematic review of all posted ideas.

4. No single idea should be evaluated until all have been summarized and are clearly understood by all participants.

As simple as it is, this technique addresses several needs. First, it gives team members time to cool off while they organize their thoughts on paper. Second, it helps rein in verbally dominant team members. Finally, when you place all ideas anonymously on the flipchart, you remove pride of authorship; in other words, team members discuss "an idea" with no personality attached.

Tool Kit

"BABY AND BATHWATER" TECHNIQUE

When people voice criticisms, they frequently make the mistake of "throwing the baby out with the bathwater"; that is, they make sweeping criticisms of everything they've heard. The following technique forces team members to reflect on those areas on which they have reached consensus, and to avoid making sweeping, generalized, critical statements.

The "baby and bathwater" tool is deceptively simple. Quite often, both parties will discover during the final step that they've overestimated the scope and severity of their disagreement. This technique also helps redirect conflict away from a personal tug-of-war and toward a joint review of topics for discussion.

Follow these steps to complete the procedure:

1. For two participants, prepare a flipchart header as shown in Exercise 4. If there are more than two, revise the header accordingly.

EXERCISE 4 • POINTS OF AGREEMENT AND DISAGREEMENT

From Linda's Point of View	From Janet's Point of View
Points on Which We Agree	Points on Which We Agree
Points on Which We Disagree	Points on Which We Disagree

2. Make the following statement to your team members: "I'm going to ask you to individually explain your views on this situation. However, before telling us about those points on which you disagree, outline those points on which you feel you're in agreement."

3. Share the following example: "I agree with you that we need to have the software in place before we can go further on the project, and that, ideally, the most effective software package would be one developed internally by our own IT department. The point on which you and I disagree concerns the *feasibility* of doing this. Our IT department is so backed up that going this route will slow our project down by three months."

4. Ask both parties to allow you to complete the chart before either one offers comments.

5. Start with one speaker and ask, "With regard to this issue, on which points do you feel the two (or three, etc.) of you are in agreement?"

6. List these points on the flipchart for review.

7. Then ask: "On what points do you disagree?"

8. Repeat Steps 5–7 with the second and any additional speakers.

9. After the entire chart has been completed, ask, "Looking at the flipchart, what do you see as your strongest points of agreement? On which points do we need to try to seek alignment?"

Tool Kit

MULTIVOTING

This technique is very useful when, after several good ideas have been developed by your team, each member seems intent on defending his or her own position. Multivoting helps overcome this roadblock by encouraging individuals to consider the worth of others' ideas.

Follow these steps to complete the procedure:

1. List all ideas or solutions on a flipchart, and then number each idea for review.

2. Tell team members they can cast five votes each for any of the ideas listed on the flipchart. They may apply all five votes to a particular item or distribute their votes among several items; however, an individual can give no more than three votes to his or her own idea.

3. Provide team members with markers and ask them to vote by placing hatch marks next to the ideas or solutions they favor. Speed up the process by having several team members approach the flipchart at the same time.

4. Tally all votes and highlight the items that received the most. If two or more items receive almost the same number of votes, ask the team to continue discussing these items until they know which solution they prefer.

Transition Chaos

Managing the Virtual Team

In business, as in society at large, image often lags behind reality. The word "team" tends to make us think of the traditional intact team, whose members share the same location and working hours and which orchestrates its activities in face-to-face meetings and personal briefings by the team leader. This image is firmly entrenched in our collective corporate psyche despite the fact that many teams today are essentially virtual teams, whose members may be separated by time and space. The rapid proliferation of virtual teams is easy to understand when you consider the contributing factors.

The most obvious one is the rise of the global marketplace; this development demands the formation of multinational teams to advance international business objectives and provide opportunities for new executive talent. Almost every company with a global presence is being challenged to design new virtual team structures that will help link corporate knowledge pools across broad geographic and organizational boundaries.

A second factor responsible for the growth of virtual teams is the increased corporate emphasis on employing cross-functional teams—to address such issues as corrective action, process improvement, and customer action—as a means of encouraging employee involvement and commitment. The move toward employee involvement is reflected in efforts to include those who traditionally have been left out of these cross-functional activities, such as second- and third-shift workers and associates at remote field sites. With the addition of these types of team members, team leaders must search for ways to overcome logistical barriers to project success.

Still another factor behind the spread of virtual teams is the rapid growth of telecommuting and other unorthodox arrangements like the staggered use of shared offices by groups of employees. Corporate cost-containment programs also compel team leaders to identify creative alternatives to the expensive and time-consuming option of flying in team members for face-to-face meetings. Concurrently, we are witnessing rapid advances in technology—for example, digital cameras for PCs—which are making it easier to maintain team connections electronically.

All these factors are forcing many teams to begin operating at least partially within a virtual framework. As a result, we can anticipate that the ability to successfully lead virtual teams will be a critical survival skill for the emerging twenty-first-century manager.

Unfortunately, not all work professionals make an easy transition to the unique demands and characteristics of virtual teams. Quite frequently, traditional teams announce their intention to become virtual teams by initiating telecommuting or the physical redistribution of team members. Sometimes, only after these actions are well under way does the team begin to realize that the traditional guidelines and assumptions no longer apply. Some teams never reach this level of understanding. Their members frantically try to maintain the same types of reporting relationships and communication patterns that worked for them in the past—with disastrous results. E-mails sent by team members to others in their organization are countermanded by mixed messages emanating from other team members. Meetings are scheduled, then delayed, then rescheduled, and attendance is sparse and unpredictable. Project objectives often seem stuck in quagmires, with no solid alignment on goals or outcomes. In the worst-case scenario, teams in this situation are frequently experienced as disjointed and dysfunctional by their own members and are viewed as such by affiliated teams. In short, the new virtual team (which, ironically, is often created to improve work efficiency and cost effectiveness) can easily find itself experiencing transition chaos as it struggles to maintain the effective integration and smooth orchestration of activities.

The Symptoms

If you're leading or participating in a virtual team, the following symptoms may indicate that your work group is experiencing transition chaos.

Communication Problems

Virtual teams that have not yet developed solid communication methods often find their decision-making process is very spotty. Members walk away from conference calls or videoconferences unsure of what agreements were reached, how decisions are supposed to be translated into team actions, or who is responsible for certain actions. Given this confusion, issues and problems that supposedly were resolved are again brought up for review during subsequent discussions, to the frustration of many team members.

To compensate for their communication problems, team members may appeal to external work associates to keep them informed of their own team's activities. When team members are blind to their group's internal activities, the team is definitely moving toward a chaotic state.

Ineffective Coordination of Both External and Internal Activities

Teams in the midst of transition chaos are unable to effectively orchestrate their activities. Suppliers receive mixed directions from different team members, coworkers waste time by unknowingly duplicating one another's actions, or tasks fall between the cracks because team members assume someone else is responsible for certain activities.

In addition, if effective check-and-control mechanisms are not built into the planning process, virtual team members will be unsure of how far they can stray from group plans without seriously jeopardizing the overall project strategy. The result can be either a team that works against itself or a team that grinds to a standstill because its members are afraid to take action.

Lack of Core Identity

Virtual teams that are also cross-functional sometimes have difficulty with defining who constitutes the actual team. Is the technical expert who contributes occasional suggestions and problem-solving advice via e-mail or phone conference a team member? How about the work associate who takes it upon herself to provide input to the team's electronic database? This problem is exacerbated when a team consists of individuals who represent different organizations, as is the case with a supplier-customer quality improvement team. In this situation, multiple management layers may feed into the team's decision-making process, leaving members confused about who needs to be contacted or informed regarding key decisions and actions. Without solid answers to these questions, the members of virtual teams will be unable to establish the types of boundaries that support team solidarity, and the team's identity can become diffused and weakened.

Case in Point: The International Sales and Support Team

On the flight into Dublin, Dara Ripley thought a lot about the leadership role she played within her company, a relatively recent start-up in the field of integrated IT network solutions. As the manager of the small, but very influential international sales and support team, Dara bore a lot of responsibility for making her company's overseas expansion a success. Because the company had only recently made inroads into international markets, Dara's small team of fifteen people was spread across Australia, Europe, and the United Kingdom. Dara herself, along with three of her teammates, covered corporate accounts for the entire United Kingdom.

Later, seated across the table from Darrell James, the senior vice president of marketing for Dublin-based Alcove Enterprises, Dara Ripley began to feel very uncomfortable. Alcove Enterprises was one of her company's biggest customers, and now this newly formed account was beginning to unravel. A few days ago, Dara had received an angry e-mail message from Darrell, claiming that her company was falling behind in the installation of a very important IT networking system. As she continued her conversation with Darrell, Dara realized that her team had failed to keep her informed of events in several areas. At one point in the discussion, Darrell became very upset because Dara was unaware of some of the promises made by her team regarding upgrades to Alcove's PC support desk. Dara knew that the very important customer sitting across from her was beginning to see her team as inefficient and disorganized. As she collected her thoughts, she promised herself that as soon as this meeting was over, she was going to call her team together and resolve their communication problem, once and for all.

The Underlying Causes

To succeed as a virtual manager, you must first understand the unique factors that can create transition chaos.

Barriers to Communication Within Teams

Virtual teams rely heavily on electronic tools such as e-mail and phone conferences to maintain communications. Without face-to-face contact, team members miss out on the many subtle nonverbal and paraverbal contextual clues that would help them interpret and respond correctly to team interactions. Does a team member's abrupt silence during a phone discussion signal disagreement, anger, frustration, or simply the need to pause and mentally regroup before responding? It's also important to remember that terse and abrupt e-mail messages lacking the subtle context of visual and verbal feedback are more likely to sound aggressive or confrontational. The response can be flaming, or hostile, e-mails, and (should others respond in kind) the flames may escalate into e-mail wars between team members.

By definition, the members of virtual teams are based in scattered geographic locations. Members of virtual teams usually have demanding and conflicting work schedules that require them to operate in an asynchronous fashion. In other words, it's fairly common for virtual team members to provide input on team decisions, tackle problems, and implement team activities with little, if any, face-to-face or simultaneous team communication. For team leaders, the inherent challenge is to establish methods of coordinating activities to allow asynchronous interactions yet minimize the possibility of communication breakdowns.

In the most challenging scenario, global team members must span not just different countries but widely different time zones as well. In addition, many international team members are continually in motion—traveling within and across national borders—which makes it difficult to anticipate the best time and place for team communication.

Transparency of Team Activities

I use the word "permeability" to describe the transparency of a virtual team's activities to others within the organization. After all, what's said behind closed doors may remain within the team's confidence, but e-mail notes and voice-mail messages somehow manage to find their way to others within (or even outside) the sender's organization. Permeability is a two-edged sword.

On the one hand, it increases pressure on the virtual team to establish clear guidelines for how, and with whom, information will be shared outside the team. On the other hand, a virtual team that can creatively manage its permeability has greater opportunities for keeping the rest of the organization apprised of its efforts and can markedly strengthen its market position within its organization.

Diverse Makeup of Teams

As a rule, virtual teams tend to be far more heterogeneous than their intact counterparts. The reasons are readily apparent. Location, time zones, and even organizational identity aren't the primary selection criteria for virtual teams that they are for intact teams. Virtual teams draw from the widest possible pool of talent within the company. In addition, cross-functional virtual teams frequently extend membership to individuals who are external to their organization, such as suppliers, consultants, and customers. The diversity quotient increases even more when we consider the makeup of international virtual teams, whose members are likely to have different cultural values and languages.

The Treatment

There's no great secret to performing effectively as a virtual team leader. It all rests on taking certain steps to adapt your communication and planning processes to the unique challenges encountered by virtual teams. Here are some suggestions for making these adaptations.

Select Effective Self-Managers

Despite all the skills and experiences you can bring to your role as a team leader, a virtual team has little chance of success if its members can't effectively self-manage their performance. The Selection Matrix, Tool #12 in your Tool Kit, will be helpful in evaluating the suitability of candidates for virtual teams.

Conduct Preliminary Discussions with Members' Managers

If you're leading a cross-functional virtual team whose members report to their own functional managers, you face a unique set of challenges. Since a virtual team requires a different style of leadership and membership and places more responsibility on team members to self-manage their activities, it's important get the full support of your members' managers. Your virtual team will seldom have opportunities for face-to-face meetings, so managers must agree to allow team members to attend all face-to-face meetings as well as phone and videoconferences. Discuss these issues early on in your team's start-up process.

Much of the work undertaken by a virtual team is electronically generated and may be hidden from the view of others in your organization. As a result, it's difficult for managers to identify what percentage of their direct reports' time is being invested in your project. Agree on a method for keeping managers posted on the estimated time required of members and for immediately notifying managers of any drastic changes in these commitments.

Explore Problems in Communication as Soon as Possible

Don't wait until your team is experiencing severe communication breakdowns to explore potential obstacles to team success. As soon as possible, encourage your team members to provide input on the following key issues:

- What communication avenues would work best for you as a team member? What unique restrictions do you face? (For example, some telecommuting members may not have access to portable printers or faxes.)

- When could you make yourself available during the next few weeks for regularly scheduled e-mail or phone discussions?

- Take the view of a troubleshooter for our team and identify some of the potential obstacles and challenges we face as we attempt to work together as a virtual team. What are your suggestions for dealing with these obstacles and challenges?

Chart 8 provides a checklist that will guide you and your team members as you explore those specialized issues that pertain to telecommuting arrangements. Chart 11 in your Tool Kit (page 93) details communication options that may meet the requirements of your team.

Develop Ground Rules for Individual Accountability

Sit down with your team and generate a list of useful ground rules for keeping project activities on track when members are widely dispersed. Suggested ground rules may include

- No team member should change milestone dates without first consulting the team leader.

CHART 8

Telecommuting Questions for Team Members and Leaders

1. Which aspects of my work can I accomplish through telecommuting? Which aspects of my work must be performed on-site?

2. Under our telecommuting agreement, will I maintain my job title, employee status, pay grade, insurance benefits, and other compensation? Or will I suddenly find I've become a contract worker?

3. Which of the following costs will my company cover? Which costs will I be expected to cover myself?

   • Lease or purchase my home office equipment and materials (computer system, fax/modem, answering machine, printer, scanner, copy machine, ergonomic furniture, and supplies)

   • Additional space required for home office operation and storage

   • Installation of dedicated phone line(s) for data and business calls

   • Monthly charges for phone or Internet service

   • Insurance for theft or damage to office equipment or job-related accidents while at home

   • Utility costs for operating computers, printers, and other equipment at home

4. What guidelines can we establish regarding my availability to the office (for example, reasons for contacting me in the evenings and on weekends)?

5. For what types of emergencies should we plan? Will our arrangement enable you or my coworkers to directly access my computer files if I'm unavailable?

6. How often should I visit the office? What is the best way to stay informed on organizational meetings and events that I should attend?

7. Will telecommuting keep me from attending in-house training programs?

8. How often and by what means should we jointly review my performance? What would be the best method for remote evaluation of my work?

9. At what point can we perform a joint review of this arrangement to see if it meets both our needs? If I feel that the arrangement isn't working, do I have the option of returning to the office?

- The team will always assume that members are on target with their project activities unless they contact the team leader to report delays or obstacles.

- Team members agree to take certain steps to inform one another of outside changes that could affect the operation of their team. Detail the steps.

- Address the challenge of team permeability by deciding which team members will be responsible for keeping executive stakeholders updated on the team's activities. How will this be done? How will your team be informed of feedback from these sponsors and stakeholders?

- Specify the kinds of organizational information and on-line systems your team members require. Explain why.

- If your team is scattered over many time zones, what meeting times would best accommodate the varied work schedules of team members?

- No "hit-and-runs." A hit-and-run is an e-mail message, usually sent after hours or on weekends, informing the project leader that a certain team activity will not be completed. People who hit and run assume they've fulfilled their team responsibility once they've sent the e-mail message and dropped their problem into someone else's lap.

Identify Points of Vulnerability

Help your team identify which team activities and project milestones, given the virtual nature of your project, are most prone to slippage and will therefore require the closest attention. These include project activities with some of the following characteristics:

- They are located along the "critical path" of major project plans, and delays or errors could hamper the completion of all downstream activities.

- They require precise coordination from all team members and are most vulnerable to miscommunications.

- They are highly variable and susceptible to any large-scale changes that could ripple through your organization.

For example, assume that your IT department is frantically trying to keep pace with an extensive project backlog while your project requires the creation of a customized software program. In this case, a potential point of vulnerability is the scheduling delay you might encounter if the IT group decides to downgrade your project's importance on its priority list.

Plan Ahead for Contingencies

Once you've identified points of vulnerability, your team should discuss strategies for addressing potential obstacles or delays. It's particularly important for a virtual team to determine the degree of initiative and personal accountability allowed for each member who wishes to individually resolve problems or revise schedules. The tools and techniques introduced in Chapter 9 can help team members troubleshoot their plans and decisions and identify options for dealing with possible difficulties.

Coordinate Milestones and Activities with Project Software

This is especially important when you're working on a project that involves high cost, diverse resources, and a time period of several weeks or months. Although there are many good software tools on the market, I'm particularly fond of Microsoft® Project. This program allows you to link related tasks so that team members can understand how delays at one point of activity will affect the entire project. It also allows you to assign team members and resource support people to projects. Furthermore, by loading the hourly pay rate of team members into the project spreadsheet, you will be able to determine the total staffing cost for a given project. You can also quickly determine when a given staff member is approaching 100 percent allocation to a given project. In addition, the software enables your team to link the activities of several different projects, allowing you to identify such problems as scheduling conflicts when the same individual has been assigned to two or more activities for a single time period.

Establish Guidelines That Encourage Communication

A few minutes of team brainstorming can usually help you compile a list of solid guidelines for fostering good team communication. Some of the following suggestions have been useful to me.

When faxing information, take the time to send out originals instead of photocopies, and keep the type size large enough for readability. This is especially important when conveying financial or other numerical data, since blurry faxes can lead to transposition errors. Also, be sure to date and number the revisions of all documents (reports, project schedules, etc.) transmitted back and forth electronically for repeated review. Otherwise, some team members may reference outdated copies.

When communicating at a distance, provide a context for sharing the information. If an extended silence occurs during a phone discussion, explain that you don't know how to interpret the team's reactions and you need their feedback. Since you may not be able to see who enters and leaves a room during a phone conference, ask members to be courteous enough to announce when they are joining or exiting a phone conference. Members should also be asked to identify any nonparticipants who are sitting in on the conference.

Always spell out the type of response you expect in your communications. Never assume recipients of your messages automatically know what to do with the information you're sending them. Is the e-mail to be read only, or are you looking for an answer to a specific question? Make your intentions known.

Whenever possible, consolidate communications. I often receive more than fifty e-mail messages within a twenty-four-hour period, many of which are follow-up messages from senders who have added thoughts or ideas to their original messages throughout the day. I find that since I respond to e-mails as I get them, my response to the first message will often later be pre-empted by the sender's subsequent messages. To eliminate this problem, ask team members to save up their comments for substantial e-mail or voice-mail messages, which they can send out to the team in consolidated "chunks."

Highlight the major points. Many e-mail systems offer color and bold print to highlight key information in your message. I use this feature to allow my recipients to skim through my messages and pick up the main points. Another option is to send out a very brief one- or two-sentence summary of any documents sent via e-mail and then include additional details as attachments.

If a team member becomes very upset during a phone or videoconference, or two team members begin to enter into a conflict, suggest that they continue these discussions with you off-line, after the conference is over. It's far easier to resolve such issues if they are not being aired in an electronic fishbowl.

Develop a Core Team Identity

A virtual team that is too permeable—too open to input from and inclusion of non–team members—may find that its identity as a team has been weakened.

CHART 9

Distinguishing Between Core and Supplemental Team Members	
Core Team Members	**Supplemental Team Members**
• Invest 20 to 50 percent of their time on the team's activities	• Invest much less time on the team's activities
• Have decision-making authority with respect to developing and changing the project plan and deliverables	• Have no decision-making authority
• Are committed to the project throughout its life cycle	• Are brought into the project from time to time to provide technical assistance or guidance
• Attend most or all team meetings	• Attend only those meetings, e-mail discussions, etc., for which they are needed to provide technical assistance
• Have final accountability for project results	• Perform a support role in the team, with little or no accountability for project results

This problem is more severe when the virtual team is cross-functional in nature. To remedy this situation, I often suggest virtual, cross-functional teams designate a core team that remains committed to the team throughout its life cycle, with support members (usually technical and knowledge experts) flowing through as required. Chart 9 outlines guidelines for distinguishing between core and supplemental members.

Use the Full Range of Electronic Tools Available

Many team leaders never utilize all the electronic tools at their disposal. Consider pursuing some of the following options:

- Create a group mail listing in your company's e-mail system so you can distribute a single e-mail message quickly to all team members.

- Become acquainted with the relevant features of your company's voice-mail system, such as the ability to distribute messages to multiple addresses.

- Many e-mail systems feature an electronic prompt that automatically notifies team members of key dates, for example, meetings and executive briefings.

- Make use of your company's electronic calendar system. Team members should have their calendars on this system to expedite the scheduling of meetings and events.

- Many videoconference centers now offer electronic whiteboards that display written information at both the sending and the receiving video sites.

Develop Electronic Facilitation Skills

Traditional facilitation skills must be applied to electronic meetings when you're leading a virtual team.

When conducting phone conferences, it's important to take the lead in facilitating discussions. This includes keeping track of time, helping participants maintain their focus during discussions, and acting as a monitor to prevent verbal collisions when team members try to talk at the same time. In addition, some participants may be overly assertive and verbose during phone conferences. Since the visual feedback that normally serves as a stop sign during face-to-face meetings will be missing in these situations, you must be able to rein them in and at the same time draw out quieter team members who may be reluctant to speak up.

Keep in mind that others in an electronic meeting may not be able to see the document you are referencing and that you could easily refer to several documents during discussions. Avoid confusion by identifying each document by its correct title, and provide page numbers if necessary.

If you're leading a cross-functional team, its members probably represent different technical groups, functions, and even organizations. If this is the case, avoid or clearly define all specialized jargon and acronyms. If your team makes extensive use of such terms, consider creating and maintaining a jargon dictionary for team review.

Make Optimum Use of Each Communication Avenue

Team leaders who are accustomed to directing intact teams have a difficult time weaning themselves from the face-to-face team meeting. When working with such leaders, I often find that they respond to every new project roadblock by scheduling another meeting. I recommend you substitute e-mail, faxes, or individual phone contacts whenever you need to do the following:

- Assess the status of tasks performed by individual team members

- Pass along team documents, research, or status reports for input from the team

- Obtain initial input project deliverables

- Assign tasks to individual team members

- Clarify technical issues that pertain only to isolated team members

- Provide background data to accelerate your team's thinking about project obstacles or problems

Managing the above types of tasks with alternative forms of communication enables you to utilize your scarce face-to-face meeting time for the following:

- Develop your team's game plan for completing key objectives

- Resolve critical team management issues, obstacles, and problems

- Recalibrate and make midcourse corrections to team plans

- Assess the impact of any large-scale changes that have occurred since your last team meeting

Aggressive use of all available electronic media can jump-start your team meeting process.

Create Graphic Models to Keep Your Team on Track

Whenever possible, illustrate your team's activities through graphic models, such as cartoons, scanning photos of product features, icon-driven project summaries, idea diagrams, or performance tracking. These methods enable team members to visualize and evaluate their progress within selected team performance areas.

Put a Human Face on Your Team

Look for creative ways to compensate for the lack of rapport and support that is readily available to intact teams. Here are a few suggestions for building team spirit.

If you're leading a temporary, cross-functional team, create a name for the team and ask members to consistently use this name in every team communication and document.

Invite team members to submit ideas for new team projects or success stories that could become interesting features in your company's corporate (hard copy or electronic) newsletter. Ask them to include photos and mini-bios for their articles. These actions may help familiarize other departments and senior managers in your organization with members of your team who are working in locations far from your corporate site.

Utilize every opportunity for communication and interaction. For example, while waiting for all members to come online during phone or videoconferences, use the dead time to make small talk with team members and discuss new developments in your department or company. Call periodically to check in with each team member to solicit ideas or find out about any problems or concerns. If possible, work visits with team members into your travel plans when you visit other company locations. On those occasions when you're able to meet together as a group, include some social activity, such as a team dinner or breakfast. Be alert for team members who seem to be withdrawing from team communications or appear increasingly unmotivated.

Each time your team overcomes a project obstacle or meets or beats the date for delivery of a project milestone, send out a congratulatory e-mail message to team members and carbon copy your senior manager. Use color and interesting fonts to liven up your message.

When team members are about to tackle extremely challenging or tedious tasks, consider using a buddy system. Pair members with other members or with outside support personnel who are located at their work sites. Even if they don't require any technical assistance, people usually find it helpful to have someone with whom to discuss ideas and other project issues. An electronic alternative, if available, is to create a team discussion database via a communication system like Lotus® Notes® or the Internet that enables team members to provide input and sustain dialogue with the entire team, regardless of each individual's location. The database can serve as a team memory that preserves the history and continuity of your project.

Another great opportunity for enhancing team spirit is to invite your manager, or selected senior managers, to sit in on team meetings. The members of your team will appreciate your extra efforts to make them visible to your executive team.

Learn from the Experience of Others

Accelerate your learning process by trying to identify the managers in your organization who have developed strong reputations as excellent virtual-project leaders. Don't hesitate to approach them for ideas and suggestions on how to overcome the barriers you've identified for your own team. In

addition, consider participating in a public seminar on how to lead distributed work teams. The American Management Association (212-586-8100)
offers several seminars on this topic. Finally, for additional information on
the subject of virtual teams, I'd like to recommend *Virtual Teams: Reaching
across Space, Time, and Organizations with Technology* by Jessica Linack and
Jeffrey Stamps (John Wiley and Sons, 1997).

Related Problems

The following chapters contain additional details about related problems
experienced by virtual teams.

Chapter 6 (The Team Divided: The Problem of Intra-Team Conflict)—
The virtual team is especially vulnerable to conflict because of the unique
stresses and demands it experiences. If you observe that your team members
have become involved in conflicts, you'll want to review this chapter.

Chapter 8 (The King Dethroned: Solving Member-Leader Conflict)—
Team leaders play a pivotal role in helping distributed teams overcome communication obstacles and coordination challenges. They provide a strong
bonding element for teams that are fragmented by space and time. If you
find that you have begun to experience problems in your relationship with
your team, you'll need to address this issue before the members of your virtual team will be able to work together successfully.

Chapter 12 (The Brittle Team: Learning to Adapt to Change)—It stands
to reason that a virtual team may find it more difficult to develop coordinated
strategies for responding to unanticipated and demanding changes, such as a
revision of the team's charter or a structural reorganization. This chapter
details techniques that can help you and your team adapt to change.

Tool Kit

SELECTION MATRIX FOR VIRTUAL TEAM MEMBERS

Virtual teams are a unique entity, and successful members of these teams possess certain competencies and personal qualities. The selection matrix shown in Chart 10 is an effective method for selecting members for your virtual team.

Take the following steps to complete this procedure:

1. Begin the discussion by reviewing the member selection criteria shown in Chart 10.

2. Next, ask your team to contribute additional qualities, if any, that they feel are important criteria for success.

3. When your team has completed its list, ask members to rate the relative importance of each selection criterion on a 1–5 scale (with 5 as the highest score). Place the team's averaged rating for each criterion in the Value column.

4. Assess each candidate with the same rating process. Spaces have been provided for four candidates (Candidates A–D).

5. Multiply Value scores by Candidate's Ratings scores for each criterion to calculate the total score for each candidate.

CHART 10

Selection Matrix for Virtual Team Members					
		CANDIDATE'S RATINGS			
Selection Criteria	**Value**	**A**	**B**	**C**	**D**
Evidence of self-management skills; ability to follow through on assignments without repeated prodding, to manage own schedule, to be consistently on time for phone, e-mail, or videoconferences, etc.					
Excellent communication skills; has the ability to present information clearly or to probe for understanding when communicating electronically					

Tool Kit

Selection Matrix for Virtual Team Members *continued*		CANDIDATE'S RATINGS			
Selection Criteria	**Value**	**A**	**B**	**C**	**D**
Experience in working as part of a virtual team, or (as a minimum requirement) experience in working with a team that was distributed across several work sites					
Experience with telecommuting or working from home, with limited contact with a field site or corporate office					
Ability to send and receive e-mail from remote locations					
Ability to prepare electronic attachments for e-mail					
Experience with the following database program: (specify)					
Ability to access the company's rental ledger, financial accounting systems, or proprietary database programs: (specify)					
Ability to operate key software programs (e.g., Microsoft® Word, PowerPoint®, Visio®, Project)					
Experience in working with groupware applications (for example, Lotus® Notes®)					
Experience with an extended international assignment					

ALTERNATIVE COMMUNICATION OPTIONS

If you're leading a virtual team, you're probably struggling with the challenge of finding the most effective means of communicating within your team. Chart 11 reviews the advantages and disadvantages of four communications methods: e-mail, phone conferences, videoconferences, and face-to-face meetings.

Tool #13

CHART 11

Checklist for Alternative Communication Options				
	E-Mails	**Phone Conferences**	**Video-conferences**	**Physical Meetings**
Advantages	Fast Saves time with on-line editing Provides an audit trail or team record Supports asynchronous communications	More personalized than e-mail Easier to administer than video Easy access for all team members while on the road	Most personalized electronic communication option Simultaneous review of video and text Provides a stronger team experience than phone or e-mail	Strongest option for team building Full context (opportunity to read between the lines and interpret visual clues) Less fatiguing than phone, video, or e-mail
Disadvantages	Impersonal Absence of contextual clues may lead to flaming or censoring of message Some systems have no option for e-mail conferences	More difficult to facilitate than videoconferences (cross-talking) Fatigue factor sets in after 60–90 minutes Greater chance for communication breakdowns for team members who don't speak English as primary language	Rental systems often three times the cost of phone conferences Irritating lag time between sending and receipt of message More difficult to administer (do all members have access to system?)	Low-status team members can be intimidated by high-status members (studies show this occurs less in e-mail communications) Major time and cost factors for setup and delivery Unfeasible for teams separated by large distances

Tool Kit

To apply this tool, complete the following steps:

1. Send this document to your team to review before your discussion.

2. Ask team members to identify the advantages or disadvantages on this checklist that are especially important to them.

3. Invite members to note additional communication concerns or problems that are not mentioned in this list.

4. Use team members' feedback to determine which communication approach would work best to maintain communication within your own team.

8

The King Dethroned

Solving Member-Leader Conflict

If I had to single out one factor that makes the difference between successful and unsuccessful teams, I would probably choose the relationship between team members and their leaders. Productive member-leader relationships can be characterized by four words: trust, external focus, balance, and adaptability. Let me briefly describe the role of each characteristic in the development of strong member-leader relationships.

Within effective teams, members trust the direction provided by their leaders. They believe their leaders act in their best interests and communicate honestly and openly on important issues. Leaders are viewed as people who consistently carry out promises and follow up on concerns. For their part, leaders trust their team members to alert them to problems and openly share their concerns. Another part of trust is that members and leaders feel they can count on each other for help and support. They believe that both parties in the relationship are giving their best efforts to the team.

With a relationship based on trust, leaders don't have to tie up large amounts of time and energy policing team activities. They limit their direction and guidance to situations in which members are attempting to tackle difficult technical or business problems, and they look for ways to encourage members to take independent action. Members, in turn, are able to avoid energy-wasting conflicts with their leaders. Because such teams have developed strong member-leader relationships, they are able to focus their time and energy outside the structure of their work groups, to identify ways of improving their performance with customers, suppliers, and other parts of the organization.

Effective teams establish a solid balance between, on one side, personal accountability and the freedom exercised by team members and, on the other, the degree of direction, control, and coaching provided by team leaders. There's no single, correct formula at work here. Within the most effective teams, control shifts continually back and forth between leaders and members in response to changes in work demands or the composition of their membership. These shifts are not a tug-of-war but are orchestrated smoothly by the whole team.

When member-leader relationships are solid, both parties are willing to adapt these relationships to meet changing needs. Leaders vary their leadership styles to suit work conditions. They recognize that within rapidly changing work environments, member-leader relationships must be constantly redefined and examined, and they are open to ways in which they can strengthen this relationship to improve team performance. For their part, members know that certain time-critical situations demand they take risks and act without clear guidance from their leaders, while other situations may require them to rely on their leaders for direction.

In coaching and facilitating a variety of teams over the past twenty years, I've frequently encountered situations in which teams were very reluctant to tackle the issue of poor member-leader relationships. This is especially true when interactions between team members and their leaders are friendly and personal. After all, if everyone on the team gets along well, how can the team have a relationship problem? To answer this question, you must first understand that the issue of member-leader relationships extends well beyond the personal relationships that exist between team members and their leader to include such issues as

- How to effectively balance member autonomy with leader control

- How members and their leaders can improve two-way communication

- How to balance the need for fast, streamlined decision making with the desire to achieve team consensus on important issues

In fact, member-leader relationships can be a significant concern for even the nicest of team leaders, due to the dynamic nature of today's work teams. In the space of a few weeks, a team may encounter any of the following situations:

- Experienced members leave, to be replaced by inexperienced new hires

- Team members are assigned new and demanding work responsibilities by their senior executives

- A recent budget revision leaves the team strapped for resources

- A corporate restructuring creates a completely different set of reporting relationships

- Team members who worked on-site become telecommuters, leaving little time for face-to-face interactions with their leaders

In short, a number of events may abruptly change the nature of the team's job demands. These changes, in turn, require leaders to look for ways to strengthen and fortify their relationships with team members.

The Symptoms

Take some time to examine your team's member-leader interactions. The following symptoms may indicate that you and your team are experiencing or may be heading for conflict in your relationship.

Team Leader Practices Micromanagement

Micromanagement is a common symptom of poor member-leader relationships. A leader who engages in micromanagement treats highly experienced and skilled professionals as if they were novices, double- or triple-checks work, or places rigid and excessive restraints on the decision-making authority of team members. To someone looking at the team from the outside, it would appear that all decisions and information are being channeled through a very narrow managerial portal. As the team leader frantically attempts to maintain tight control over an ever increasing array of projects and problems, work efforts slow down significantly.

Communication Problems

Troubled member-leader relationships are sometimes characterized by the completely opposite condition, when team leaders provide insufficient direction to their teams. Team members may receive vague or ambiguous instructions on projects. They may also discover that the team leader has failed to relay instructions or provide an overall context that enables them to understand the larger work issues involved. For their part, team members may not keep their leader informed of emerging problems and may even conceal mistakes and fail to disclose difficult situations. Eventually, these small failures in communication may result in unpleasant surprises for both the team's leader and its members.

There may be a high level of tension in the few, limited communications that do take place between team members and their leader. Team members may be defensive, guarded, and hesitant about sharing their concerns, while the team leader appears confrontational and demanding. Under these conditions, conversations are likely to be stilted and cautious, not a free-flowing exchange of ideas.

Team Stress Level Rises

Because team members depend on their leader for feedback, coaching, guidance, and recognition, deteriorating member-leader relationships produce a high level of stress. A tense and hostile relationship between team members and their leader may cause some members to view the leader's office as enemy territory. In addition, the team leader plays an important role in guiding members through times of volatile organizational change. Members who lack strong bonds with their leader are less prepared to deal with such change and will regard it as a stressful, unmanageable experience.

In time, team members will begin to display all the classic symptoms of work burnout, such as low energy level and the inability to concentrate on complicated tasks. When conversing with other work groups, they may appear tense and curt. A concurrent symptom is a rise in absenteeism among team members, which is usually characterized by frequent one- or two-day absences.

Lack of Trust Within the Team

Team members and their leaders may experience increased levels of mistrust. When this happens, team members will respond to their team leader's suggestions or explanations of altered requirements with a great deal of skepticism and suspicion, while their leader may be dissatisfied with the team's justifications of poor performance or missed milestones. Both parties will covertly probe behind the other's defenses to try to find out the real story. As time goes on, team members and their leader may respond to the deteriorating situation by curtailing all communication.

At this point, team members may begin to circumvent the team leader and turn to experienced coworkers or senior-level mentors for information and guidance. In the worst-case scenario, members will formally complain about their leader to senior executives or HR departments.

"Us Versus You" Syndrome

Eventually, when the relationship is on its final legs, team members and their leader separate into opposing camps. In discussions with other work groups, both sides will complain to their respective peers about the difficulties they're experiencing with the other party.

In some cases, team members begin to view their leader as no longer part of the team. When the team leader walks into a room, informal conversations will cease or become very guarded. Team members may even make a covert pact with one another to keep their team leader out of discussions involving performance problems or work issues.

Personnel Problems Increase

When the lines of communication between team members and leaders are strained or completely severed, team members may feel they have no choice but to bring their complaints to senior-level managers or the HR department, while team leaders may feel that the best way to fix broken relationships is to get rid of a few key troublemakers. Either of these two responses creates innumerable personnel problems, and the group's overall reputation can be badly damaged. If the situation becomes unbearable, valued players, including the team leader, may decide to leave the team. In addition, the team may acquire such a negative reputation that job candidates won't be willing to join it.

Case in Point: The Service Repair Team

Three years ago, Jeff was hired by his company's vice president of customer support to lead the department's service repair team. At the time, the vice president asked Jeff to provide "firm direction and order" because several team members were relatively inexperienced and the company was in the process of introducing major changes to its customer service operations. Jeff performed very effectively within this position by establishing firm technical direction and clear performance standards. As team members strengthened their technical skills, their performance quickly improved. Last year, the team's bench strength was further enhanced through a reorganization that added several highly experienced members to the group.

Unfortunately, although the team's skill base had become quite strong, Jeff's leadership style remained largely unchanged. He continued to exercise the same degree of control and direction he had used three years before. His directive leadership style was particularly irritating to experienced team members who had transferred in from other teams and were used to working with less guidance and direction. In addition, during the past year, the team had grown from six members to twenty-three and the number of customers serviced by the team had almost doubled. Jeff's standard practice of making daily visits to each site to direct repair teams was creating operational bottlenecks and contributing to a lack of overall coordination of the group's work.

Not too long ago, one team member summed up the situation this way: "Jeff just can't continue to manage our team the same way he did in the beginning." Although many team members had offered suggestions for improving the scheduling and management of their team's workload, they didn't feel Jeff was receptive to their ideas. The team wanted to discuss this problem with Jeff but were hesitant about voicing their concerns. They knew, however, that sooner or later someone would have to broach the topic.

The Underlying Causes

Deterioration in member-leader relationships occurs over time and for a variety of reasons. Examine the situation within your own team to determine if any of the following conditions apply.

Inappropriate Leadership Styles

Each organization has a characteristic culture, which is created out of the norms of behavior that define a valued associate or a skillful leader.

Some workplaces expect their leaders to be aggressive and willing to apply a bulldog's determination toward achieving business objectives. Other organizations place a much higher value on the ability of leaders and associates to build long-term work relationships with customers and other groups. In this latter type of organization, leaders who meet objectives by damaging relationships are seldom tolerated.

Certain work environments are characterized by a high degree of energy; their employees approach their jobs with fanatical zeal and think nothing of working evenings or weekends. In such organizations, the line between personal and work spaces is blurred. Team members and leaders routinely send or receive e-mail messages or cell phone calls at home, and those who place family or personal needs above work requirements are viewed as disloyal. Other companies pride themselves on balancing work and family life. Their associates think nothing of asking managers to make work accommodations that will allow them to take care of personal or family business.

Many companies' environments are extremely formal. A business suit is the uniform of the day, and communications are formal. In such companies, associates wouldn't think of dropping in to speak informally with senior managers. Fancy Microsoft® PowerPoint® presentations are delivered at briefings, and staff meetings are heavily laced with protocol. Other companies are characterized by casual business attire, informal communications, and discussions on a first-name basis at all levels.

It's easy to see that different leadership styles are suited to different work environments and cultures. The team leader who comes from a very directive, task-focused, "climb up the walls with bare knuckles to get the job done" work environment is likely to run into a lot of resistance if he or she is brought in to take over a team that is accustomed to a highly participative and relationship-based leadership style. One of the most common sources of member-leader conflict is a mismatch between the expectations of team members and leadership styles.

Limited Accessibility

Team members and leaders sometimes have difficulty developing strong relationships because each side simply lacks ready access to the other. They may be separated by geography, work shifts, or heavy travel schedules that make face-to-face meetings impossible. In addition, team leaders may be spread too thin, expected to exert overwhelming amounts of control, or so busy addressing problems at higher levels in the organization that they have very little time to spare for their team members.

Personal Conflicts

Occasionally member-leader relationships may be seriously eroded as a result of long-term personal conflicts between certain team members and their leader. These team members may attempt to enlist the support and sympathy of coworkers or may stage covert actions designed to hamstring the team leader. The real problem here is not that personal conflicts exist within the team, since all teams are subject to occasional conflict. The underlying concern is that this kind of one-on-one conflict may become a staging ground for a series of broader battles that can seriously weaken or destroy a team.

Lack of Alignment within the Team

Sometimes, team members are not aligned with their leaders regarding the value or feasibility of business objectives, the relative priorities that should be placed on competing projects, or the performance expectations used for member evaluations.

For example, I know of one international sales and marketing firm that demonstrated a very good customer growth rate for several years. Unfortunately, to secure their contracts, sales representatives often committed the company to service agreements that were extremely unprofitable and difficult to implement. A new manager was brought on board to redirect the team's activities. This leader tried to convince her team to make dramatic changes to the terms and conditions in the customer agreements. At each stage of the process, this leader met with an enormous amount of resistance from her staff. Eventually, she won over her team, but not before she was forced to terminate two team members who had steadfastly dug in their heels and refused to change their sales approach.

Inappropriate Level of Control

Leaders feel pressured to maintain control of team decisions and to ensure that members approach their work in a structured and orderly fashion. Team members who are new to a team or who are relatively inexperienced in a particular work function may welcome a high degree of close-quarters coaching. As they gain experience, these same individuals will want to have more say in their team's operations and depend less on their leader for day-to-day direction. It is vital to a team's success that its leader knows how to exercise an appropriate level of control.

If leaders exert excessive control, members can't exercise their full range of skills and will feel dominated and restricted. At the same time, leaders waste time and inhibit team initiative by overmanaging jobs. However, if leaders offer insufficient direction, new and inexperienced members may not receive the feedback and coaching they need to strengthen key work skills; at the same time, experienced members will be unable to follow standard work methods or meet team performance standards. In both cases, poor work coordination will most likely result in errors.

The Treatment

Members and leaders must be able to agree on a leadership process that encourages members to exercise their own judgment while ensuring adherence to set guidelines and attainment of team goals. Some of the following suggestions may be helpful as you develop your own system.

Recognize the Needs of Team Members and Leaders

Leaders and members are sometimes reluctant to ask each other for support and assistance. For example, some leaders regard it as a sign of weakness to ask their teams for technical advice or assistance, even when team members have the specialized skills their leaders lack. Likewise, team members sometimes incorrectly assume that their leaders are unwilling to share information about matters such as impending large-scale changes in the organizational structure or customer relationships.

In today's rapidly changing work environment, the members and leaders of high-performing teams recognize the importance of continually redefining the types of support and assistance they need from each other. For example, the issue of mutual support and assistance becomes especially relevant whenever the following situations occur:

- New, inexperienced members join the team

- The team takes on difficult work projects

- Some members leave and their work must be redistributed among the rest of the team

- The team expands its charter to include additional work functions

- Team members are required to master new skills, equipment, or work procedures

- The company undergoes reorganization

On the other hand, team members and leaders gradually require less support and assistance from each other under the following conditions:

- The team contains a greater proportion of skilled members

- The team builds support networks within the organization

- Work procedures become familiar

- Maturity and knowledge develop over time

Teams are dynamic structures, and team leaders and members must reevaluate their support needs periodically to meet changing organizational and business conditions.

Secure Mutual Support

Once you and your team understand the value of offering mutual support and assistance, you may want to use the following four-step process as a guideline:

1. Identify support needs

2. Explore ways to provide support

3. Select support options

4. Develop a support action plan

Identify Support Needs

This first step involves specifying the types of support and assistance you and your team members are seeking. In doing so, it's important to avoid vague language. A team leader who says, "You need to be more proactive," doesn't really communicate a lot to the team. Likewise, the team member who tells her leader, "You need to give us more autonomy," may feel she's clearly expressing a need, when, in fact, she's forcing her leader to try to interpret an ambiguously worded concern.

Tools #14 and #15 (Needs Checklist for Team Members and Needs Checklist for Team Leaders) in the Tool Kit section can help you and your team establish an effective, open dialogue on this issue.

Explore Ways to Provide Support

Your team may run into obstacles that make it difficult for you or your team members to provide the requested support. For example, suppose your team depends heavily on a certain software program, but only one team member has been trained in its use. What if this person were having more and more difficulty in keeping up with the team's needs for the use of this software? In that case, members of your team might identify "training in the XYZ software system" as an area in which they could use additional support from you, their team leader. You, however, are aware that your team is currently putting in a lot of overtime, which means it wouldn't be a good idea to release everyone to attend a formal training class. In addition, your team has little money left in its budget for training.

To overcome these kinds of roadblocks, you must be prepared to work with your team to explore ways of providing mutual support. Thus, a brainstorming session by our hypothetical team could yield the following solutions:

- Select only one team member to attend an off-site training class

- Find out if inexpensive training classes are available through local community colleges or trade schools

- See if additional funds are available through the company's tuition reimbursement program

- Ask for one-on-one or small-group coaching assistance from the IT department or from employees in other departments who have already been trained on this software

- Explore the possibility of having the skilled team member informally train/coach a few other individuals while working with the software package

- See if the team can purchase a self-directed CD-ROM or Web-based training package that can be used on the employees' own time

As you've been reading, you may have identified very different options that would enable this team to meet its training needs. With careful consideration, it's quite possible to come up with creative ways of providing support while working within your team's scheduling and cost limitations. During your team discussion, take the time to fully explore options for eliminating obstacles to mutual support.

Select Support Options

In this step, your team reviews alternative support options and selects those that best meet its needs.

Develop a Support Action Plan

At this point, your team may be tempted to terminate its discussion. I strongly advise against this, for the only thing you've accomplished so far is to arrive at a list of possible actions that could provide the requested support and assistance. Without some solid planning, these actions may never be implemented.

Tool #16 in your Tool Kit, the Team Support Chart, can help expedite this planning process.

Resolve Personal Conflicts

If you're having serious personal conflicts with a few key team members, other members of your team may easily find themselves caught up in these battles. Therefore, it's very important to resolve personal conflicts as quickly as possible to prevent them from expanding and drawing in neutral team members. You may find it useful to review the conflict-resolution techniques outlined in Chapter 6.

Identify Communication Hot Spots

Every team has a few areas of special concern that can severely damage member-leader relationships if left unaddressed. Examples include

- How choice assignments are assigned to team members

- How work is allocated among team members

- How team budgets and resources are distributed

- How members represent your team to other work groups or customers

- How commitments are made to senior managers

Invite team members to help you identify hot spots within your team that require special attention.

Obtain Feedback on Your Leadership Style

We all like to think we're relatively objective and have a realistic idea of how we appear to others. In truth, there are several reasons why it may be very difficult for you to get an accurate read on your leadership style.

First, we're often so engrossed in resolving technical and business problems that it's difficult to detach ourselves from the situation and clinically observe our behavior. In addition, we humans are not so much rational creatures as we are rationalizing creatures; in other words, we can always be counted upon to come with a good excuse for our own behavior. If we're creating problems for other people on our teams, we may find it difficult to honestly admit our role in initiating the conflict.

You should also keep in mind that most of the feedback you receive on your leadership style probably comes from a few dominant, vocal members of your team who may not truly represent the views of your entire team.

Finally, there is a phenomenon I refer to as "image lag." Speaking simply, this means that once we form a self-image, it is fairly impervious to change. Quite often, a person's self-image lags several months or years behind actual changes in appearance or behavior. When you look in the mirror, the person you see may not be the person you are today but the person you were a few months ago. A good friend of mine recently completed an intense workout and diet program that lasted six months. Still, when she stands in front of the mirror, she sees the same "overweight" person who's been looking back at her for the past several years. It will take a while for her new self-image to register.

For these reasons, you may want to try some of the following approaches to develop an accurate assessment of your leadership style.

Ask Team Members for Feedback

The easiest way to obtain the desired information is to let team members know you welcome their feedback. If this represents an unusual action on your part, don't be surprised when the first couple of invitations are either ignored or rejected. Team members may also respond by "throwing you a bone"—in other words, they may start off by providing you with innocuous and guarded feedback in order to test your reaction to their input. If you feel that team members are reluctant to provide critical feedback on your leadership style, consider asking a peer in another work team (someone who has closely observed your interactions with your team) to give you feedback on how you come across to your team.

Participate in a 360-Degree Review

One way to overcome your team members' reluctance to share feedback is to participate in a 360-degree review session in which you, team members, and coworkers provide structured feedback on many aspects of your leadership behavior. A typical 360-degree profile may involve a questionnaire that covers forty to sixty leadership behaviors. Each grouping of data (feedback provided by your team members, your manager, or peer-level leaders in your organization) is consolidated into a single report that displays averaged scores for all relevant areas. In many cases, this data is collected and brought back to you by a trained coach, who can help you interpret your scores, target leadership strengths and development needs, and suggest options for improving your leadership style.

For information on more extensive 360-degree profiles, I recommend contacting one of these two consulting groups, both of which have extensive experience in developing 360-degree profiles: Lominger Limited, Inc. (612-544-0573), or the Center for Creative Leadership (336-288-7210).

You may want to begin with Exercise 8 in your Tool Kit, a simple questionnaire that will help you gather basic feedback from your team and coworkers.

Learn to Leverage Your Leadership Style

Once you've obtained feedback on your leadership style, consider how to leverage that style to your team's benefit. One of the most solid tenets of leadership theory is the concept of situational leadership, which is based on the idea that the effectiveness of a given leadership style varies according to the type of work situation in which that style is applied. As illustrated in this chapter's Case in Point, a very controlling and directive leadership style might be necessary for a team leader who must make rapid changes in team performance while leading a very inexperienced team. On the other hand, this same leadership style would prove stifling to an experienced team.

Since leadership style is often learned over the course of several years, it can be very difficult to change. Accordingly, leveraging your style doesn't mean completely changing your interpersonal approach, but rather making some behavioral modifications to enhance its effectiveness with your team. For example, if your team feels you're too cold and aloof, that doesn't mean you must immediately transform yourself into a "warm and fuzzy" kind of person; instead, you could try to set aside some time each week during lunch or coffee breaks to engage team members in small talk. Likewise, if your team feels that you are too directive, you might try to determine the types of situations (such as coaching, directing inexperienced team members, or guiding your team during emergencies) in which this approach works for you, as well as those situations in which it is problematic.

Gain Alignment on Expectations with Team Members

Quite often, member-leader relationships begin to degrade because the team doesn't have a clear understanding of its leader's performance expectations. There are several reasons why such situations occur.

Your team may never have had the opportunity to sit down and openly discuss these expectations, or perhaps you, as the team leader, felt you only had time to provide a bare-bones sketch of an assignment or project but not enough to detail clearly what you expect with certain jobs. To compound the problem, leaders sometimes assume they have supplied their teams with complete information on projects or responsibilities because there are no questions from team members. "No questions" translates mistakenly into "no problems."

Alternatively, leaders may communicate their expectations but use very vague and misleading language. For example, requesting that a project be completed "as soon as possible" gives team members no idea of a firm completion date. At the same time, team members may use fuzzy language when confirming their understanding of their leader's expectations.

And finally, your expectations may have changed significantly over time as you attempt to meet the changing requirements of your customers or senior managers. It's possible you never passed this crucial information on to your team.

If any of these situations exist in your own team, it's important to find ways of helping your team to better understand your expectations. As a starting point for team discussion, team members should pinpoint the types of performance expectations on which they need additional clarification. Ask team members to complete the Leader Expectations Checklist, Exercise 9 in your Tool Kit. In addition, I recommend you look ahead and review the suggestions in Chapters 10 and 11.

Improve Team Members' Access to You

Team effectiveness suffers when team members and leaders lack ready access to each other. It's extremely ironic that the members and leaders of high-performing teams are usually so spread out on assignments that it's difficult for them to meet regularly. There are a number of actions you can take to improve this situation, such as:

- Request that your company provide a cellular phone or paging service for each member of your team

- Make sure all team members can reach one another during emergency situations at a special after-hours phone number

- Offer to meet with team members over breakfast, at lunch, or after work (I've found I'm able to keep my current manager's full attention by setting up early morning meetings at our neighborhood Starbucks)

- Use electronic calendars to confirm schedules

- Use e-mail distribution lists to maintain communications

You may also want to consult Chapter 7, which contains additional suggestions for meeting this challenge.

Balance Consensus with Direction

A common cause of member-leader conflict is the difficulty of finding the proper balance in decision-making authority. There's no rule book that can tell a team leader when to strive for team consensus, obtain limited team input, or impose a unilateral decision.

In general, most team members prefer work environments in which they're free to do the following:

- Fully utilize their skills

- Use their judgment and initiative in making decisions

- Control their work areas

- Clearly define, and act within, the limits of their authority

At the same time, leaders want to establish control systems that favor effective team performance. They're most interested in the following conditions:

- Standard procedures and work methods are followed

- The team supplies prompt and error-free work to customers

- Methods are in place to ensure timely tracking and follow-up on assignments

Here are five steps you can take to explore ways of balancing team decision making:

1. Identify areas for review

2. Describe and rate the desired changes

3. Develop change strategies

4. Select the best strategy

5. Set a time for follow-up

Identify Areas for Review

Begin by identifying work areas in which the lack of effective team decision making represents a major performance problem. Some possible areas for review are

- How much authority should team members have when making commitments to customers, resolving vendor problems, correcting problems that occur on jobs, or deciding when to deviate from accepted work methods?

- How involved do team members want to be in setting team goals, establishing team priorities, scheduling jobs, matching people to assignments, or identifying areas for improving team performance?

During the first part of your team review session, set aside time to identify those work areas that you would like to discuss with your own team.

Describe and Rate the Desired Changes

Next, discuss the types of changes your team would like to make to its decision-making process. Consider your own ideas as well as those of team members.

The Team Decision Style Chart, Exercise 7 in your Tool Kit, can be very helpful at this point (see Chart 14 on page 119 for an example of a completed chart). This chart gives team members the opportunity to compare, in terms of four alternative styles of team decision making, their current method of making team decisions and their ideal method of making decisions. Please note that team members may not concur on the degree of decision-making control required within certain key work areas. This is to be expected. One of the most important outcomes of this exercise is that team members are able to reach greater alignment on their involvement in team decision making. Use your Team Decision Style Chart to rate the relative importance of each work area identified for discussion. That way, if your team has limited time available, you'll be able to focus on the most significant areas.

Develop Change Strategies

This step involves identifying viable change strategies for each decision area identified for improvement by your team. If, for example, your team wants to become more involved in the selection of new coworkers, change strategies might include

- Allowing team members to jointly compile a list of criteria (desired experience, personal characteristics, and technical skills) for evaluating candidates for team membership

- Including team members in the process of screening résumés and internal job applications

- Pairing up to conduct the first wave of job selection interviews

Chart 12 outlines five alternative strategies for negotiating member-leader authority.

CHART 12

Alternative Strategies for Negotiating Member-Leader Authority

Establish Rotational Leadership

One way to balance authority within a team is to assign team members responsibility for certain work areas on a rotating basis. In our hypothetical example, the team might have proposed that team members take turns tracking variances that show up in the monthly budget reports from the finance department. The team leader could train the first team member to perform this task, and that person could then train his or her replacement.

Phase In Delegation

Sometimes team members are reluctant to take on new responsibilities because they lack experience in managing these areas. One way to overcome this obstacle is to have the leader delegate larger portions of the work area to the team over time.

For example, if team members have never before been responsible for selecting new team members, their leader could phase in this responsibility by taking the following steps over several months:

• Ask team members to develop a list of performance criteria for job candidates.

• After team members have had an opportunity to successfully perform this task, train them to conduct preliminary job interviews.

• Finally, coach team members on how to evaluate the relative standing of various job candidates. After they receive this coaching, incorporate their joint input into the final selection of new team members.

Establish Team Review Cycles

One way to increase member autonomy is to create opportunities for team members to provide input on the team leader's decisions. This may involve asking team members to troubleshoot their leader's plans and suggest methods for overcoming obstacles. To use this technique, teams will have to decide on the types of decisions they'll review and how often these team reviews will take place.

Develop Guidelines for Action

Address team decision-making authority by establishing standard team guidelines for action. For example, the members and leader of a purchasing team might agree that purchasing agents are free to negotiate contracts with suppliers below a given dollar value, but any contracts exceeding the specified dollar value will require authorization from the team leader.

Create Team Control Systems

Some teams have found it useful to set up visual control systems for monitoring their overall performance on work quality and productivity. Team control systems may range from simple posted control charts to software programs that enable members to track complicated work performance. Such control systems allow teams to review the performance of individual team members and set guidelines for their review of performance issues.

Select the Best Strategy

In this step, you must work with your team to select the best overall strategies for establishing member-leader authority in selected work areas. At the same time, identify the action steps your team will take to implement these alternatives.

Set a Time for Follow-Up

The final step is to schedule a follow-up meeting to discuss the effectiveness of the changes you've made to your team decision-making process. The issue of member-leader authority is often a sensitive area for review. Specifying a follow-up period assures team members that any changes they propose will not be implemented in a haphazard fashion.

Create an Early Warning System

Perhaps you're frequently upset with your team members because they don't alert you to problems. In the same way, they may believe that you fail to keep them apprised of changing developments in your company. If you'd like to resolve these types of problems, you may want to set aside time during one of your staff meetings to create an early warning system for your team. Chapter 9 offers a number of suggestions for designing these systems.

Related Problems

Chapter 6 (The Team Divided: The Problem of Intra-Team Conflict)—Personal conflicts between the team leader and dominant team members sometimes expand and engulf other members of the team. This chapter provides guidelines for resolving such conflicts.

Chapter 7 (Transition Chaos: Managing the Virtual Team)—Distributed work teams face many unique communication barriers. You may find it useful to explore this chapter if you feel that some of the difficulties in your team relationships are caused by this type of communication problem.

Chapter 9 (Painted into a Corner: Developing Better Foresight)—If communications have broken down between yourself and your team, it will be very difficult to anticipate and plan team strategies for dealing with emerging threats and opportunities. This chapter provides structured tools for resolving the situation.

Chapter 10 (The Broken Compass: Finding a Sense of Direction)—
Written vision statements, objectives, and performance standards are the
conceptual "glue" that helps hold a team together. A team that's experiencing a strained relationship with its leader may have difficulty articulating a
common description of its desired long-term direction. If your team feels
somewhat directionless, you may find it helpful to review the suggestions
outlined in this chapter.

Tool Kit

NEEDS CHECKLISTS FOR TEAM MEMBERS AND TEAM LEADERS

Tools
#14 & #15

Members of your team can use Tool #14, the Needs Checklist for Team Members (Exercise 5), to detail the areas in which they would like you to provide them with more support and assistance. This checklist can be completed by selected team members or by your team as a whole. Tool #15, the Needs Checklist for Team Leaders (Exercise 6), provides a similar checklist for the team leader.

EXERCISE 5 • NEEDS CHECKLIST FOR TEAM MEMBERS

Types of Support Needed	Examples
As team members, we are looking to you for the following kinds of support:	
• Informing us of organizational changes	
• Running interference for our team with other work groups	
• Representing our team to senior management	
• Providing needed resource support	
• Providing coaching or instruction on technical or administrative skills	
• Providing developmental and training support	
• Troubleshooting; taking the time to help us plan and test our ideas and spot potential problems before they expand beyond our control	
• Helping us resolve conflicts between certain team members	
• Pitching in and helping us during times of peak workload	
• Making our successes known to senior management	
• Other needs: _____	

Tool Kit

EXERCISE 6 • NEEDS CHECKLIST FOR TEAM LEADERS

Types of Support Needed	Examples
As the team leader, I am looking to you for the following kinds of support: • Committing to team decisions, even when you don't agree with them • Maintaining a positive image when representing our team to other work groups, suppliers, or customers • Being willing to take on extra work when we are struggling through peak workloads • Providing help when it's needed by other team members • Providing me or other team members with assistance in developing specialized technical skills • Helping our team identify innovative opportunities for improvement • Being my eyes and ears; keeping me informed of new developments or emerging problems • Assisting me in some of my administrative leadership functions • Challenging my ideas rather than rubber-stamping them • Other needs: _____	

Here are some guidelines for conducting these procedures:

1. Each checklist has a column that provides space for actual or hypothetical examples of the kind of assistance a team member needs and the type of payoff that would result. For instance, a team member might check off the need statement that says "Providing needed resource support" and could then use the second column to elaborate on this problem, by writing; "Currently only two members of our team have laptop computers. Given the long hours we're putting in on our work projects, if we all had laptops, we could work from home and perform document exchanges when we're on the road."

2. Before scheduling a meeting to discuss the results of these check-lists, I recommend you set aside a few days to review them. One way to do this is to have someone collect the checklists (team members should have the option of remaining anonymous) and make copies for distribution to everyone on the team. This provides all team members with the opportunity to reflect privately on the team's overall concerns and to see whether the needs they identified are shared by other team members.

3. The first part of your team discussion should focus on reviewing your team's overall comments and identifying those support needs that are listed as key issues by several team members.

4. I also encourage you to share with your team the support needs you identified for critical review on your own checklist.

Tool Kit

Tool #16

TEAM SUPPORT CHART

The Team Support Chart is a means of specifying and recording team actions for improving mutual support within your team. The completed example shown in Chart 13 describes possible action items for a team that's attempting to improve its members' proficiency with a software training program. The support action plan provides information on six factors:

1. What action will be carried out
2. Which team members will receive this support or assistance
3. Which team members will be responsible for ensuring this assistance is provided
4. When the process will begin
5. When the process will be completed
6. The date for a follow-up discussion with the team

CHART 13

Team Support Chart: Plan for Learning New Software

Support to Be Provided	Team Member(s) Who Will Receive this Support	Team Member(s) Who Will Provide this Support	Start Date of Process	Completion Date of Process	Date for Follow-Up Discussion
Attend training program offered by community college	Bob B. Carlos G. Sally T.	Rex T.	9/15	10/27	11/19
Attend after-hours coaching sessions on system	Bob B. Linda H.	Julie S.	11/4	11/18	11/19

Tool Kit

TEAM DECISION STYLE CHART

Balanced decision making is a crucial factor in effective member-leader relationships. The Team Decision Style Chart enables a team to compare its current decision-making process with its ideal decision-making process by asking team members and their leader to select among four alternative styles of team decision making. Chart 14 shows an example of a Team Decision Style Chart that has been completed by a hypothetical work team. Exercise 7 provides a blank chart for your own team.

CHART 14

Team Decision Style Chart

Work Areas	DECISION-MAKING OPTIONS				Importance
	Leader Only	Leader with Input	Team Consensus	Individual Members	
Preparing our annual budget	C - - - - -	- -➤D			High
Selecting new team members	C - - - - -	- - - - - - - - - - -	- -➤D		Moderate
Making a commitment to customers on delivery dates			D◄- - - - - - - -	- - - -C	High

Tool Kit

EXERCISE 7 • TEAM DECISION STYLE CHART

Work Areas	DECISION-MAKING OPTIONS				Importance
	Leader Only	Leader with Input	Team Consensus	Individual Members	

Team Decision Style Chart

Complete the chart by taking the following steps:

1. In the Work Areas column, describe those work areas that you would like your team to review.

2. When filling out the area labeled "Decision-Making Options," use a C to indicate how decisions are currently made and a D to indicate the option that is desired by your team. The four decision-making options are

- Leader Only (the team leader makes decisions without input from the team)

- Leader with Input (the team leader makes decisions after obtaining input from the team)
- Team Consensus (the team arrives at decisions through review and consensus)
- Individual Members (decisions are made by individual team members)

3. In the example shown in Chart 14, one of the work areas selected for review is "Preparing our annual budget." Team members feel that this decision is currently made by the team leader without input from them, but they prefer to be included in the process before the budget is finalized by the team leader.

4. You should also be aware that team members may not agree on how much influence they should have in certain key work areas. This is natural and can be valuable in itself. One of the most important results of engaging in this exercise is that team members may be able to reach greater alignment on effective degrees of member-leader control in specific decision-making areas.

5. Once your team has completed the Team Decision Style Chart, it may be useful to go back and summarize the need for change in each of the identified work areas. For example, given our hypothetical team's identified needs, the team leader could make the following comments on the annual budget: "Because team members currently have no input on our annual budget, we often run into situations in which key resource requirements are overlooked by the team leader. Sometimes, we have had to curtail projects due to lack of resources." You may want to provide similar details for your team.

Tool Kit

Tool #18

LEADER FEEDBACK QUESTIONNAIRE

The questionnaire in Exercise 8 will help you find out how your team members view your leadership style. Using their feedback, you will be able to determine the steps you should take to become a stronger team leader.

When completing the questionnaire, I recommend that you adhere to the following guidelines:

1. Give your team a clear explanation of what you hope to gain from this questionnaire.

2. Encourage team members to provide honest, candid feedback—in other words, a warts-and-all description of your leadership style. Assure them that all feedback will be submitted anonymously to one member of your team, who will consolidate the ratings into a single report.

3. It's often helpful to complete the questionnaire yourself, as if you were seeing yourself through the eyes of your team members. Keep this self-assessment separate from your team's scores and refer to it later to identify blind spots (performance areas in which your self-ratings differ significantly from the ratings of your team).

4. Some team members may claim their feedback isn't valid because they work with you on a limited basis, they are somewhat new to the team, or they're the most junior-level members of the team. Let them know that all feedback is valid—it's just as important to see how you come across to new members of the team (first impressions are sometimes lasting impressions) as it is to see how you are viewed by experienced team members.

5. When you've had an opportunity to review the final report, meet with your team to discuss your conclusions. Regardless of whether or not you choose to distribute copies of the completed responses, you should at least identify for your team the two primary leadership behaviors that are your strengths and the two behaviors that represent your greatest development needs.

6. Feel free to ask team members for clarification on certain issues if you're having trouble understanding the reasons why you received certain rating scores.

7. Don't feel as if you have to walk into the meeting armed with detailed solutions for areas identified as in need of improvement. Sometimes there's great value in telling your team, "I'm not really sure how to resolve this problem, but I'm open to your suggestions."

Tool Kit

EXERCISE 8 • LEADER FEEDBACK QUESTIONNAIRE

Using a five-point scale, rate your team leader's performance on each of the following questions. A rating of 5 means the leader performs extremely well on that factor, a rating of 3 represents a moderate level of satisfaction, and a rating of 1 indicates an area requiring significant improvement.

Team Dimension	Feedback Questions *To what extent does your team leader do the following:*	Rating
Information sharing	1. Pass on to the team important information provided by customers, senior managers, and other work groups?	
	2. Pass on to others the concerns, issues, and questions raised by team members?	
Direction	3. Provide clear direction on projects?	
	4. Provide clear feedback on work priorities?	
Team building	5. Encourage open communication within the team?	
	6. Help the team build effective relationships within itself and with other work groups?	
Planning	7. Develop thorough project plans?	
	8. Provide sufficient flexibility in the planning process?	
Empowerment	9. Give you a free hand in determining how you perform your work?	
	10. Solicit your input and feedback on key decisions?	
Conflict resolution	11. Help resolve conflicts between team members?	
	12. Effectively manage conflicts between the team and other work groups?	
Resource utilization	13. Make effective use of available resources?	
	14. Help overcome resource constraints?	
Feedback and coaching	15. Provide clear feedback on your performance?	
	16. Provide needed coaching on how to perform work more effectively?	
Professional development	17. Provide opportunities (training, seminars) for building your skills?	
	18. Provide stretch assignments that test and develop your skills?	
Personal growth	19. Remain open to feedback from the team about his/her performance?	
	20. Model professional development by continually attempting to strengthen his/her skills?	

21. What is the single most effective aspect of your leader's leadership style? What would you *not* want this person to change?

22. What one change could your leader make to his/her behavior that would help you perform even more effectively as a team?

8. At the end of the discussion, remember to thank team members for their input and their willingness to provide honest feedback.

9. For many team members, the true test of your intentions will be whether you make an effort to follow up on any proposed improvement suggestions. For this reason, it's very important to translate these suggestions into solid action.

10. Wait several weeks, and then solicit additional feedback from team members regarding any changes they've noticed in your behavior.

11. Finally, approximately twelve to sixteen weeks after your initial meeting, conduct a follow-up session to discuss whether the improvement actions you've undertaken have made a difference in your team's view of your leadership style.

LEADER EXPECTATIONS CHECKLIST

One of the underlying causes of member-leader conflict is that members lack a clear understanding of the leader's performance expectations. In attempting to resolve this issue, the team leader faces the challenge of distinguishing between a variety of performance components (such as objectives, standards, and priorities) that may not be well understood by team members. The checklist in Exercise 9 lists seven performance areas in which a team often has difficulty discerning the leader's expectations. Ask your team members to anonymously complete this checklist and present you with the consolidated results so that you can determine those areas in which your expectations require more precise definition.

> **Tool**
> **#19**

EXERCISE 9 • LEADER EXPECTATIONS CHECKLIST

Listed below are some of the problems frequently encountered by team members who are trying to interpret their leaders' expectations. Review the list after it has been completed by team members and check off the problem areas that are relevant to your own team. Be prepared to discuss your conclusions during your next team review session.

❑ **Work Methods:** Understanding our leader's expectations regarding required work methods and procedures when completing jobs or projects

❑ **Time frames:** Understanding due dates for the completion of projects; determining when dates have slipped and which completion dates are final and nonnegotiable

❑ **Work responsibilities:** Understanding each team member's role when we are assigned to a given job or responsibility

❑ **Customer/supplier interface:** Understanding our leader's expectations when dealing with supplier problems or customer complaints or requests; understanding how far we should go to build effective relationships with other work groups

❑ **Work priorities:** Understanding which jobs take priority and the changes in work priorities; being able to clearly differentiate between hot jobs and other jobs

❑ **Performance expectations:** Understanding what our leader expects in the way of desired outcomes, what it means to do a good job, and the degree of effort we are expected to put into a job (as opposed to overworking low-priority jobs)

❑ **Resources:** Understanding what resources (facilities, support staff, equipment, software, budget) have been allocated to perform a job and how much control we have over resource decisions

Strengthening
Team Focus

Painted into a Corner

Developing Better Foresight

It's not uncommon for teams to run into occasional unanticipated challenges. Considering the times in which we live, team leaders can't possibly plan for every eventuality. On the other hand, if you find your team being repeatedly ambushed by unforeseen events, you may need to develop stronger skills in the areas of foresight and planning.

High-performing teams know their success depends on securing timely, accurate information about circumstances that could affect their performance. We can think of significant change events either as threats or as opportunities, both of which are represented in Chart 15.

Threats are those obstacles or pitfalls that can impede your team's progress, or stop it completely dead in its tracks. Opportunities are favorable occurrences, which, if seized quickly, can ensure your team's success or accelerate its progress toward its objectives. To perform effectively, your team needs to be able to anticipate both kinds of changes.

The failure to anticipate threats reduces your team's ability to deal effectively with these events when they do occur. In addition, the longer the reaction time after the onset of a threat, the greater the cost to your company in terms of lost work time, recovery actions, budget overruns, or customer

CHART 15

Team Threats and Opportunities	
Threats	**Opportunities**
• **Resource/staffing shortfalls:** Discovering that anticipated staff or resources are not forthcoming, or that staff or resources have unexpectedly been diverted from your project.	• **Increased availability of resources/ staff:** Receiving a windfall in the form of additional staff or resources, or discovering that existing staff members have more time than expected to invest in the project.
• **Information blockages:** Being denied access to required information, or discovering that vital information is not available.	• **Emerging needs:** Experiencing additional customers or expanding needs of current customers.
• **Organizational change efforts:** Encountering a large-scale business or organizational change that places team projects on hold or forces you to consider a major revision to your project design.	• **Organizational change efforts:** Encountering a large-scale business or organizational change that accelerates the pace of your projects or fortifies your team objectives.
• **Loss of a team sponsor:** Having your sponsor withdraw from a project prior to completion due to a transfer, new job assignment, or pressing responsibilities.	• **Addition of new sponsors:** Having new sponsors come into the picture and offer additional support or advice.
• **Encountering a "blocker":** Discovering a senior manager whose actions may block the team's efforts.	• **Opportunities to strengthen your team's bench:** Becoming aware of training options, benchmark reviews, or development opportunities.

complaints. Likewise, missed opportunities don't lie dormant. They are frequently snatched up by your competitors, who may be quite capable of profiting from a team's lack of foresight.

Four Types of Response to Change

It's important to understand that foresight implies more than a willingness to look ahead. A team must also be able to respond quickly and with flexibility to changes in its environment. Depending on a team's position in relation to the qualities of speed and flexibility, we can place it into one of the following categories: entrenched, reactive, proactive, and preemptive. These four categories are illustrated in Figure 2.

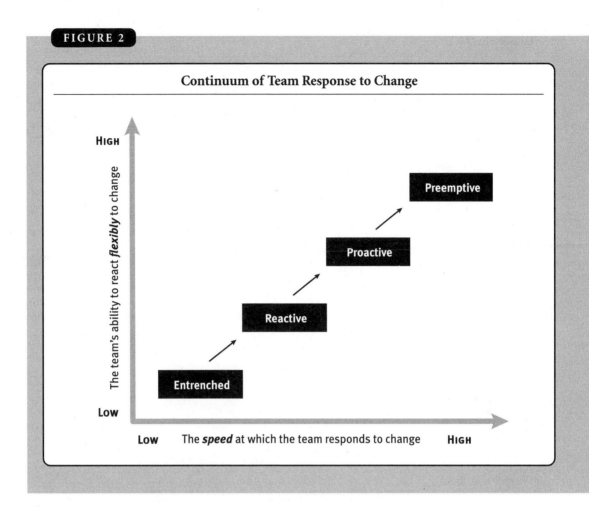

FIGURE 2

Continuum of Team Response to Change

The team's ability to react *flexibly* to change — High / Low

The *speed* at which the team responds to change — Low / High

Entrenched — Reactive — Proactive — Preemptive

Entrenched teams live in denial. When faced with major change, they either ignore it or convince themselves that it's just a temporary aberration. They believe that, sooner or later, things will get back to normal. It goes without saying that entrenched teams are extremely rigid. Once they chart out a course, they proceed in a lockstep manner, regardless of any new and contrary information that may suggest the need for midcourse corrections.

Reactive teams are slow to respond to change and usually take action only after the situation is obvious. They demonstrate a minimal amount of flexibility in that they attempt to make some small adjustments to their plans. With these teams, preventive planning is virtually nonexistent.

Proactive teams try to get out ahead of change and consider the possible implications of events that are just starting to take place. However, they are hampered by a kind of team myopia—they look ahead only to events that are

coming into view on the horizon and seldom consider the business implications of large-scale changes, only those that directly affect their own operations.

Preemptive teams have long-term vision. Regardless of their day-to-
day work pressures, they continually scan the horizon to track trends and
changes that can affect not only their own operations but the overall performance of their companies. They invest a considerable amount of effort in
thinking through and preparing for all contingencies, and whenever possible, they attempt to influence the course of business events. They anticipate
and try to shape change instead of just waiting to react to it.

The Symptoms

As you read the following symptoms, consider which of the above four categories best describes your own team.

Ineffective Approach to Problems and Opportunities

Teams that suffer from lack of foresight are more likely to be jolted by unpleasant surprises. Without an efficient early warning system, such teams are
frequently blindsided by problems. In addition, they employ a reactive
approach that allows problems to mushroom out of control before they're
finally addressed. Thus, a team might begin to deal with its inability to track
a growing budget variance only after these discrepancies accumulate into a
significant end-of-year cost overrun, or an increase in customer complaints
might go unnoticed until the company begins to lose customer accounts.

When dealing with the positive aspects of change events, teams that are
weak on foresight become aware only in retrospect that they missed the boat on
major opportunities. For a clear example, refer to this chapter's Case in Point.

Focus on the Past

Reactive teams focus their energies on the past rather than the future. This
symptom can take a variety of forms. In casual discussions, the team may
talk about where it's been, not where it's going. Team members tend to
deflect questions about planning or future actions and are quick to explain
that they're too busy putting out fires to address long-range planning. Quite
often, such teams develop revisionist histories in which they remember the
"good old days" under a previous CEO or organizational structure without
objectively recalling both negative and positive changes that have occurred
within their organizations.

Inability to Assess the Impact of Change

A team that lacks foresight often miscalculates the impact of external and internal change. Team members might see a variety of potential problems in an impending merger but never consider the growth opportunities that are also part of this organizational change. That is, they focus on only half of the change equation (threats) while ignoring the other half (opportunities). The members of this same team would be unlikely to think through the long-term impact of their actions. They could, for example, revise their work methods and then discover six months later that their attempt at increased efficiency created significant quality problems for other departments.

Case in Point: The Marketing Team

A marketing team took two years to study the feasibility of opening a business-to-business e-commerce site for its company. Because the company was a stranger to the e-commerce market, and few competitors had entered the market, the team wrote off this opportunity. In doing so, they minimized the significance of trend information provided to them by other subsidiaries within their company and largely ignored an external consulting firm's recommendation that the company develop an immediate pilot venture into e-commerce.

Two years later, when the marketing team finally decided to proceed, this e-market niche was flooded with a host of competitors. By failing to act quickly, the team lost a significant first-mover advantage. In addition, the lack of foresight and planning forced this team into a sudden scramble to develop e-commerce marketing, sales, and distribution plans. The company has had to make enormous expenditures on advertising to distinguish itself within a now crowded field and must perform belated calculations on how its entry into e-commerce will affect the rest of the operation, including the deployment of its national sales force.

The Underlying Causes

The inability to look ahead may result from a number of different situations and attitudes. You may recognize some characteristics of your team in the following descriptions.

Failure to Establish or Utilize External Sensing Array

Some teams have an extended sensing array. They are heavily networked within their industries and professional groups and keep current on emerging trends within their fields. They are also internally networked and make an effort to stay in contact with others in their companies who can keep them current on organizational changes that might affect their groups. When teams exhibit a lack of foresight, it's often because they have neglected to establish the types of networks that can alert them to important changes in their work environments.

Every team faces problems that must be resolved immediately. However, when a team diverts all its attention and resources to tackling the problem of the day, its members tend to lose sight of the bigger picture. No matter how pressured a team is feeling, it needs to continually channel at least part of its energy into scanning ahead to understand the overall business environment within which it is operating.

Victim Mentality

The victim mentality is both a symptom and an underlying cause of the lack of team foresight. A reactive team is easy to spot because its members talk as if they are passive victims of forces beyond their control. They spend hours discussing the unfair actions of their senior managers or the negative repercussions of a business change that "came out of the blue." In all cases, they view these events as something that happened without warning and over which they have no control.

Once in place, the victim mentality feeds on itself. Team members who think of themselves as victims tend to attract like-minded people to the team. They socialize with others who support their perceptions of their own helplessness and the unfairness of others. A victim mentality fuels a self-fulfilling prophecy, because assuming they are helpless victims discourages team members from trying to anticipate and manage change (after all, what good would it do?). These actions, in turn, make the team less prepared to deal with future events—a situation that further solidifies its victim position.

Resistance to New Information

Teams are sometimes resistant to new information that contradicts their current belief systems. This is especially true for teams whose members experience a high degree of team loyalty and take an elitist and insular "us versus them" position with respect to others in the organization. Not wanting to appear disloyal, the members of such teams sometimes hesitate to share information that might be contrary to the team's set objectives, positions, and norms. Groupthink like this can lead even the best-performing teams to filter out potentially dangerous problems, which may leave them vulnerable to developing circumstances.

Static Planning

Lack of foresight may also be found in teams that formulate thorough plans but consider only a very narrow set of contingencies. Such teams are analogous to campers who assume there will be consistently sunny weather. They put a lot of work into designing Plan A but completely neglect to come up with a backup plan. Teams like this tend to follow their plans in a rigid, inflexible manner. They don't understand that a plan is a living document, which should be continually reexamined in light of changing business conditions.

The Treatment

Team members and leaders can improve their teams' ability to foresee and handle problems, and to take full advantage of opportunities, by implementing several strategies.

Create an Early Warning System

Early warning systems enable teams to prepare for large-scale changes and possible problems and allow them to concentrate on prevention instead of trying desperately to resolve one difficult situation after another.

Problems and changes tend to gather momentum and become harder to control as they develop, much like a snowball that gains mass and speed as it travels downhill. As their influence spreads, they soon affect other areas outside the team and may eventually extend beyond the range of the team's control. For example, if a manufacturing team fails to identify product defects that occur in its production process, these defects will eventually come to the attention of customers, resulting in increased warranty costs and lost sales. Early warning systems enable teams to tackle problems before they become too big to manage.

It's impossible for individual team members to keep track of all potential problems and changes that could affect their teams. By providing others with critical updates, team members help close information gaps between different team members and develop a more complete picture of their work environment.

There are several steps you can take to set up a formal process for tracking emerging trends and business and organizational developments that could affect your team's performance.

Start by asking, "What are the major business drivers that shape and influence the performance of our work team?" Then ask, "For each of these factors, what are the most important trends that can shape our performance?" For an HR recruiting team, such a trend might involve changes in tracking and compiling systems for electronic ads and résumés or integrating the use of Internet job sites with reliance on traditional executive recruiting firms. Next, determine the best vehicles for tracking these trends. They could be professional or trade chat rooms on the Internet, professional or trade seminars, or planning meetings with key organizational leaders, external consultants, or university researchers who are at the crest of important change curves. Finally, determine how to allocate accountability for trend tracking among your team members. You might assign a particular individual to a specified tracking vehicle— for instance, news articles delivered through your corporate clipping service—or ask a member to represent your team on important cross-functional project review meetings.

Expose Your Team to Other Points of View

Create situations that force team members to question their assumptions about the future—especially those that, if wrong, could end up being disastrous for them. If team members attend meetings conducted by other departments, they may be able to better understand the broader changes that are taking place within your organization.

Consider bringing your team into contact with departmental or outside experts who could help troubleshoot your planning processes. For example, before your team advances too far in planning an IT-related solution, ask a specialist from your IT group to join you to offer input and advice. You might also call upon senior managers, peers in related corporate functions, recognized leaders in your industry, and new hires who have recently been imported from your competitors. Outside consultants can also play a valuable troubleshooting role and often have the advantage of their past experience with a variety of organizations that have already progressed through the same change scenarios.

Implement a Thorough Troubleshooting Process

This means identifying the preventive and corrective actions your team should take to plan for the future. Preventive actions allow you to shape the outcome or affect the likelihood of an event, while corrective actions help you manage changes once they are under way.

Aside from assisting your team with assessing potential threats and opportunities, the troubleshooting process provides a number of other benefits. First, it represents a vehicle for developing user-friendly, graphic overviews of the potential obstacles and opportunities associated with your project. This kind of review process makes it easy for your team to tackle the assessment of a project or decision in incremental stages as well as to look back and analyze the success of past decisions. In addition, these exercises can be used to supply your stakeholders with a quick outline of your team's thought processes while also gaining their input. And finally, the simple act of mapping out obstacles and opportunities can help teams view challenges as more manageable because they have been examined and understood. Both types of planning activities are discussed in Tools 20 through 22 in your Tool Kit for this chapter.

Develop the Art of Scenario Planning

If rigid planning is one reason for a lack of foresight, then one of the logical solutions is to create a more robust and flexible planning process. Useful approaches to achieving this goal can be found in Tools 24 and 25, which are located in the Tool Kit for Chapter 10.

Related Problems

Chapter 10 (The Broken Compass: Finding a Sense of Direction)—Developing a sense of long-term direction encourages team members to continually scan their environment for changes that could affect their performance. In addition, a team that takes an overall view of its operation and its industry in general acquires a better understanding of the broader implications of change.

Chapter 11 (The Missing Scorecard: Strengthening Accountability)—Scorecards prompt teams to take note of performance trends that could affect their success, thus contributing to team foresight.

Chapter 14 (Reversals: Dealing with Setbacks)—Developing plans to prevent potential setbacks and planning corrective actions to remedy reversals are two components of foresight. Without foresight, a team is hampered in its ability to deal effectively with setbacks.

Chapter 17 (Our Own Worst Enemy: Strengthening Customer Relationships)—Without foresight, a team will have difficulty anticipating and preventing customer problems or taking note of changes in its customer base that may signal new opportunities.

Tool Kit

Tool #20	**EARLY WARNING CHART** Use the Early Warning Chart in Exercise 10 to help your team establish its own monitoring system.

EXERCISE 10 • EARLY WARNING CHART

Areas for Monitoring	Red Flags	Suggested Guidelines	Suggested Follow-up Actions

Schedule some time during a team meeting to complete the following four steps:

1. Use the first column to list the types of tasks and project areas that should be closely tracked for changes and potential problems by team members. When attempting to define areas for monitoring, many teams have found it useful to consider the following criteria:

   • **Importance:** Teams should give special attention to work areas that have the greatest impact on their performance.

   • **Volatility:** Teams should closely monitor those work areas that are subject to sudden, unpredictable changes.

- **Past experience:** Teams should identify past situations in which they were caught off guard by sudden problems or changes and try to determine why they were unable to anticipate these events.

2. In this step, your team identifies "red flags," or indicators that signal sudden changes or problems. Common indicators might include

- Sudden increase in customer complaints

- Sudden increase in delayed payments from a major account

- Loss or gain of a major corporate contract

- Proposed large-scale changes for a function's work methods or processes

Once again, ask your team what indicators would be helpful in monitoring important changes within each of the work areas listed in your chart and describe these indicators in the Red Flags column.

3. Ask your team to agree on and establish guidelines for monitoring key work areas and red flags. Team guidelines usually address the following issues:

- Will a single team member or the entire team be responsible for monitoring selected work areas?

- Should the team leader be the only one alerted to emerging problems or changes, or should the entire team be placed on alert?

- At what point should the team or team leader be alerted to changes? In other words, what degree of urgency do we assign to the change areas we have identified?

Working with your team, describe any guidelines or suggestions for jointly monitoring the selected change areas in the Suggested Guidelines column.

4. Finally, your team should develop procedures for following up on the actions and guidelines you identified in steps 1–3. During the follow-up session, your team should review the success of your tracking system by asking the following questions:

- Have we improved our ability to anticipate and plan for problems or changes within this work area? Are we still encountering nasty surprises? If so, what do we need to change about our monitoring system?

- How quickly are we able to alert ourselves to problems? Are there ways of further reducing the time between the occurrence of problems or changes and the point at which our team is first alerted to them?

Tool Kit

- Are we supplying the right people within and outside our team with necessary information?
- Are we getting accurate information on problems and changes?
- Are we getting complete information on problems and changes?
- How could we further improve our early warning system?

Ask team members to summarize their responses to these questions in the Suggested Follow-up Actions column.

Tool Kit

Tool #21

THREATS ANALYSIS

In troubleshooting any major team activity, such as the completion of a key project, it's easy to feel overwhelmed by the sheer complexity of the many challenges your team could encounter. One means of helping team members maintain their focus on the most important aspects of a change event is to guide them through a systematic review of potential threats and opportunities. The following three tools will help you perform this assessment.

Chart 16 shows a threats analysis performed by a cross-functional team charged with planning the reorganization of its company's operations department. Note that the team has chosen to perform this analysis for each step of the reorganization project (for simplicity, Chart 16 shows only steps 1, 5, and 8).

First, the team identified potential threats that could interfere with the successful completion of steps 1, 5, and 8. The team then evaluated (as high, medium, or low) both the probability of potential problems and the relative impact of each threat on the project. The team used the Trigger column to write in events that could be early warning signs for these problems. Based on this chart, the single most important problem for the team is that of "identifying changing functional and business requirements," and it has been rated high in terms of both probability and impact. The team now knows that it will encounter its most important threat during the completion of the first step of its project.

Looking at Chart 16, you can see that the team has tried to identify the preventive actions as well as the corrective actions it could take should these problems occur. Usually, a rigorous questioning process can help your team identify appropriate preventive and corrective actions. Exercise 10 appears on p. 138.

Tool Kit

CHART 16

Threats Analysis for Departmental Reorganization

Project Steps	Potential Problems	Probability of Occurrence	Impact of Occurrence	Trigger	Corrective Actions	Preventive Actions
Step 1: Identify changing functional and business requirements	Invalid requirements caused by inaccurate business forecast	M	H	Requirements don't match fourth-quarter business forecast	Recalibrate and adjust structure at midyear	Obtain rough forecast from strategic planning department
Step 5: Assess current bench strength against new requirements	Incomplete assessment due to lack of data	H	M	Lack of executive alignment on competencies of incumbents	Midyear recalibration of structure	Update all performance appraisals and use assessment center to independently assess skills
Step 8: Notify redundant staff of transfer or termination options and establish time frame for personnel decisions	Staff could contest decisions	L	M	Anger, resentment, and confusion at time of notification	Meet with selected staff to review options (timetable for actions) that might increase acceptance	Consult legal department on severance and transfer agreements, test approach on employee focus group

Tool Kit

OPPORTUNITIES ASSESSMENT

Teams naturally tend to become so preoccupied with all the things that could go wrong with a project that they miss out on opportunities for improving their chances for success. The Opportunities Assessment is an effective way to counter this preoccupation by capturing ideas for maximizing the success of a project and exploring ways to extend the benefits that could be derived from it.

To return to our illustrative example, Chart 17 shows the cross-functional team's assessment of the opportunities that could arise during steps 1 and 5 of its project. The team has also used this chart to rate the relative probability of each of these opportunities as well as their potential impact.

CHART 17

	Opportunities Assessment for Departmental Reorganization				
Project Step	**Potential Opportunities**	**Probability of Occurrence**	**Impact of Occurrence**	**How to Encourage This Event**	**How to Exploit This Event**
Step 1: Identify new functional and business requirements	Ability to obtain internal benchmark data from other plants	M	H	Make inquiries to HR director of other plan, with push from our president	Use data to verify design assumptions and dramatically shorten time for planning reorganization
Step 5: Assess current bench strength against requirements	Can extract data from 360-degree competency study if completed sooner than expected	L	M	Explain how moving up completion date would benefit our project	Would provide data to independently support performance appraisal findings

Tool Kit

In the final phase of the exercise, team members have identified what they can do to increase the likelihood of potential opportunities and identify ways of exploiting these opportunities should they occur.

The following questions can help your team encourage opportunities:

1. Who, within or outside our team, is in the best position to bring about this opportunity?

2. Is there a critical time period within which we need to pursue this event?

3. What other steps can we take to improve the likelihood of this event?

The following questions can help your team exploit opportunities:

1. How can we modify this opportunity to make it more useful for our project?

2. How can we use this opportunity to generate other positive out comes for our team?

3. How can we apply this opportunity to other areas within our organization?

Apart from troubleshooting major projects, teams can also assess the threats and opportunities associated with key decisions. In the example shown in Chart 18, a small consulting team has assessed the comparative desirability of developing proposals on two different projects.

Assuming that the revenue stream from these two projects would be about the same and the team has the capabilities to go after only one of them, the team has decided to identify the relative threats and opportunities associated with each decision.

The team used a five-point scale to rate the threats and opportunities in terms of their perceived impact (I) and probability of occurrence (P). Multiplying these numbers results in a total score (T) for each threat or opportunity.

When the total opportunity scores are compared to the total threat scores, we can see that option B is the winner.

Tool Kit

CHART 18

	Opportunities/Threats Matrix for Two Comparable Projects							
	Option A: Pursue Proposal with Company A	I	P	T	**Option B: Pursue Proposal with Company B**	I	P	T
Threats and Disadvantages	1. Customer has a history of extensive revisions to project plans that result in high costs and project delays.	4	4	16	1. Customer has a history of delayed payments to other vendors, a key point if we were to continue to have a cash-flow problem.	5	4	20
	2. Distant location would mean a lot of travel time.	2	4	8	2. Extensive contractual requirements would place a large administrative burden on us. Some initial up-front costs here might not be recouped if the contract were terminated in the initial stages.	4	4	16
	3. We would have to make a complete commitment to the entire program, which would represent a big drain on our cash flow.	5	5	25				

Tool Kit

Tool #23

CHANGE EVENTS TECHNIQUE

Up to this point, I've introduced you to team tools that involve discrete change events that are at least partially within the control of your team. By contrast, the Change Events Technique begins with a review of large-scale changes that lie well beyond your team and then moves inward to assess how these events could influence your team's success. Because this technique forces teams to shift their focus of attention from external events to the teams themselves, I sometimes refer to it as the Outside-In Exercise.

Figure 3 illustrates how this technique has been applied by a cross-functional management-associate team that has been given the responsibility for introducing self-directed work teams to a selected plant site. Self-directed

FIGURE 3

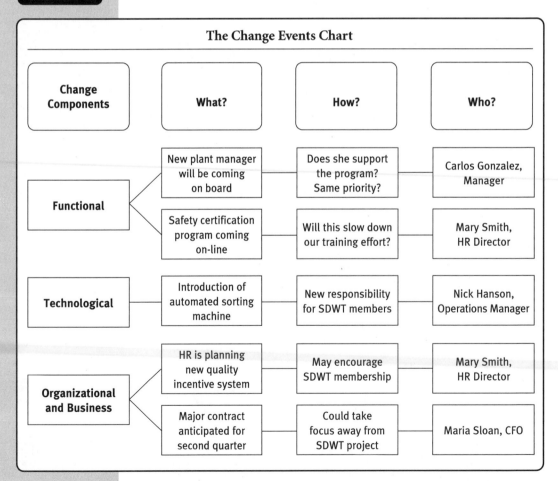

The Change Events Chart

Change Components	What?	How?	Who?
Functional	New plant manager will be coming on board	Does she support the program? Same priority?	Carlos Gonzalez, Manager
	Safety certification program coming on-line	Will this slow down our training effort?	Mary Smith, HR Director
Technological	Introduction of automated sorting machine	New responsibility for SDWT members	Nick Hanson, Operations Manager
Organizational and Business	HR is planning new quality incentive system	May encourage SDWT membership	Mary Smith, HR Director
	Major contract anticipated for second quarter	Could take focus away from SDWT project	Maria Sloan, CFO

work teams are groups that are trained to function as semiautonomous and self-managed teams and whose members gradually learn to take on responsibilities that are traditionally reserved for managers.

To lead your team through the Change Events Technique, complete the following steps:

1. To begin, I find it easier to analyze large-scale changes if they're first broken down into three subcomponents:

   - Functional changes that affect the operation of discrete work functions

   - Technological changes that become a factor

   - Broader organizational and business changes that must be addressed

   List these three change components on the left side of your flipchart, as illustrated in Figure 3.

2. Next, have your team brainstorm the types of changes associated with each of these three change components. In the example shown in Figure 3, one such change concerns the imminent introduction of computerized sorting machines.

3. Once your team has finished brainstorming, ask team members to complete the How column by describing the possible effect of each identified change event on the project. Include both potential obstacles and opportunities.

4. Complete the Who column, indicating the person within or outside your organization who is considered the most knowledgeable about, or responsible for, each change event.

5. As the final step in the exercise, ask team members to circle the changes they feel are most likely to affect the team's long-term success. Then consider whether it's feasible to use some of the other tools that were introduced previously in this chapter to better prepare your team to address these changes.

One of the ways your team can avoid getting "painted into a corner" is to troubleshoot potential obstacles and explore ways to overcome them. The chart in Exercise 11 provides a method for performing this type of troubleshooting. Use the questions listed in the Preventive Action Plan section to help your team explore steps it can take to prevent the occurrence of problems. Write your answers in the space provided in the right column. In the same way, use the questions in the Corrective Action Plan section to identify team options for correcting difficult problems, should they occur.

Tool Kit

EXERCISE 11 • DEVELOPING PREVENTIVE AND CORRECTIVE ACTION PLANS

Preventive Action Plan

1. What actions could we take to prevent this problem? How potent are these actions?

2. If several options are available, which would be most useful?

3. What is the most effective timing for these actions? By what point in our project do we need to have them in place?

4. Are we currently capable of taking these actions? If not, what steps are necessary to prepare for them (additional training, resources, information, etc.)?

5. Who within or outside our team will be responsible for implementing these actions, and how will they report back to our team?

Steps Your Team Will Take

Corrective Action Plan

1. What actions could we take to minimize the impact of this problem or eliminate it once it occurs?

2. Of all available actions, which would be the most potent? Which could be implemented most quickly and have the most beneficial effect?

3. Are we currently capable of taking these actions? If not, what steps are necessary to prepare for them (additional training, resources, information, etc.)?

4. How quickly could we put these actions into effect? What could we do to shorten delivery time?

5. Who within or outside our team will be responsible for implementing these actions and how will they report back to our team?

Steps Your Team Will Take

The Broken Compass

Finding a Sense of Direction

Take a team, shake up its reporting structure, and change its membership. Next, give that team a hefty load of projects and accountabilities, leaving members to sort out what's most important from this morass of accountabilities. To make things even more interesting, dramatically change the charter and function of the business unit that houses this team. Now, place all these events within the context of a fast-paced organization, one that is rapidly changing its markets, services, and structure. In today's volatile work environment, scenarios like this are increasingly common. What happens next, however, depends a lot on whether the team has developed a clear sense of its long-term direction.

For teams that are working with well-constructed vision statements, targeted long-term goals, and clearly delineated priorities, these challenges may be frustrating, but they're not overwhelming. Like small but sturdy boats knocked about by a turbulent storm, such teams manage to stay on track because they've developed very effective radar systems for checking their current position in relation to their long-term goals. As a result, they're able to make quick adjustments whenever they discover that they are veering off course. More important, their team members are motivated because they believe their day-to-day activities are closely linked to the overall goals of their organizations.

On the other hand, when teams try to function without a sense of long-term direction, the future can appear murky and uncertain. Under such conditions, team members may begin to feel that their actions lack purpose or meaning. They may experience greater difficulty in sifting through competing priorities and determining what's *really* important and where they can most effectively focus their attention.

If a team is disoriented, it will find itself caught in the middle of departmental tug-of-wars as its members try to meet the competing needs of different work functions. Not knowing their team's priorities, they will try to meet all requests. In the end, they will manage only to disappoint their customers, frustrate their coworkers, and waste their own time and resources.

Some team members will invest large amounts of energy on activities that appear to their coworkers to be of little or no value. Given these disagreements, if the team experiences shortages, conflicts may ensue as to the allocation of scarce resources. Other team members will start projects, only to have their team leader put the projects on hold to reassign them to new projects. Eventually, some team members may drag their heels or withhold their cooperation, thinking that if they wait long enough, a project or assignment will simply go away of its own accord.

If the situation isn't resolved, the best and brightest members of the team are likely to leave. After all, high-potential performers are motivated by a strong need for achievement. Within a directionless team, such members may be working sixty hours a week—yet after several months, they will have little to show for their efforts.

On the other hand, mediocre performers love directionless teams. The directionless team becomes the favored organizational ecosystem for the shiftless and irresponsible, because they know they can easily hide their lack of skill, ability, or effort behind the team's internal confusion. Such individuals know they can survive (and maybe even prosper) within a directionless team, if they just keep their heads down and perform the set of routine activities to which they've been assigned. They understand that their performance will never be gauged against the team's objectives, nor will their work activities be closely evaluated to see if they truly add value at the end of the day. As a result, a directionless team is in danger of attracting the incompetent while driving away talented performers. In short, if a team cannot establish a clear sense of direction, the results can be confusion, chaos, and complacency.

The Symptoms

At some point in its existence, every team reaches a crossroad where the future looks uncertain and chaotic. If you are concerned that your team may be attempting to navigate with a "broken compass," look for the following symptoms.

Big-Picture Blur

The first way to spot a directionless team is to ask yourself if its members lack a clear overall picture of their desired future. Because they're unable to visualize a scenario for success, they don't understand how their separate day-to-day activities are of any value in supporting the performance of large-scale business objectives, and they often simply go through the motions to perform their functions. For the average team member, the experience is a bit like trying to visualize the planned redesign of a room by looking through the keyhole.

Because team members don't have a good understanding of how their individual functions fit together, they can't respond to questions or address issues that lie outside their immediate field of vision. You've probably experienced this if you've ever made a phone call to ask a simple question and received a response such as, "Sorry, but I can't answer that. Sally's the only person who knows the answer and she's on vacation for two weeks." This limited point of view plays an important role in discouraging team accountability, for if team members don't understand the jobs of their coworkers or know anything about their projects, it becomes a lot easier to define their own jobs as just those work activities that take place within their own cubicles. To an outside observer, such a work group looks like a series of disconnected, isolated workers, not a coherent team.

Excessive Dependence on Team Leader

I refer to this symptom as the "wheelbarrow syndrome" because a wheelbarrow is a strong and stable tool, but it only goes as far as it is pushed. Like a wheelbarrow, team members who lack a sense of direction are forced to stop frequently and wait for marching orders, rather than taking the initiative and determining the proper course of action. This jerky, hesitant, start-and-stop action with its accompanying overdependence on the team leader is one of the characteristics that most defines directionless teams.

Team Members Display a High Level of Anxiety

Because the team's future appears unpredictable and chaotic, members may experience a high degree of stress, anxiety, and helplessness. It's important to note here that this anxiety isn't focused on events that have already taken place. Instead, it's based on feelings of helplessness and vulnerability in the face of a bewildering and potentially overwhelming future.

Conflicting Priorities

Because team members don't have a picture of the future to guide them, they have difficulty assigning priorities among competing projects or account-abilities. This ambivalence is likely to reveal itself in a variety of ways.

Team members may feel they are working at cross-purposes and, accordingly, may push personal objectives at the cost of the team's overall success. They may also hesitate to commit themselves to their projects because they don't know how important those projects are in relation to their overall responsibilities. In the worst-case scenario, team members will simply throw up their hands in the face of what they see as an unmanageable workload. In such a situation, the inability to make quick, definitive decisions about competing priorities means that the team will achieve very few of its goals.

The Underlying Causes

As with the other team roadblocks covered in this book, the problem of lack of direction can result from a number of interacting causes. Carefully review this section with your team to determine which of the following factors may be contributing to its lack of direction.

Accelerated Change

Even teams with a solid game plan can lose their direction when they're overwhelmed by change. For example, a work group may suddenly be presented with a new set of business challenges, such as working around a severe resource crunch or taking on a very different charter. In a similar vein, a team might find itself operating within an organization that is rapidly transforming its static-state, low-change work setting into a dynamic high-change environment. The introduction of a new CEO or senior team, a major organizational shake-up, and a corporate merger are but three scenarios that can force teams to question their direction and focus. Quite often, an organization's executives will outline very broad and sweeping changes that are coming down the path, such as entries into new markets or the formation of unique partnerships with vendors or competitors. Many work teams experience a subsequent period of instability as they attempt to decipher how these changes are likely to affect their performance.

Isolation from the Organizational Mainstream

Teams are more likely to be waylaid by the onset of large-scale organizational change if they're isolated from their company's informal communication networks or cut off from the long-term planning process of their senior managers. For obvious reasons, teams that operate in isolation are far more likely to be the last to know if significant changes are heading in their company's direction.

Lack of Alignment

Teams may also experience difficulties in establishing long-term direction if their members hold very different views about their collective future and the long-term strategy needed to maximize their chances for success. This situation often follows a change in leadership. The new leader may have a set of goals and performance expectations that does not match that of his or her predecessor but may never specify these differences. Unfortunately, team members usually don't have opportunities to openly discuss these issues. Team members may only realize that their ideas of vision and purpose are out of alignment when they find themselves fighting over competing initiatives.

Weak Direction from the Team Leader

Please don't misinterpret what I'm saying here. I'm not stating that team leaders should do the thinking for their teams. I certainly hope most organizations have evolved past the point where they expect their team leaders to sit alone in their offices, in solitary wisdom, crafting objectives and long-terms goals that are then force-fed to their teams. I think most of us would accept the view that in today's workplace, the most effective leader is one who attempts to work collectively with team members to forge a picture of their desired future. At the same time, team leaders play a number of roles that are critical to the success of long-term goal setting.

First, they often serve as a vital communication link between their teams and the rest of the organization. The team leader is also in a better position to observe how each team member's activities relate to the team's overall work efforts. Finally, team leaders are likely to have gained valuable experience and knowledge regarding the workings of their organizations and industries. Such experience often provides the team members with the perspective they need to interpret the broader impact of their decisions and activities. Without this direction, a team will be operating in an information vacuum and will have difficulty achieving a clear sense of its overall direction.

Nebulous Planning

Occasionally, I find that team members may have discussed and reached alignment on their common future but have never taken the time to clearly articulate the details of the actions required to achieve it. Just as a homeowner might have a rough idea of what a dream house should look like but lack an orderly blueprint for building the structure, many teams fail to create an organizational blueprint for defining their future and guiding their long-term efforts. As a result, long-term plans may be vaguely referenced but never effectively executed.

Lack of Midcourse Corrections

Team planning activities are a bit like diets. I know many people who read the latest diet books and then put together a detailed dietary plan, only to find that two months later they are once again afraid to look at their bathroom scales. In the same way, teams sometimes mistakenly assume that once they craft a vision statement or strategic plan, they can put their plans on the shelf and let these tools continue to passively work their magic without the need for additional intervention.

The problem, of course, is that teams are dynamic entities that are continually changing and adapting to new circumstances. Although vision statements and strategic plans do serve a valuable direction-setting function, they only work if the team takes its plans out once a month to determine where it stands in relation to those plans. Many times, such a review will show that a team has drifted off course and needs to alter its direction. The team might also realize that circumstances have changed dramatically and the original plans no longer fit its requirements, in which case, team members need to set aside some time to alter them. Teams that fail to perform such midcourse corrections end up with their day-to-day work activities increasingly out of sync with their future plans.

Belief in Their Own Helplessness

Sometimes, when I talk about the importance of teams defining their visions and establishing long-term goals, I encounter a great deal of cynicism from experienced team leaders and members. Over time, these individuals have completely bought into the idea that they are powerless to shape their teams' future direction. Of all the underlying causes, this is the most difficult to address, since skill deficiencies and knowledge gaps are far easier to resolve than dysfunctional beliefs. Once established, this belief sets in motion a number of behaviors that turn it into a self-fulfilling prophecy.

Team members who feel powerless don't take time to discuss their long-term future because they assume the future is unpredictable and uncontrollable. Such teams stop scanning ahead, and they're the last to hear of impending organizational or business changes that will affect their performance. As a result, they find themselves scrambling to address these changes long after other work groups in the organization have taken adaptive action. Powerless teams also don't see the point in sorting through priorities, since they believe their efforts will be totally wasted. Instead, they shuttle back and forth among competing priorities, a situation that only adds to their stress level. When a team tries to function under these stressful conditions, its belief in its own powerlessness feeds upon itself in a continuous self-eroding cycle.

Weak Relationships with Senior Executives

Senior managers provide a top-level perspective on their organizations. They can help teams understand the long-term payoff for projects that might appear irrelevant or meaningless. They're often the first to know of shifts in the company's direction and tend to keep a close watch on marketplace and industry trends. Even if you sincerely believe your senior managers are totally clueless when it comes to sensing the direction of your company, the one indisputable fact is that your executives have the power to support or hamper your team's goals and work efforts. Their commitment to your team's long-term direction is indispensable to its survival.

Lack of External Sensing Array

As explained earlier, in Chapter 9, a team's ability to set its direction is directly related to its ability to look down the path and foresee emerging changes. If a team has not developed a method of systematically scanning the horizon to track organizational changes and industry trends, it will be trying to plot its course using nothing but hindsight. This is a recipe for disaster.

Case in Point: The Training Team

In preparation for its annual budget review, the members of Alpha Company's training team decided to go off-site and spend the day discussing their staffing and funding requirements for the upcoming year. As team members continued their discussion, it became apparent that they had very different views on where the team needed to focus its attention.

Carlos: "As I mentioned, I'm asking for $80,000 to pilot our first Web-based training program. In the last company I worked for, we made incredible progress by converting stand-up training to Web-based training, and the total savings—"

Gloria: "We've been over this before, Carlos. That was the last company you worked for. This is a completely different situation. We've made a lot of progress over the past few years, using our training classes to get close to our customers, and I don't think we should do anything that would detract from that relationship. Besides, our real focus should be extending the options we're providing in the areas of customer service and sales training. That's where we add the most value."

Barbara (Team Leader): "You both have good points, but obviously, given the financial crunch our company's in, we don't have the funds for everything. One option might be to simply allocate an equal amount of money to stand-up and Web-based training."

Dave: "Well, that sounds good. But I seem to remember that at our last meeting of the CEO Forum, I got the distinct impression that John was counting on us to expand our delivery of 360-degree feedback profiling and executive coaching sessions to our executives, and as you know, we're talking about quite a bit of money here. Based on the three bids I received from outside consulting firms, the least this is going to cost us would be a little over $100,000—and that's only taking it down to the director level."

Jill: "We've been at this discussion for two hours and we don't seem to be getting anywhere. Seems to me, the reason we can't reach agreement on budget is that we don't agree on where we should be headed over the next three years as a training team. Until we get this question answered, we're stuck!"

The Treatment

There are several steps you can take to help your team establish a clear direction. Carefully review the following section to determine which action steps are most applicable to the challenges faced by your team.

Scan the Horizon

Begin by mapping out organizational change factors that are likely to have a serious effect on your team's future direction. You might want to try some of the following approaches:

- Assign team members to sit in on the staff meetings of affiliated work groups

- Invite your senior managers (all of them, not just those directly above you in the reporting chain) to meet with your team at different times to share their views on the company's future direction

- Ask to be placed on your company's news-clippings list, and share all the latest media coverage on your company with your team

- Invite key corporate customers and suppliers to share their views on your organization's future direction

- Review customer surveys that can shed light on any important changes in your customers' requirements

- Distribute pertinent materials to your team, such as copies of your company's annual report, marketing plan, strategic plan, manpower forecast, and product development plan—all of which provide valuable information on corporate direction

Tool #24 and Tool #25 in the Tool Kit at the end of this chapter introduce structured methods for guiding your team through its scan of the future. I also strongly recommend reviewing the suggestions and tools in Chapter 9.

Identify Industry-Wide Changes

While you are looking *inside* your company to detect future changes that are likely to affect your performance, you should also look *outside* your company to identify industry-wide changes that are shaping the future of your field.

Consider sending your team on a scavenger hunt for significant industry trends. For example, one team member could be asked to consult back issues of leading business and trade journals for articles that might provide clues to industry trends. Another could be your team's liaison to professional organizations, which frequently perform annual surveys to track key trends. A third could be asked to utilize trade and professional networks and news groups on the Internet. A fourth could make use of contacts with customers, vendors, or external consultants—all of whom would be able to fill in different parts of the puzzle regarding emerging industry trends.

In addition, you might consider several other approaches.

- Attend professional and trade seminars that focus on key trends in your industry

- Have team members join professional Internet chat rooms where they can track emerging trends

- Sponsor a futures forum, composed of yourself and the team leaders of other comparable functions within leading local organizations, for the purpose of exchanging views on emerging trends within your industry

At some point, call your team together for a meeting that focuses on profiling these trends and consolidating them into a composite picture of the changes taking place in your professional field or industry.

Create a Blueprint

Schedule time to go off-site with the other members of your team to exchange views on your team's core mission, its long-term vision, and your strategy for realizing this vision. From this dialogue, help team members construct a written blueprint for guiding their long-term efforts. This blueprint requires at least four components: a team mission statement, a vision document, team objectives, and written criteria for quickly sorting team priorities. Your Tool Kit contains exercises that can help your team develop these components.

Periodically Check Your Work against the Blueprint

Once these elements are in place, your team should periodically self-audit its work to determine whether projects and work activities are aligned with its long-term strategy. Every ongoing team activity should be represented in your strategy document.

Another aspect of checking your work entails confirming your team's operating assumptions with your manager. Work with your team to develop a list of potential three-year objectives, and then ask your manager to provide feedback regarding the relative value he or she would assign to each one. In addition, make it a point to hold quarterly meetings with your manager to discuss your team's direction. At this time, provide your manager with a one-page summary outlining where your team is investing the bulk of its activity and how team members plan to refocus their attention over the next quarter.

Send Clear Signals About Work Priorities

If your team is foundering because team members are having difficulty understanding your priorities, work on sending clearer signals. Begin with your objective-setting process by limiting each team member to a maximum of three objectives. I know, you can't possibly do this with so many important priorities in front of you. On the other hand, if you look back, you will probably find that only a few of the previous year's objectives were crucial to your team's success. Make some hard decisions, and then act on them. If you see members of your team engaged in conflicts over priorities, don't hesitate to arbitrate. Periodically review your team's objectives and ask members to tell you to what degree their day-to-day work activities are centered on these objectives.

Audit Performance Criteria

Another step you can take is to audit the types of performance criteria your team uses to track its performance. As a standard rule of thumb, 80 percent of your team's work efforts should be focused on no more than three criteria. Thus, an accounts receivable department may track the percentage of payments in arrears by thirty or sixty days, while an IT help desk might track both the time-to-response for service calls and the percentage of calls that are resolved successfully without the need for call-backs (rework). Additional suggestions for setting team performance standards can be found in Chapter 11.

Provide a Teamwide View

Share copies of your own list of yearly objectives with team members, and ask them to provide copies of their own objectives to the rest of the team and to you. Meet periodically to discuss progress on teamwide objectives and obtain updates on how team members are performing in terms of individual objectives. Use these meetings as opportunities for soliciting suggestions from coworkers on how to tackle tough problems or work around project obstacles. If team members understand each individual's role in supporting the team, they'll be able to view the team's success as their own.

Construct a Vision Summary

During the last few years, much has been written on the "vision statement," perhaps too much, for I feel the term has been vastly overused and has lost a lot of its utility. In fact, the concept of constructing a team vision has become a favorite target for Dilbert™ and other cartoons that enjoy poking fun at the latest in corporate fads.

Part of the problem is that the term "vision statement" is an oxymoron, a seemingly contradictory combination of opposing words, much like "jumbo shrimp." A vision statement is supposed to be a succinct statement that captures a group's future direction, yet I've never encountered an organization or team that's been able to compress a description of its future direction into a single sentence.

In addition, the concept of direction implies a choice among competing options. For a company, this means determining where to focus its markets within different customer segments and where to advance in the area of technology and services. For a team, it means formulating a clear picture of how to develop its strength as an organizational contributor. Unfortunately, many organizations and teams are so afraid of foreclosing on options that instead of writing a sharply focused description of their desired futures, they end up creating vague and meaningless tag lines such as "To be number one in our field" or "To be the product innovator within our industry." Teams also encounter problems if they don't do their homework and instead attempt to pull a vision statement out of thin air, with the result that the statement is totally disconnected from future trends.

Finally, it goes without saying that a vision summary should be future focused. While this sounds rather self-evident, it is amazing how many teams view their vision statements as simple extrapolations of the past. A team looks back over the last three to five years of its history and asks, "How can we do better at this?" In actuality, a vision summary may direct a team along a completely different line of thinking, as it challenges team members to explore new ways of applying their strengths and capabilities.

Related Problems

Chapter 8 (The King Dethroned: Solving Member-Leader Conflict)—Team leaders play a significant role in helping their teams establish a firm sense of direction, assess work priorities, and balance long-term strategic objectives with short-term tactical requirements. If the relationship between you and your team has deteriorated, this could contribute to the team's lack of direction.

Chapter 9 (Painted into a Corner: Developing Better Foresight)—The absence of a long-term game plan is one of the main reasons for a team's inability to anticipate future threats and opportunities. I strongly recommend that you carefully review this chapter along with the current chapter.

Chapter 11 (The Missing Scorecard: Strengthening Accountability)—If your team lacks a sense of mission and purpose, it won't be able to identify performance activities that need tracking. It's impossible for a team to establish a performance scorecard without first knowing the direction of its long-term efforts. Before moving ahead to Chapter 11, be sure your team has made sufficient headway in defining its team mission, objectives, and priorities.

Chapter 15 (Cast Adrift: Securing Senior-Management Sponsorship)—The loss of senior-level sponsorship is both a symptom and a cause of lack of direction. First of all, senior managers perform a valuable function in sharing organizational goals and keeping team members informed of large-scale business and organizational changes. On the other hand, a team's credibility is partly derived from its ability to construct a viable, long-term game plan. Any team that sits passively and waits for its executive staff to offer direction will lose substantial credibility in its organization.

Tool Kit

Tool #24

SCENARIO FORECAST*

This tool encourages your team to think outside the box by trying to anticipate a variety of large-scale changes that could affect your organization and team. It goes beyond the simple, straight-line extrapolation of a company's projected performance to show how different factors can interact to produce powerful change scenarios. When done correctly, this technique forces management teams to develop business plans that can accommodate a variety of interacting change factors. It also provides a valuable tool for building alignment among managers on future opportunities and threats. Still another benefit is that scenario forecasting helps team members better understand how their disagreements on key issues are often based on very different assumptions about the future.

During the first three steps of this process, it's important to obtain input from those who can expose your top leadership team to different assumptions and inputs. These individuals might include technical leaders who have a reputation for accurately tracking industry trends, industry leaders, and even key customers and vendors. This is an area in which a trained outside consultant can often be helpful in testing those assumptions and providing needed facilitation support for your team discussion. Chart 19 outlines the steps taken to create a scenario forecast for a hypothetical strategic planning team operating within a U.S. petroleum company. Chart 20 shows the four scenarios developed by this team.

One of the most potent applications of scenario forecasting is to help a team look far into the future to consider the implications of how different change scenarios might affect its performance. One such implication involves the types of competencies that will be required of a team. Chart 21 displays examples of how four different types of business changes could influence the types of competencies required by different teams.

*Adapted from *Executive Resource Management* by Robert W. Barner. Copyright © 2000 Davies-Black Publishing. Reprinted with permission.

Tool Kit

CHART 19

How to Complete a Scenario Forecast

1. **Identify influencing factors:** With your team, brainstorm a list of external factors that are likely to shape the business environment in which your company operates. For example, a strategic planning team for a U.S.-based petrochemical company might include factors such as changes in environmental regulations pertaining to petrochemical removal, disposal, and transport; domestic gasoline consumption levels; and petrochemical production levels in other countries, including OPEC members.

2. **Rate influencing factors:** Rate each factor on a scale of 1–10 (with 10 being the highest) in terms of degree of impact and scope of change. "Degree of impact" refers to how intensely changes in this area may affect your company's performance. A score of 10 means this factor could have a major impact on your business performance. "Scope of change" refers to the amount of change this factor is likely to undergo over the next two years. A rating of 10 means that you believe a factor will change substantially over the next two years.

3. **Identify key influencing factors:** Multiply each factor's rating for degree of impact with that for scope of change. You should have a scoring range that extends from 1 (1 x 1 = 1) to 100 (10 x 10 = 100). Select from your list the two factors with the highest overall scores. These are your key influencing factors.

4. **Create alternative scenarios:** Describe two other possible scenarios for each factor. For the petrochemical company, domestic gas consumption is a key influencing factor. As a result, one future scenario might be "increased business and leisure travel create a 15% increase in gasoline consumption over the next 2 years," while an alternative might be "domestic economic pressures cause a 20% reduction in business and leisure travel over the next 2 years." Create optimistic and pessimistic scenarios, but avoid highly improbable scenarios.

5. **Combine scenarios:** Integrate your scenarios into a combined scenario matrix as shown in Chart 20. Next, create a title that best describes the combined scenario represented in each cell of the matrix. In the example presented in Chart 20, "Golden Window" indicates the window of opportunity created for increased gasoline sales, given a strong increase in domestic gasoline consumption and a simultaneous decrease in worldwide production.

6. **Describe each combined scenario:** Create a one- to two-page summary describing the details of the combined scenarios in the four cells, including the sequence of actions that would likely lead to each combined scenario.

7. **Assess probability:** Use all available information to assess the relative probability for the occurrence of each combined scenario. In the example shown in Chart 20, there's an estimated probability of 16% that the Golden Window scenario will occur during the next two years.

8. **Assess the implications:** Ask team members to jointly identify the implications of the four combined scenarios for your business strategy.

Tool Kit

CHART 20

Scenario Matrix

Scenarios Related to Worldwide Production	Scenarios Related to Domestic Consumption	
20% *increase* in worldwide petrochemical production	Everyone Wins (24%)	Sharp Fall (36%)
10% *decrease* in worldwide petrochemical production	Golden Window (16%)	Export Express (24%)

CHART 21

Scenario Forecasts and Executive Competencies

Scenario Forecasts	Implications for Competency Requirements
We will undergo a major shift from the defense to the commercial market, with 70% of revenues coming from commercial sales in 5 years, compared to 30% today.	• Less emphasis on importing executives with military backgrounds and experience in marketing to the military • Need to import or develop marketing executives with strong skills in customer focus and commercial marketing and sales
Within the next 5- to 10-year period, more than 50% of our revenues will come from new product developments.	• Need executives with ability to manage fast product development and design for manufacturing • Need executives who can perform effectively in marketing, production, and legal so we can shrink development times
We anticipate streamlining our direct overhead expenses, with our entire field support and audit functions outsourced to external providers.	• Require leadership competencies in negotiating and managing large outsourced work functions • Need organizational development executives who can help us plan a smooth transition from in-house to outsourced work functions
We will open our first e-commerce site on the Internet next year, with the goal of having 15% of all sales coming through the Internet within the next 4 years.	• Need IT executives who are able to identify appropriate e-commerce target markets and manage Web site design, including integration of inventory, tracking, credit, and billing

Tool Kit

RUNNING THE GAUNTLET TECHNIQUE*

Tool #25

This technique can help your team evaluate its readiness for successfully pursuing different business objectives, given the alternative change scenarios that were developed with Tool #24. By using this tool, you'll be able to test the robustness of your business objectives against three or four short-term business scenarios.

To better understand what I mean, consider an individual preparing for an extended camping trip. Someone planning for a narrow set of contingencies may take only a few bare essentials, such as a sleeping bag, tent, flashlight, and matches, whereas the person who develops a sturdier plan will bring along a variety of supplies—perhaps foul-weather gear, a cookstove, water purification tablets, a first aid kit—to cope with a wider range of environmental conditions. In the same way, when your team is establishing business objectives, team members can use this technique to determine how well your business plans incorporated the types of changes created by alternate change scenarios.

Chart 22 shows how this application could be used with four scenarios developed by our hypothetical strategic planning team. This team has discovered that in undertaking its first objective, it is well prepared to handle any of the four potential business scenarios. On the other hand, objective 3 is not very promising since the team has rated its readiness to execute this objective as "low" in three of the four scenarios. Looking at this example from another perspective, we can see that the Export Express is the overall scenario for which this team is least prepared, while it is most prepared to deal with the Golden Window scenario.

Work teams often incorporate into their plans a set of implicit assumptions—a Plan A—which is based on their conviction that a given scenario will occur, while at the same time, they ignore the need to plan for other contingencies. This tool forces teams to examine their operating assumptions and evaluate the overall strength of their plans.

CHART 22

Running the Gauntlet				
Alternative Scenarios	**Everyone Wins**	**Golden Window**	**Sharp Fall**	**Export Express**
Objective 1	High	High	High	Moderate
Objective 2	Moderate	Moderate	Low	Low
Objective 3	Low	Moderate	Low	Low

*Adapted from *Executive Resource Management* by Robert W. Barner. Copyright © 2000 Davies-Black Publishing. Reprinted with permission.

Tool Kit

Tool #26

TEAM VISION SUMMARY

An effective vision summary—a detailed, one-page statement of how the team hopes to evolve and develop over time—is built from a careful analysis of changing patterns in the team's industry, customer base, competitors, and value-added products and services. Of special note here is the word "competitor." If your work team directly supports other departments within your company, you may feel you have no competitors. In actuality, a competitor is any group within or outside your organization (an existing group or one that might form after a reorganization) that could assume your group's normal functions. Your customers may even become your competitors by deciding they could provide your team's services in-house. (See Chapter 17 for suggestions on strengthening customer relationships.) A vision summary also addresses the team's view of its evolving role within the organization. In this technique, I'll introduce a structured process for crafting a vision summary that addresses both components.

There are five steps involved in constructing your vision summary:

1. Describe anticipated changes in your customer base and market, competitors, and industry. These are not the changes you hope will occur but those you feel will most probably occur, given present trends. Exercise 12 will help your team members think through potential changes to your customer base and market. The worksheet in Exercise 13 applies to potential changes in your competitors. Exercise 14 provides a third worksheet for evaluating potential changes in your field and industry. I recommend asking the members of your team to complete these three worksheets individually over several days before meeting together to combine their views into a consolidated summary of anticipated future events.

2. Describe anticipated changes in your team's future organizational role. Once again, at this point, you're being asked to describe how organizational and business pressures are likely to shape the structure of your team. Exercise 15 provides a worksheet for gathering input from your team. The worksheet also asks for a description of your team's desired organizational role, or the role your team would like to play in the future, as well as any changes you foresee in the types of products and services you provide to your internal and external clients.

Tool Kit

EXERCISE 12 • ASSESSING CHANGES IN CUSTOMER BASE AND MARKET

Questions You Need to Answer	Your Team's Responses
What additional customers might your team be serving over the next 3–5 years?	
Which of these customer segments are likely to assume far greater importance for your team?	
Which of your current customer groups are likely to become less important or will cease to be served by your team?	
What changes do you anticipate in your customers' requirements? How will their expectations of your team change over time?	
What products and services do your customers want that your team isn't currently providing and will need to provide in the future?	

Tool Kit

EXERCISE 13 • ASSESSING CHANGES IN COMPETITORS

Questions You Need to Answer	Your Team's Responses
Currently, who are your team's primary internal and external competitors?	
What new competitors are likely to emerge over the next 3–5 years?	
What product or services gaps could these competitors fill (customer needs not currently being addressed by your team)?	
What distinct cost, service delivery, or relationship advantages could these competitors provide that might place your team at a serious competitive disadvantage?	
What activities could your team undertake over the next few years to meet the potential challenges posed by your competitors (strengthen lines of communication with customers, improve service delivery, etc.)?	

Tool Kit

EXERCISE 14 • ASSESSING CHANGES IN YOUR FIELD AND INDUSTRY

Questions You Need to Answer	Your Team's Responses
What new technological developments will dramatically alter the shape of your field over the next 3–5 years?	
What new technical and functional competencies are being sought by managers in your field? What competencies are likely to be in short supply over the next 3–5 years?	
What existing technical and functional competencies are becoming far less important? (Example: Typesetters are no longer required in newspaper production)	
How is the role of your work function changing in other organizations? (Example: HR teams are gradually taking on the role of adviser to senior management regarding executive selection, placement, and development)	
What major changes are occurring within your industry that could dramatically affect the demands on your team over the next few years?	

Tool Kit

Questions You Need to Answer	Your Team's Responses
What likely changes in your company's business arena over the next 3–5 years could affect its expectations of your work team?	
What changes are likely to occur in your company's organizational structure over the next 3–5 years? How will these changes affect your work team?	
How are your company's expectations for your team likely to change over the next few years? (Example: Do you foresee a severe tightening in quality performance standards? Are you likely to encounter severe cost pressures?)	
Over the next few years, how is your team's organizational role likely to change?	
Ideally, how would you like to see your team's organizational role evolve over the next 3–5 years? What new functions or responsibilities do you want to manage? What changes do you want to see in your team's service delivery over time?	

Tool Kit

3. Summarize all the information gathered in the first two steps in a one-page vision summary that describes your team's desired future direction. Chart 23 shows a vision summary crafted for a hypothetical training team.

CHART 23

Vision Summary for Training Team

Our overall vision is to help raise the performance capability of our organization and to become, over the next few years, the benchmark for state-of-the-art performance delivery systems among our competitors.

Our team intends to expand our service delivery function over the next 3–5 years to cover not only our internal customer base but our external customers as well. At the same time, we will evolve from a cost center to a discrete profit-and-loss center, with the goal of generating a net profit on all training activities undertaken by our team.

With these changes, our team will develop from a domestic training team into a truly international one. Currently, we provide only limited and sporadic service to our international employees and customers. Our goal over the next five years is to shift at least 30% of our base training activities toward this international market in order to support our company's goal of becoming the premier international provider of corporate financial and investment services. We know that such a transition will require integrating bilingual trainers and a higher degree of flexible program delivery into our training programs.

We realize that, to accomplish these aims, we must invest heavily in stand-alone Web-based training and training delivered through the recently expanded corporate intranet site. We are just beginning to pilot in this area but have set the goal of having at least 25% of all training programs available on the Web or intranet over the next five years.

With regard to our executive development efforts, our intention is to build a seamless executive assessment and development system that will provide our executives and managers with a clear understanding of their respective leadership strengths and weaknesses and will direct them through a program of development activities tied directly to identified performance improvement areas. To achieve this aim, we intend to introduce our managers and executives to the concept of 360-degree profiling. Within 12 months, we will create our first corporation-wide roll-up of executive competencies and development gaps and will match this data against the organizational requirements spelled out in our corporate strategic plan. We also intend to assume the role of development coach by extending executive activities beyond the classroom to include structured development assignments, third-party coaching by one of our staff, the creation of a formalized mentoring program, and a fast-track program for identified high-potential talent.

Tool Kit

CHART 24

4. Identify key team performance gaps (e.g., team competencies, knowledge, team structure) and any organizational obstacles (e.g., current reputation of your team, nonsupportive senior manager) that must be surmounted before your team can fulfill its desired vision. Chart 24 provides an example based on our hypothetical training team.

Performance Gap Summary for Training Team

Identified Performance Gaps	Current Situation	Desired Future Situation
What technical or functional skill gaps must be closed before your team can pursue its vision?	We're relying on an outside consultant to guide us in the design and delivery of our Web-based training pilots.	We will hire a manager of Web-based development and two technical support people to direct this function. We will also invest approximately $100k in technical start-up costs.
What knowledge gaps will your team need to close to pursue its vision?	We don't have the expertise to decide when Web-based training provides advantages over classroom training and have only limited, anecdotal information on our customers' requirements. We don't understand cultural factors that could affect training delivery in our new Pacific Rim ventures.	We will conduct best-practice reviews and use our new manager's expertise with Web-based development to make these decisions. We will incorporate questions on training requirements into our annual customer service audit and will develop cultural familiarity through partnerships with our international marketing team.
In what ways must your team's structure and composition change?	All training design and delivery activities are currently performed by a single team of trainers. Only one person is allocated to the area of executive assessment and design.	We may need to break out a special design team devoted entirely to Web-based development. This area should be a three-person function within the next two years.
What organizational obstacles will you need to overcome? What steps could you take to overcome them?	Our senior executive is uncertain about the potential applications of Web-based training. Our senior vice president of customer support is concerned about our ability to manage training delivery to external customers.	We will ask a representative of a company that is advanced in this area to make a presentation to our senior executive on the advantages to be gained from this option. We will suggest to our customer service executive that this function be co-managed by a member of his staff.

5. Test the feasibility and robustness of your team vision summary by inviting input from one or two managers who are familiar with your team's operation and whose judgment you respect. With the help of these objective observers and team members, answer the following questions:

- Is the summary you've constructed specific to your team? If the summary is so vague and generalized that it could pertain to any team, it needs to be rewritten.

- Have you taken into account all of the broader organizational and industry-related changes that are likely to occur over the next few years? (Here's where your outside observers can be of great help.) Has your team accurately assessed the probable effect of these changes on your work team?

- Is your vision summary exciting? Does it capture the commitment of your work team?

- Is your vision summary wrapped in fancy jargon and obscure language, or is it something that can be understood easily by team members and internal customers?

- Does your vision summary enhance your team's understanding of the types of choices or tradeoffs involved in meeting the needs of various customers?

- Does your vision summary paint a clear and vivid picture of your team's desired future?

11

The Missing Scorecard

Strengthening Accountability

Have you ever wondered why some teams seem to flail around ineffectively while others consistently meet their objectives? It's not uncommon to see teams start off with a flourish, only to reveal that they're confused, disorganized, or, at worst, totally aimless. Quite often, ineffectual teams lack a well-defined scorecard for evaluating success. Unless teams have clearly articulated and agreed on their performance metrics for measuring success, how can members, leaders, and senior management measure their performance? A solid and explicit performance scorecard is essential to the success of any team. This is true regardless of whether the team in question is a traditional manager-led team or a temporary cross-functional one.

Consider the following example, involving someone we'll call Judy Stuckee, an employee who has just agreed to take on the leadership of a new cross-functional process-improvement project.

Manager: "Judy, as I'm sure you're aware, our customer fulfillment process is really causing problems with our customers. As it stands now, it's grossly ineffective. We have a great product, but we make our customers jump through hoops just to sign on with us. I've been talking to our senior team about this problem, and we'd like you to take on the job of exploring improvements to the current process. You'll be able to put together your own team. This includes your own work group and also personnel from other departments if you feel they could contribute substantially to this project. Everyone will be told that this is a top priority. How do you feel about the assignment so far?"

Judy: "It sounds exciting. Improving our customer fulfillment process could generate a number of benefits for our company. When would I start, and how much time should I plan on allocating to the project?"

Manager: "We'd like you to start immediately. As for time, my guess is that it would involve about 50 percent of your time over the next few months. Better count on off-loading some of your responsibilities to Bill and Natasha. Any other questions?"

Judy: "No. I'll probably have some later on, but I think I'm ready to give it a try."

Manager: "Great! Why don't you plan on getting back to me in a few weeks, after you've assembled your team, to give me a progress check on where you stand?"

At first, everything we've heard sounds fine. The manager has described the project, and Judy believes she's ready to put her team together. A closer look, however, reveals that Judy's team is about to collide with a brick wall, because she has failed to reach agreement with her manager regarding the performance factors against which she and her team are to be measured.

The manager has described the current customer fulfillment process as "grossly ineffective," but what does that really mean? Does it take too long to fill an order once it's been taken from a customer? Does the process add too much to the overall cost of the company's products? Are the wrong products shipped out, or are the correct products shipped to the wrong addresses? If team members don't understand the types of improvements their senior managers hope to achieve with the project, they won't be able to focus their efforts on the most important improvement opportunities.

A well-constructed performance scorecard is vital to the success of any team. Without a clear set of standards against which to measure its performance, a team won't be able to evaluate its success or accurately gauge the effectiveness of any improvements to its work processes.

The Symptoms

Teams that are unsure of how to measure their performance display some of the following symptoms. Review this section with other team members, and with selected managers who have a good "outside-in" view of your work group, to determine which symptoms are applicable to your team.

Focus on Activities, Not Results

Without access to effective measurement systems, teams are forced to develop rough guesstimates about their performance, based on the amount of time and attention invested in different activities. Unfortunately, such activity-based evaluations can easily fool teams into believing they're making valuable organizational contributions when their employers are actually deriving little from their activities.

Thus, a corporate training team may brag about the numbers of hours of training they have provided yet be unable to demonstrate whether this training improved performance throughout the organization. In the same way, the members of a sales team may convince themselves they're achieving better results simply because they're making more sales calls, although in reality, a simple review of sales volume and revenue might show the team's performance has been steadily declining over the past two years.

Lack of Direction or Motivation

According to an old adage, "What gets measured gets attended to." Well-designed scorecards help team members focus on the most important work activities instead of scattering their efforts among a dozen or so competing ones. Similarly, it's hard to stay interested in a game if you can't tell the score. Team members who are trying to function without solid measurement systems are often unmotivated and apathetic. From their point of view, a team that doesn't track their performance doesn't really care about getting results.

Difficulty Recovering from and Analyzing Setbacks

Even the best of teams encounter occasional performance setbacks. When faced with reversals, teams with reliable scorecards in place are able to put the situation in perspective by reminding themselves of the steady improvement they've made over the long run. Teams that haven't established performance measurement systems find it difficult to adopt such a long-term perspective and may well become demoralized when faced with reversals.

Scorecards provide teams with a means of identifying factors that contribute to performance problems. For example, at what point did on-time delivery become a problem? Is there a pattern emerging in customer complaints? At what point did production begin to decline? What was happening during this time period that might explain the onset of the customer service problem? Teams that lack effective scorecards are usually at a loss to explain why certain performance problems are occurring.

Case in Point: The Auto Dealership

An international automobile manufacturer found that its dealerships consistently outperformed their competitors in revenues from auto lease sales but scored only moderately well in the area of customer service. Further investigation showed that many complaints occurred after customers signed their lease and returned to the dealership for their first scheduled service call. Customers expressed concern that whenever they attempted to contact their sales agents about problems with their vehicles, they were immediately directed to the service department; at this point, members of the sales teams washed their hands of any problems. The reason for this behavior was that sales agents' commissions were based totally on their sales revenue, the only aspect of their performance that was tracked. In addition, the sales group received only sketchy feedback on service complaints through the company's customer satisfaction audit system.

To correct this problem, the automobile manufacturer created a customer feedback form that included questions about the customers' views of their sales agents' ability to address service problems. In addition, sales agents' commission plans were modified to integrate service satisfaction scores obtained from customers. Soon after this program was initiated, the company observed a huge jump in customer satisfaction scores and, shortly thereafter, a significant increase in repeat business.

The Underlying Causes

Well-defined scorecards allow teams to measure significant areas of their performance. Sometimes, however, teams encounter factors that make it difficult for them to develop or utilize such scorecards. As you review this section, try to determine whether any of these causes is relevant to your team.

Failure to Identify Important Outputs

It's pointless to select a measuring instrument unless you know what you're trying to measure. A ruler might serve well for measuring a person's height, but it's a poor tool for determining the speed of a car. For a team, it's vital to identify the most important outputs before creating a performance scorecard. Outputs can be defined as those products and services the team generates to meet the needs of its internal and external customers. Representative outputs include databases, reports, technical assistance, training programs, equipment procurement, contracts, and market research studies. A team that has not determined its most important outputs has not yet identified those that should be tracked and evaluated out of the hundreds of functions it performs.

Fear of Failure

Many people avoid routine medical checkups because they're afraid of what they might find out about their health. In the same way, some teams shy away from setting up performance measures because they fear that, once established, these evaluation tools will be used in a punitive or malicious way by their team leaders or senior managers. Team leaders can help team members overcome this fear by engaging in a frank discussion about the potential benefits of measuring the group's performance, while at the same time conveying their sensitivity to any concerns raised by team members.

Failure to Take the Customer into Account

Teams sometimes severely weaken their team evaluation process by failing to include measures that focus specifically on customer satisfaction. Sometimes a team is reluctant to learn how customers view its performance; in other words, no news is good news. In other situations, a team may be so absorbed in its own perspective that it fails to consider that it might not have an accurate idea of the customer's-eye view of its performance. Finally, there are many teams that aren't sure how to proceed in evaluating customer satisfaction. Whatever the reasons, the absence of customer performance measures is always a severe weakness in any performance scorecard system.

Inability to Agree on Ground Rules

Teams sometimes find that although they would like to create performance scorecards, they can't agree on when and how to measure their performance. Some team members may want to take such detailed measurements that they become engrossed in the minutiae of the process, while others may feel that any measurement at all infringes on their freedom. While some team members may want to display team performance results on wall charts for easy viewing, others may be leery of disclosing potential performance problems to individuals outside the team. These different points of view are not insurmountable but do require diligent efforts toward resolution on the part of all team members.

The Treatment

Follow these eight sequential steps to help your team create a performance scorecard:

1. Convince your team of the value of a scorecard

2. Reach agreement on what is to be measured

3. Identify useful performance measures

4. Obtain commitment from stakeholders

5. Decide on a method of implementation

6. Perform a baseline evaluation

7. Track improvement over time

8. Identify knowledge gained

Convince Your Team of the Value of a Scorecard

Ask your team to read this chapter and determine if they've noticed any of the symptoms related to the lack of a scorecard in your team. Rather than attempt sweeping changes in this area, see if your team can agree on the single most important team performance area that currently lacks a scorecard process. Then see if they can agree on the need for establishing a team measurement process for this area. Finally, discuss the types of ground rules that would make them feel more at ease with the use of performance scorecards. Representative ground rules might include

- Scorecard measures will be identified and monitored by the team.

- Scorecard measures will be restricted to team performance and will not be used to evaluate the performance of individual team members.

- The scorecard will only be used and reviewed by the team.

- The scorecard will be piloted for a period of three months and continued beyond this time only if the team is comfortable with the use of this tool.

Reach Agreement on What Is to Be Measured

Working with your team, determine which of your many team responsibilities should be measured and tracked. As a general guideline, try to select a performance area that has a strong impact on your team's overall success, and one that is directly visible to your customers.

Identify Useful Performance Measures

Performance measures can be divided into two categories. For your team's ongoing daily responsibilities, the evaluation should center on the most important outputs (products and services) provided to internal and external customers. The three standard measures for outputs are

1. Efficiency: How productively your team uses staff, time, and resources

2. Quality: The degree to which your team's work is error free and meets quality standards

3. Customer satisfaction: The degree to which your team meets customer requirements

Chart 25 shows examples of how these measures can be used to evaluate ongoing responsibilities.

You may also use these three measures to evaluate the outcomes of key projects completed by your team, as shown in Chart 26.

In addition to these three factors, you might also consider a fourth evaluation criterion, process effectiveness, when evaluating important projects. Process effectiveness is the degree to which team members and their leader work together effectively to plan and implement the project. Chart 27 provides an example of how the four measures of quality, customer satisfaction, efficiency, and process effectiveness have been used to evaluate a facilities project.

Obtain Commitment from Stakeholders

Once your team has identified which performance area should be measured and by what types of criteria, it's essential to discuss your plans with your stakeholders. Your manager and your customers are two primary stakeholders. Both should agree with you on the importance of the performance areas selected by your team and the validity of the measurement process you've identified. When discussing your scorecard with your stakeholders, try to

CHART 25

Team Scorecards for Ongoing Responsibilities	
Type of Team	**Alternative Evaluation Methods**
Customer Satisfaction Measures	
Corporate training team	• Customer satisfaction feedback obtained through surveys, interviews, or focus groups
IT help desk	• Complaint-activity trend reports • Follow-up audits of service calls
Customer service team	• Positive/negative feedback received within focus groups
Quality Measures	
Corporate recruiting team	• Voluntary termination rates for high-performing employees, covering a 12-month follow-up period from date of hire • Interim performance appraisals for employees 6 months after date of hire
Automotive service center	• Percentage of call-backs due to incomplete or faulty service
Finance department	• Percentage of error-free billings
Efficiency Measures	
Hospital admissions team	• Time required for processing new admissions
IT help desk	• Percentage of emergency call responses within 30 minutes
Shipping department	• Percentage of on-time deliveries

CHART 26

Scorecards for Team Projects	
Type of Project	**Alternative Evaluation Methods**
Project involving changes to company policy	• Employee satisfaction surveys • Employee satisfaction interviews • Tests on comprehension of new policy guidelines • Comparison of employee complaints related to policy issue, before and after policy change
Process improvement project	Prechange and postchange reviews comparing • Cycle time and steps required to complete the process • Non-value-added steps included in the process • Costs associated with the completion of the process • Average number of errors made while completing the process
Production efficiency project	• Reductions in unscheduled downtime • Increases in product yield and corresponding decreases in scrap rates

remain open to any input they might provide on ways of improving your evaluation process.

Decide on a Method of Implementation

This means determining how and when your team will measure, track, and communicate the results of its performance evaluation. Another important aspect of data collection involves identifying the types of metrics, or tools and methods, to be used by your team to measure its performance. For example, assume that the length of time needed to fill positions is the measure of a corporate recruiting team's efficiency. Accordingly, this team might select

CHART 27

Scorecard for Evaluating a Facilities Project

Project Quality	
Success criteria:	The move should enable us to maximize space and equipment utilization while minimizing disruptions such as unscheduled downtime
Evaluation factors:	Unscheduled downtime, work delays, rework, or temporary storage costs due to • Phone or computer lines not connected on time • Equipment and furniture not delivered on time or to the right location

Customer Satisfaction	
Success criteria:	Satisfaction of internal customers (user departments) in terms of timely information on the move, minimal disruptions to work effectiveness, and satisfaction with the completion of move-related activities
Evaluation factors:	Evaluation of employee satisfaction feedback questionnaire

Project Efficiency	
Success criteria:	• Cost: Total project cost, including equipment, travel, software, staff, etc. • Time: Total time required for the completion of the project • Resources: Additional, unplanned resources required for project completion
Evaluation factors:	• Cost: Variance from projected budget • Time: Variance from projected schedule • Resources: Cost for additional, unplanned resources

Process Effectiveness	
Success criteria:	• Team performance: Effectiveness in achieving project goals. • Leader performance: Effectiveness in leading the project
Evaluation factors:	• Team feedback form: Team members rate their perceived strengths and weaknesses, and overall performance, using self-evaluation rating form • Leader feedback form: Project leader and team members rate leader performance using leader-evaluation form

as its metric a log that compares the time and date a position is posted with the time and date that position is filled, as verified by the date on which a new hire starts work. Chart 28 shows the metrics used to measure three different performance areas. Tool 27 in your Tool Kit outlines a methodology for collecting and tracking team performance data.

Perform a Baseline Evaluation

A baseline evaluation determines your team's current performance in a given area before improvement suggestions are implemented. Comparing your baseline evaluation with subsequent evaluations is the only way to determine whether the changes you've made have actually improved your team's performance.

Figure 4 shows both a baseline and a subsequent evaluation for a help-desk team that targeted the area of call responsiveness. The team tracked its performance for one week of activity and then implemented a centralized dispatching process the next week. By comparing response times during the baseline period to its performance during the second week, the team was able to confirm that the dispatching experiment yielded significant improvement.

CHART 28

Success Criteria and Metrics

Responsibility	Success Criteria	Possible Metrics
Administration team: Planning a facilities move	• Timeliness • Cost • Operational efficiency	• Variance from project milestone schedules • Variance from project cost estimate • Days of downtime attributable to move
Human resources team: Resolving a high-turnover problem	• Employee turnover rates	• Changes in voluntary turnover rates for exceptional employees during a 12-month period
Accounts receivable team: Improving billing efficiency	• Billing errors • Timeliness	• Comparison of >30 days' outstanding billings for the 12-month period following project implementation • Comparison of time and steps required to process bills before and after project

Track Improvement over Time

In this step, you'll track your team's performance to see whether it's improving gradually over time. Such tracking can also help you identify important performance trends. For example, let's consider a hospital admissions team that's tracking the time required for admitting new patients. A three-week study of admission times might show a consistent increase during the peak period of 6–8 P.M. With this information, the team can begin to develop strategies to address the situation, such as adding temporary help during this two-hour period each evening.

Identify Knowledge Gained

The last step in establishing a performance scorecard is to encourage team members to periodically step back from their work to review the lessons

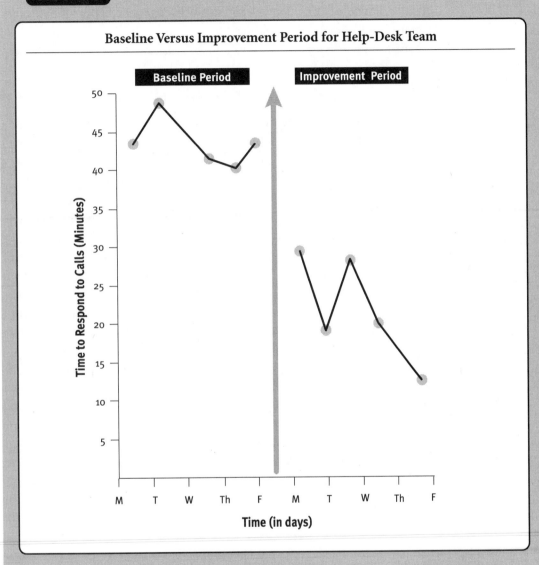

FIGURE 4

Baseline Versus Improvement Period for Help-Desk Team

they've gleaned from their evaluation process. A great time to perform this step is immediately after the completion of a team project. Your Tool Kit contains guidelines for completing this step, as well as a Lessons Learned Questionnaire that can be used to gather feedback from your team members.

Related Problems

Chapter 9 (Painted into a Corner: Developing Better Foresight)—A good scorecard helps a team anticipate and decipher performance trends that could indicate new opportunities or threats. The absence of a performance measurement process reduces a team's ability to profit through foresight.

Chapter 10 (The Broken Compass: Finding a Sense of Direction)—A team must determine its direction, mission, and priorities before it can create a performance measurement system. The lack of direction consequently contributes to an ineffective scorecard process. If you have not yet reviewed Chapter 10, you might find it useful to do so before proceeding with the rest of this chapter.

Chapter 14 (Reversals: Dealing with Setbacks)—Without a performance measurement system, it's difficult for a team to adopt a long-term perspective and place temporary setbacks in a realistic context. Keep this in mind if you intend to explore the problem of dealing with reversals.

Chapter 17 (Our Own Worst Enemy: Strengthening Customer Relationships)—When a team doesn't measure its performance against customer expectations, an effective response is difficult. If some of the customer-related symptoms mentioned earlier in this chapter pertain to your team, you may find it helpful to review Chapter 17.

Tool Kit

The first two tools in this section offer alternative methods of collecting team performance data. Each method is suited to a different category of team performance.

TALLY LOG

Use a simple tally log if the performance area you would like to measure consists of quantifiable events, such as

- How often telephones are answered by the third ring
- What number of packages are shipped on time
- Amount of service complaints from customers

The example shown in Chart 29 documents customer complaints for a hypothetical call center.

CHART 29

Customer Complaint Log									
Mon.	**Tues.**	**Wed.**	**Thur.**	**Fri.**	**Mon.**	**Tues.**	**Wed.**	**Thur.**	**Fri.**
I I	I I		I	︦H︦H	I	I I	I	I I	I I I I

The reason for collecting data is to look for patterns and discover what they reveal about team performance. In the above example, it appears there is something unique about Fridays that creates a significant increase in customer complaints.

Tool Kit

DATA COLLECTION CHART

The problem with the tally system in Chart 29 is that it assumes a consistent volume of work for the team. In our call center example, we don't know whether the increase in complaints on Friday is due to the fact that the team approaches its work differently on that day or because call activity typically rises then. One way to account for this uncertainty is to review the information against the backdrop of total daily call activity during this time period. Exercise 16 provides a data collection form for your team.

Chart 30 shows how this form was completed by a sales development team, which is attempting to understand the types of complaints it currently receives regarding service contracts. While the team knows that its customers feel these contracts are hard to understand and somewhat misleading, team members lack specific information that would help them determine how to make effective improvements.

EXERCISE 16 • TEAM DATA COLLECTION FORM

Questions We Need to Ask	with others?
What aspect of team performance will we be evaluating?	**Our Answers to These Questions**
What exactly will we be measuring or tracking?	
What do we hope to learn from this information?	
How do we hope to benefit from this information?	
Who on (or outside) our team will collect evaluation data?	
How frequently and over what period of time will information be collected?	
How will the information we gather be documented?	
How will this information be formatted for review?	
How and when will this information be shared	

Tool Kit

CHART 30

Team Data Collection Form for Sales Development Team

Questions We Need to Ask	Our Answers to These Questions
What aspect of team performance will we be evaluating?	• Our service contracts
What exactly will we be measuring or tracking?	Following contract signing: • The number and types of follow-up questions asked by customers • Complaints voiced by customers about misinterpretations of the contract
What do we hope to learn from this information?	• Which aspects of our service contract process are confusing to our customers?
How do we hope to benefit from this information?	• Learn how we can simplify contracts or design user-friendly communication vehicles to create a stand-alone contract process, thus eliminating needless follow-up activity and increasing customer satisfaction
Who on (or outside) our team will collect evaluation data?	• Every team member
How frequently and over what period of time will this information be collected?	• With every occurrence, and continuing for 30 days, starting July 1
How will we document the information we gather?	• Phone logs maintained individually by each member of our team
How will this information be formatted for review?	• Phone logs will be consolidated by our team coordinator, with questions and complaints classified according to type
	• We will develop a trend line to determine whether complaint activity is increasing, decreasing, or holding steady over time
How and when will this information be shared with others?	• We will provide senior management with a summary report and our recommendations for change

Tool Kit

LESSONS LEARNED SESSION

Teams frequently find themselves so caught up in completing one project and moving on to another that they never bother to stop and gather the knowledge they have gained from working on a given project. Your approach to this final discussion is very important. Without the appropriate stage setting, team members may be overly concerned that their purpose is to assign blame or find fault. In fact, this tool is meant to focus on the *team's* experience, not the performance of individual team members. It's the last opportunity for your team to take a look at its collective experience and distill a formula for improving performance on future projects. Many of the guidelines and suggestions I've shared in this book are the result of lessons I've obtained from such sessions.

I recommend you follow these steps when conducting your own Lessons Learned Session.

1. Thank all team members again for their contributions to your project and explain that this last meeting is intended to help members apply to future projects the knowledge they've gained through their recent team experience.

2. Ask your team to select for discussion five of the questions listed in the Lessons Learned Questionnaire (Chart 31). If time permits, you may expand the discussion to include additional questions.

3. Title a sheet of flipchart paper with the first of these questions. Record members' responses to these questions on the flipchart. Title the next sheet of paper with the second question, record responses, and continue until all questions have been addressed.

4. Team members may have very different views regarding their responses to certain questions. Highlight for further discussion those items on which there is no definite consensus.

5. Assign each team member the task of consolidating the team's responses to each question into one or two sentences.

6. Consider printing this consolidated list of lessons learned to serve as a reference guide for use with future projects.

Tool Kit

CHART 31

Lessons Learned Questionnaire

1. In what project performance areas—schedule, cost, quality—do we feel our team has performed exceptionally well?

2. What actions, techniques, and tools did we use that could be applied to future projects?

3. On which aspects of our project did we not perform as well as expected?

4. In retrospect, what would we have done differently—scheduling, budgeting, resource planning—to improve our performance?

5. What unique skills did our team bring to this project that are applicable to other projects?

6. In retrospect, what additional skills do we need to graft onto our team?

7. What unanticipated challenges did we encounter on this project?

8. What have we learned from addressing these challenges?

9. In summary, what are some of the most important things we've learned from participating in this project?

10. What steps could we take to share the lessons we've learned with other teams?

Dealing with the Challenges of Change

The Brittle Team

Learning to Adapt to Change

Rapid, highly unpredictable change is a consistent feature of today's corporate landscape. Whether we're talking about the large-scale changes inherent in corporate restructurings or mergers, or the thousands of microchanges that accompany such actions as redefining team charters or replacing team leaders, all change tests the adaptive capacity of professional work teams.

I would argue that the ability to creatively adapt to change is a megaskill that supplies underlying support for team performance. By way of analogy, consider the dinosaur. For hundreds of millions of years, dinosaurs were at the top of the food chain, dominating almost every available environment on the planet. They eventually died out, not because they were overtaken by a more ferocious predator, but because they couldn't adapt to dramatic changes in the global climate. In the same way, even the most productive teams may find themselves devolving into organizational dinosaurs if they fail to cope effectively with change.

At this point in the discussion, I'm sure a few skeptical readers are thinking, "The whole idea of change management is unrealistic. The changes that *my team* is currently experiencing are simply too large to control." My response to this statement is that effective teams know they may not be able to *control* change, but they can certainly prepare for it and manage its impact on their work functions. They are able to do this because successful change managers display the following change-survival traits:

- Ability to *anticipate change,* accurately assess the impact, and identify which specific change factors may seriously affect their team's performance

- Ability to *respond flexibly* and creatively to change, especially to unfamiliar situations that may require new types of solutions

- Ability to *maintain their focus* during periods of change and to use their business strategy and objectives as organizational lodestones to guide their teams through disruptive change

- Ability to *cope with the stress* that often accompanies rapid change, which often involves factors beyond their control

- *Proactive approach* to change, such as acquiring new competencies and business information to avoid technical obsolescence

In contrast, brittle teams lack the resilience and tenacity to cope effectively with rapid change. When waves of change batter an organization, some teams manage to ride the crest while others are trapped in the undertow. Brittle teams are usually slow to understand the implications of change, and their reaction time is even slower. When they do react, their responses are maladaptive—that is, they work against the team's survival. The danger is, of course, that since large-scale change now permeates every aspect of our business environment, individuals who haven't mastered the megaskill of resilience will find it difficult to perform well in almost any organization.

The Symptoms

Within every team, the inability to adapt to change reveals itself in many different ways. As you read through the following symptoms, try to determine which of these behaviors apply to your team.

Anxiety About the Unknown Future

Stress is an increasingly common factor for all teams. Within brittle teams, however, an excessive amount of stress is associated with the vague anxiety that accompanies an uncertain and possibly threatening future, not with events that have already occurred.

The key distinction is the difference between fear and anxiety. Fear is attached to a real, known set of events. Anxiety is that vague sense of apprehension arising from a fear that has not yet taken form. For many people, coping with anxiety is a bit like trying to cut through fog with a butter knife. When teams focus on vague worries, you'll observe members fretting over possible scenarios by making comments such as "but what if the restructuring results in a downsizing for our department?" rather than directing their energy toward dealing with the manageable aspects of change. It's reasonable to assume that every team will encounter at least one large-scale change that produces a lot of anxiety. For brittle teams, however, anxiety is the prevailing, habitual response to any new and demanding situation.

Lack of Foresight

A team's ability to adapt to change depends to a large extent on its ability to anticipate changes in its work environment and to determine the difference between innocuous events, serious threats, or significant opportunities (see Chapter 9). Brittle teams don't display a great deal of foresight. They usually don't see a change until they come face-to-face with it, and even then they have difficulty identifying, out of a variety of change events, those that can significantly affect their performance.

Cognitive Denial and Self-Imposed Isolation

Another common response of brittle teams is the tendency to meet impending change with blanket denial. Despite abundant information to the contrary, team members will staunchly insist that a large-scale change will never take place, or that somehow something will happen to alter the course of events. To outside observers, it will appear that team members have their heads buried in the sand.

Once change does occur, brittle teams respond to the resulting stress by trying to ignore the process and cutting themselves off from the organizational flow of information. In my second book, *Crossing the Minefield* (AMACOM Press, 1994), I referred to these individuals as "entrenched bunkers," for, like soldiers trapped in a war zone, they bury themselves in concrete bunkers to wait until "the whole thing blows over." They try to convince themselves that a major, permanent change is only a temporary aberration—a fad or a freak event that should be ignored and allowed to correct itself over time.

Slow or Poorly Coordinated Response to Change

As an analogy, think of an organization as a train running down the track toward change. Some teams take the role of organizational engine, others are freight cars, and the brittle team brings up the rear as the caboose. Brittle teams are very slow to respond to change, and when they do, their responses are weak and ineffective. The members of a brittle team don't take the time to analyze the change, to determine the factors behind it, and to identify those aspects that could be modified or to which the team might successfully adapt. In addition, the high degree of stress experienced by such teams makes it difficult for them to visualize adaptive options. Instead, for many team members, the change event is likely to be perceived as a complex, convoluted, and potentially overwhelming experience.

Active Resistance to Change

The members of a brittle team have a difficult time distinguishing between changes that are just beginning to surface (and, hence, are still somewhat controllable) and those that are well under way. This problem is compounded by the team's lack of foresight. Inevitably, the team fails to note an emerging change event (or intentionally ignores it) until it is bearing down on them. At this point, they leap into action and try to resist it—an approach that's about as effective as jumping in front of a speeding truck with a stop sign in your hand.

Case in Point: The Purchasing Team

For the last hour, the purchasing team at Beta Corporation had been making excellent progress in its review of a number of team projects. Martha, the team leader, was about to wrap up the meeting when one of her team members presented a concern for discussion:

Fred: "So what's this I hear about the new Dextronic contract? I was listening to a couple of our engineering people at lunch, and they said it was going to involve some major work."

Martha: "Sorry, Fred, I don't know much about it. Why are you so concerned?"

Fred: "Well, we've been asked to come up with our staffing plans for next year, and I'd like to know how the contract is going to affect our staffing requirements."

Linda: "Fred's right. I'm putting in a lot of overtime as it is. If we're going to be hit with a drastic increase in our workload over the next few months, it would be nice to begin planning for that now."

Shelly: "Aside from the impact on our workload, we need to know more about the contract. What's it for? What's the projected duration of the contract? How much of the work will be going to us versus our sister facility? It's kind of embarrassing when we continue to be the last ones informed of these things. It makes other departments wonder whether we're really tied in with the workings of our company."

Ravin: "My concerns lie in a completely different direction. The last time we worked with Dextronic, we encountered some major problems with our suppliers. If you remember, Dextronic was upset that some of our second-tier suppliers didn't have formal quality improvement programs in place. Our team ended up stuck in the middle of a lot of fights between our engineering department and Dextronic's quality assurance department. Martha, I think this situation happened before you came on board, so you may not be familiar with it, but it was a real mess."

Martha: "Well, I didn't realize that the possibility of getting this contract was such a big issue for all of you. Why don't you make a list of questions about the contract, and I'll see if I can get you some answers during the next senior staff meeting."

Underlying Causes

If you find that your team is exhibiting some or all of the symptoms you have just reviewed, your next step should be to determine the underlying causes of the problem. Teams may find themselves unprepared for change and unable to cope effectively with new situations for a number of reasons. Review the following to determine which of these causes are relevant to your team.

Information Vacuums

As explained earlier, self-imposed isolation is a common symptom of teams that are having difficulty dealing with change. At the same time, isolation can also be a principal cause of poor adaptation to change.

Take, for example, a team that's stranded in the organizational boondocks, located so far out of the mainstream of the company's informal, internal networks that it's the last to hear of impending changes. Another version of this problem involves teams that cut themselves off from their

professional and technical fields and are simply unaware of new developments. Teams that keep abreast of internal organizational changes but fail to
maintain their networks with customers, suppliers, outsource providers,
and consultants are also functioning in isolation. External groups offer
invaluable and uniquely objective views of a team's organization that could
enhance its ability to anticipate and respond more effectively to change.

Sometimes, team leaders themselves help create information vacuums
by failing to keep their teams apprised of significant upcoming events. Team
leaders play a critical role in guiding their work groups through disruptive
change. They are the primary connecting link between teams and senior
managers and are frequently in a better position to interpret the impact of
impending change. When team leaders don't accept this responsibility, their
teams will be less prepared to adapt to change.

Defensive Attachment to the Past

Teams that are having difficulty adjusting to change try to defend themselves by hanging on to the past. When faced with change, they cling fanat-
ically to the technical competencies, solutions ("It worked in '94, so why
can't we do it again?"), and beliefs ("This marketing research is a bunch of
crap! What makes them think our customers' service expectations are
changing?") that worked for them in the past. The brittle team's answer to a
unique and challenging situation is to apply the tried-and-true approach,
even if it's not remotely applicable to the approaching change event.

I observed this situation firsthand a few years ago, when the IT director
of the company for which I work continued to resist the transition from the
OS/2® operating platform to a new system based on Microsoft® and Lotus®
software. The IT director had been instrumental in selecting the OS/2 system
and clung to his belief in its superiority even though it was increasingly inadequate for our needs and the replacement system was being pushed by every
member of our senior staff, including our newly installed CEO. The deadlock
ended with the replacement of the IT director and part of his team, for
although this individual was a brilliant technical specialist, he lacked a basic
understanding of the company's business strategy and requirements.

Ignorance of the Mechanics of Change

Recently, I had a discussion with a good friend who is a team leader at a large
financial services company. He told me about a management presentation he
had attended a few weeks earlier, in which the company's IT director outlined

her plans for major revisions to the organization's server network. My friend had several concerns regarding the feasibility of the proposed project time line but confided to me that he didn't feel comfortable expressing these concerns at the meeting because he wasn't an IT expert and didn't want to sound foolish.

I've seen this type of scenario played out time and time again in many organizations. Team members hear about plans for a large-scale change that is about to occur in their company, but they're reluctant to venture out and aggressively gather the information they need to make informed decisions. They don't want to look ignorant, so as a result, they remain ignorant and lose out on an opportunity to effectively manage the change.

Feeling Overwhelmed by the Complexity of Major Changes

So far, for the sake of simplicity, I've approached the subject of change as if it were a series of isolated events. In reality, of course, things are usually a little more complicated.

Consider the following chain of events. A change in market strategy leads a company to rethink its organizational structure. Proposed revisions to that structure reveal huge competency gaps in the company's senior management. A review of these gaps suggests that the company lacks the talent it needs to pursue its business objectives. The company initiates an aggressive search for outside talent while it roots through the lower strata of the organization in search of buried leadership talent. As new leaders come on board, they put in place a number of their own changes, forcing their departments and business sections to reevaluate their current objectives, budgets, and staffing allocations. Many of these changes occur close together in time, meaning that a few teams may be facing a confusing array of overlapping changes. For some, the prospect is overwhelming. They simply give up, hide in their bunkers, and wait for the danger to pass.

Failure to Consider the Ripple Effect of Changes

Many team leaders focus their attention almost exclusively on changes that originate *outside* their work areas, yet neglect to consider the effect of the many changes they initiate within their own organizations.

Thus, an HR team might propose changes to systems for job posting or performance appraisal without gathering input from key stakeholders about the effect these changes may have on those downstream. Such managers are poor change stewards because they don't understand that an important part of their leadership role involves analyzing the more subtle, long-term effects of proposed changes to organizational and business systems. In the end, the resistance and hostility they encounter from poorly considered changes place them in a weaker negotiating position in their organizations. The widespread reaction among management is likely to be that team leaders who can't direct changes in their own backyards are not qualified to offer advice on proposed changes to other work functions.

The Treatment

The strategies you employ to help your team anticipate and manage stress depend, in part, on such factors as your team's experience level, degree of cohesion, and overall adaptability. Keep these factors in mind as you attempt to determine which of the following improvement actions are appropriate for your team.

Conduct Frequent Fire Drills

Although you can't prepare for every eventuality, you can identify those events that are highly probable and represent significant potential threats and opportunities. You can also guide your team in developing preventive and corrective actions to address these events.

For a recent example, consider the extensive preparations that many companies underwent in upgrading or replacing old software to prevent Y2K problems. As the millennial new year approached, many companies supplemented these actions by providing twenty-four-hour coverage for their IT and customer support help desks and by developing third-level contingency plans for customers who might suffer extreme service disruptions. Chapter 9 provides a number of suggestions and tools that can help your team deal more effectively with potential threats and opportunities.

Avoid Creating Unnecessary Stress

During times of rapid change, your team is likely to experience at least a moderate degree of stress. Although you might not be able to eliminate this change-related stress entirely, you can make small adjustments to your management style to ensure that you don't needlessly add to this stress level.

If you're a type A person—driven, intense, and aggressive—work on tempering your style. Cut back on the amount of coffee you drink and track your stress buildup over the course of a typical day. Try to schedule meetings with team members for times when your stress level is still fairly low.

For many managers, this may mean conducting sessions early in the morning, before they've been boxed in by e-mail and voice-mail messages. Try to remember that your team members take their signal from you. If you appear highly stressed and out of control, your team may begin to doubt its ability to handle the situation. Now is the time to slow down and appear calm and organized before you attempt to give direction. Be wary of reacting with loud and abusive behavior when you run into work problems. Instead of jumping right to the attack, try to get some answers first. In addition, avoid such actions as pitting team members against one another in win-lose competitions. Other leadership behaviors that can create unnecessary team stress include vacillating on decisions, procrastinating on actions, withholding information, and failing to confront wild rumors.

Finally, check in with your team periodically to inquire about their stress level. If certain team members appear to be burning out, ask the entire team to help you develop a plan for balancing the workload more fairly. For additional suggestions on how to manage work-related stress, refer to my book *Lifeboat Strategies: How to Keep Your Career above Water during Tough Times . . . or Any Time,* available via the Internet through iUniverse.com.

Make the Unknown Manageable

One way to reduce the stress associated with a complex change event is to chop it up into bite-size pieces that are easier to examine and understand. The more ill-defined and nebulous a change, the more we tend to fill in the details with our imaginations, sometimes by envisioning the worst possible course of events. Tool #30 in your Tool Kit can help your team separate those aspects of an impending change event that are subject to your team's influence and control from those that are not.

Learn from Others Who Have Been There

When you think about it for a moment, almost any change event you can envision has already been weathered by some other organization. Instead of convincing ourselves that our change event is unique and unprecedented, why not make use of the collective experience of other organizations?

To better understand how this works, consider the following example. A few years ago, I was given the task of preparing an organization for the introduction of an ISO 9000 program. I soon realized that few people in the company really understood the tremendous amount of money and coordinated effort involved in the introduction of this program. To address the problem, I brought in a senior line director from a noncompetitive company, who gave senior managers a very candid presentation outlining his company's procedures for ISO 9000 certification and the initial difficulties he and other executive-level managers had faced in trying to grasp the true scope of this effort.

If you're about to guide your team through a difficult change, why attempt to reinvent the wheel? Contact people who have already been through similar change events and who are known to have managed them effectively. They may be your counterparts in other companies, or they may be hidden within your own organization. They may even be outside consultants who have guided many companies through a similar type of change. This course of action offers several advantages:

- Opportunity to learn from the mistakes of others

- Access to excellent troubleshooters who can help you identify the weaknesses in your change-management plans

- Fresh pairs of eyes with no personal agendas to push who can provide calm, detached points of view

In addition, these external experts may provide support and enhanced credibility as you attempt to convince senior management of the merits of your change-management proposal. Remember the old adage: "A prophet is never respected in his own country." Sometimes senior managers are more willing to listen to advice when it comes from the outside.

Learn to Identify Signs of Organizational Change

A few years ago, I moved from Florida to Maryland and experienced northern weather for the first time. During my first winter, a grizzled old native asked me if I'd purchased a snow shovel. I told him I didn't think there was any hurry. After all, the latest local weather report indicated we still had a few weeks until heavy snow would be upon us. My friend just laughed and proceeded to tell me about several nature signs that suggested we were in for heavy snowfall. He was right. To the eyes of this experienced native, the warning signs were plain to see.

In the same way, large-scale organizational change events don't just appear overnight. They usually follow a number of precursors—subtle but significant warning signs that suggest your organization is about to experience a change in direction. Tool #31 in your Tool Kit can help your team learn to spot these warning signs.

Consider the Potential Long-Term Effects

As I've explained earlier in this chapter, when you initiate a major change event, you must think through its implications and how it might affect others in your organization. If you develop a reputation for being an effective change catalyst, others are more apt to follow your recommendations when change-related issues are up for negotiation. Tool #32 in your Tool Kit provides a method for systematically assessing the potential impact of large-scale business initiatives.

Overcome Resistance to Change

Never make the mistake of underestimating the degree of resistance you will meet when trying to initiate change. Part of your planning process should include identifying the concerns that are likely to be raised by resistant individuals in your organization and the steps you can take to overcome their concerns. Tool #33 in your Tool Kit provides suggestions for overcoming resistance to change and a chart to guide you in applying these suggestions to the changes your own team is currently facing. In addition, the following pages outline several techniques you can use for overcoming resistance to change.

Build Ownership and Support

One effective method of eliminating resistance is to look for ways to foster a sense of ownership among your detractors. You can do this by

- Involving them in the design of your project

- Integrating their input into your project plan

- Capturing agreement by increments, by convincing blockers to support the first few steps of your plan while agreeing that any additional support will be contingent upon the success of your initial project results

Lower the Risk Level for Change

Look for ways to make the changes generated by your project less threatening to others in your organization. One way to do this would be to suggest that you try out your business initiative on a limited basis with a small pilot group. Another option would be to incorporate a test-and-review period into your project plan. If the question of who controls the project appears to be an important issue, invite potential blockers to take part in the project review process, or even consider enlisting their support as cosponsors. If they claim they don't have the time to participate in these activities, ask them for the names of people who they feel would be good project advisers or reviewers. Another approach to working around the issue of control involves developing a formal control system that makes your project appear less formidable and more manageable, such as process flowcharts, sign-off documentation, or formal review checkpoints.

Identify a Surrogate

Consider whether part of the resistance you're experiencing is a direct response to *you* as the project leader. (Yes, I know, you're a lovable person and everyone should be grateful that you're leading your team, but perhaps, just perhaps, you've made some enemies along the way.) If this is the case, you may be better off having a team member or sponsor pitch your project to your detractors.

Do Your Homework

Be prepared to provide evidence that your project is well designed and your recommended changes are well considered. For instance, make sure you've considered questions such as the following:

- Do you have surveys or interview data indicating how the business initiative will be received by customers and employees?

- Do you have access to financial data that justifies the cost of your project?

- Which of your team members or project sponsors could be seen as knowledgeable experts on the business initiative you are attempting to put into place?

- Has your project team followed the recommendations of these experts?

- Have you considered performing a best-practices study to demonstrate that certain world-class organizations have already undertaken the changes proposed by your team and that these organizations have met with exceptional results?

Choose the Time and Place for Your Battles

Many project leaders make the mistake of viewing their projects as strictly task-focused events. They're confident that if they're armed with sufficient facts and solid logic, they'll be able to sway even the most adamant blocker. Unfortunately for this approach, blockers are not completely logical and objective, like the Vulcans in *Star Trek;* they're human beings and come complete with all the usual human insecurities and emotions.

You're apt to find blockers entering into their first discussion of your project predisposed toward anger, frustration, or anxiety. If you're talking to a person who tends to spout off without first getting the facts, it's especially important to consider your approach. As uncomfortable as it might be, I always recommend that your best choice is to set up a series of private one-on-one meetings before facing your opponents in a public forum. Private meetings enable you to address at least some of their concerns while defusing their emotions. It also shows that you're making an effort to gain their support and gives you time to identify and prepare for any objections that might surface later during public review. Finally, if your blocker is very influential, a private discussion provides an opportunity for damage control before this person attempts to sway the opinions of others in your organization.

Begin Your Discussion on a Positive Note

Once you've selected the best time and place for your meeting, your next task is to determine your approach. I recommend that you open the meeting with a brief statement that sets the stage for a productive, amiable discussion. For example: "Jeff, thanks for meeting with me today to discuss the change in personnel policy our team is considering. I wanted to hear your views on this project and see if we can incorporate your ideas and concerns into our project planning process."

Identify the Concerns Behind the Objections

After you've set the stage, be prepared to sit back and listen. Try to hear your blocker out completely before coming back with any arguments or rebuttals. Remember, you aren't involved in a debating contest. You only win if you leave this person's office with more support than you had when you entered. Another step you can take to ensure the success of this meeting is to probe patiently for the true concerns and needs that lie behind your blocker's initial objections. There are four questions you can ask to uncover these concerns:

- "At this point in the project, what are some of your main concerns?"

- "What do you feel we need to do to make this initiative a success?"

- "What do you want to see happening in this situation? From your perspective, what are the desired outcomes of this project?"

- "What can I do to gain your support?"

Build a Base for Negotiations with a Progressive Review of Project Issues

Engage your blockers in dialogue to find out how to secure their support. A suggested technique for creating this dialogue is the progressive review of project issues.

Begin by describing the opportunity, challenge, or problem that led to your project. Before you can move forward with negotiations, your blockers must be able to agree with you on the validity and significance of the business requirements that have created the need for your project. Once you've gained this initial agreement, move on to a discussion of the validity, feasibility, and necessity of your project objectives.

Your next step is to reach agreement regarding your project success criteria. Do your adversaries agree with you that your success criteria constitute a reasonable method for evaluating the success of your project? Do they understand and support your project measurement process? If they do, try to secure support for your project plan. It stands to reason that if they agree with you on the above points, then the only remaining area of concern would be the approach you plan to take to achieve your objectives.

Trade Minor Concessions for Support

Occasionally, you'll find that you are able to secure support from potential blockers if you're willing to make minor adjustments to your project plan. While your first response might be to resist such concessions, ask yourself whether they would significantly interfere with your project outcomes. Examples of reasonable accommodations might include

- Adjusting your project timetable

- Building additional safeguards into your project, such as review sessions or sign-off points

- Revising your project so that it also supports your blockers' personal performance objectives

- Adding to your team a few individuals whom your blocker considers highly credible or enlisting them as resource experts

- Selecting a different location or population group for the initial test of your project.

Don't make the mistake of immediately refusing these kinds of minor requests if you can trade your cooperation for much-needed support. Successful project leaders know the value of winning over potential blockers and make substantial efforts to do so.

Related Problems

Chapter 8 (The King Dethroned: Solving Member-Leader Conflict)—Without strong relationships between team members and their leaders, communication is limited and ineffective. As a result, team members and leaders will be less inclined to perform the type of rapid information exchange that is often necessary when they are trying to keep pace with turbulent change.

Chapter 9 (Painted into a Corner: Developing Better Foresight)—The ability to look ahead and detect emerging threats and opportunities is a prerequisite to effective stress management. I strongly recommend reviewing Chapter 9 along with this chapter to obtain a more complete picture of the potential performance issues facing your team.

Chapter 10 (The Broken Compass: Finding a Sense of Direction)—A team's charter, objectives, and knowledge of its company's business strategy help keep the team on course even if it is being buffeted by stressful change events.

Chapter 13 (Stuck in a Rut: How to Foster Innovation)—Your ability to manage change influences your ability to successfully carry an innovation from management to implementation. The Tool Kit for this chapter introduces two tools for directing innovative projects.

Chapter 14 (Reversals: Dealing with Setbacks)—When you think about it, a setback is one of the major change events a team can encounter. The ability to manage change and the ability to deal with setbacks both depend upon a team's flexibility and tenacity. If your team is presently experiencing a setback, you may find it helpful to review Chapter 14 and this chapter at the same time.

Tool Kit

CHANGE MANAGEMENT GRID

Your team can use a change management grid to identify critical information gaps about an emerging change event and determine the steps you can take to manage it. Chart 32 shows how this grid might look if it were completed by a hypothetical corporate training team that has just learned its company will soon be expanding into a new market area (auto sales). A blank chart has been provided for your own use in Exercise 17.

Note that the top row of the grid contains three categories: Known, Unknown, and Sources.

- Known aspects are solid facts, not assumptions or guesses on the part of your team. In our example, the training team knows a number of facts, including the location of the new sales office (Auburn Hills) and the time frame for the staffing of this office (six months).

- Unknown aspects of the hypothetical change event in Chart 32 include the types of customer-based training that will be required as part of the corporate contract and the amount of funds allocated for training.

- Sources provide necessary information for your team. In our example, the training team identified the company's director of contract administration as the best source for information on specialized training since this individual will be closely involved with contract compliance.

The second row of the chart covers three additional categories: Within Our Control, Subject to Our Influence, and Beyond Our Control.

- The first category covers aspects of the change event that are completely within the team's control. Members of the training team included in Chart 32 the format of training delivery as one of the items they felt they could control.

- Although unable to control certain events, a team may still be able to influence the decisions and actions of other individuals and work groups. In our example, the training team has decided that although it won't be in a position to decide whether training components are outsourced to another supplier, it can influence the selection of such vendors.

- Finally, some aspects of the change event will be beyond the team's control. In Chart 32, the training team knows it has no control over training programs that are mandated by the contract.

Tool Kit

CHART 32

Change Management Grid for Expansion into a New Market		
Known	**Unknown**	**Sources**
• Our company is planning to expand into the U.S. auto market over the next 6 months • We have secured a contract with Ford Motor Company • This market sector will be based in Auburn Hills, MI. • First year of operation will involve a staff of 150 • No training needs have yet been identified for this employee group.	• What training will this group require over the next year? • What customer-based training (e.g., completion of customer's quality assurance course) will these employees be expected to complete? • What is the expected staff size in year two? • What training (ISO 9000) will be mandatory? What will be optional? • What training funds have been budgeted for this department? • Which managers will be heading up this operation?	• New VP of auto market • Director of contract administration • VP of human resources • Director of contract administration • New VP of auto market • New VP of auto market or VP of humanr resources
Within Our Control	**Subject to Our Influence**	**Beyond Our Control**
• Selection of staff allocated to this project • Delivery format for training • Design and delivery of corporate-mandated training	• Timing/scheduling of training • Criteria we use to evaluate training • Our recommendations regarding an outsourced training supplier • Recommendations for supplemental budget to meet these needs	• Training requirements mandated by the contract • Amount of auto staff time available to participate in training

Tool Kit

EXERCISE 17 • CHANGE MANAGEMENT GRID

Change Management Grid

Known	Unknown	Sources

Within Our Control	Subject to Our Influence	Beyond Our Control

Tool Kit

CHANGE ANALYSIS CHART

To help your team navigate through stressful situations, you must first be able to identify change indicators that act as a type of organizational weather vane by indicating significant changes in your company's direction. The Change Analysis Chart shown in Exercise 18 identifies nine key indicators that tend to signal the onset of organizational change.* My recommendation is to begin by inviting each member of your team to take a day or so to respond individually to the questions presented in the chart. At a later date, set aside two hours to meet as a group and discuss your responses. During your team discussion, compare your individual observations and look for any recurring patterns in the data.

EXERCISE 18 • CHANGE ANALYSIS CHART

The change event you are tracking:

Change Indicators	Your Observations
Topics of Interest • On what topics is attention currently focused within executive-level meetings? • On what issues is your manager beginning to spend an increasing amount of time?	
Paths of Influence • To what functions have your most influential managers been reassigned? • Which functions have been handed off to mediocre performers? • Which functions have recently been given approval to hire "A players" from the outside?	
Sources of Organizational Pride • Which programs/functions have been highlighted in your company's newsletters or annual report? • Which programs/functions have been recently paraded in front of key customers, the media, or your board of directors?	

Continued

Tool Kit

Change Indicators	Your Observations
What Is Rewarded • Which functions are now receiving top priority from your senior managers? • Which functions/projects receive the greatest weight on your managers' bonus objectives? • In which functions are budgets rapidly growing or shrinking?	
Shifts in Skills Emphasis • What leadership and technical competencies are being aggressively sought by your company? • What new technologies/products are being closely monitored? • Which functions have recently received increased funds for training?	
Organizational Pioneers • Who within your company would you consider as at the cutting edge in your field? • Where are these individuals currently focusing their attention?	
Outside Influences • Which consultants are being courted by your senior managers? • What feedback on impending changes are you receiving from external customers and suppliers? • What trends are being avidly discussed in leading technical and business journals?	
Areas of Sensitivity • Which work areas are being micromanaged by your boss? • What topics are suddenly off-limits to your inquiries? • Within which functions/projects do people quickly jump on emerging problems?	

Change Indicators	Your Observations
Organizational Mirrors • What world-class corporate performers is your company attempting to track? • What are these companies currently pursuing that is of such interest to your senior managers?	

Tool Kit

Tool #32

TEAM ADAPTATION DIAGRAM

Every large-scale change event forces individuals and teams to reevaluate the emphasis they place on competing priorities. The Team Adaptation Table shown in Exercise 19 helps teams evaluate major changes in terms of seven different types of trade-offs that must frequently be made to accommodate competing priorities.

EXERCISE 19 • TEAM ADAPTATION TABLE

What large-scale change is your team facing?

Category	Past Situation	Future Situation
Information	Outdated:	Opportune:
Competencies	Obsolete:	State-of-the-art:
Experience	Irrelevant:	Applicable:
Networks	Static:	Dynamic:
Issues	Declining:	Emerging:
Customers	Tangential:	Central:
Requirements	Head nods:	Hot buttons:

Tool Kit

The table lists seven categories for analysis in two different situations—the past and your projection of the future. Take the following steps to apply this table:

1. Briefly describe, in the space provided at the top of the table, the large-scale change that is affecting your team.

2. Use the following seven categories to help team members explore how the change is likely to affect your team's approach in the future.

   - **Information:** What information and resources (journals, Internet sites, conferences and seminars, technical knowledge, proprietary knowledge related to the workings of your company) will become outdated with the impending change? What information will be very opportune?

   - **Competencies:** What competencies will become obsolete? What competencies will be regarded as state-of-the art?

   - **Experience:** What type of experience will become increasingly irrelevant? What experience will be more applicable to the new challenges you will face in dealing with the change?

   - **Networks:** What professional networks appear to be static, or less connected to the focus of change in your area? What professional networks are viewed as more dynamic, or closest to the center of action in your field?

   - **Issues:** What work issues will decline in importance with the onset of change? What work issues will emerge as increasingly important?

   - **Customers:** Given the anticipated change, which customers will become more tangential to your team's success? Which customers will assume a more central role?

   - **Requirements:** Which aspects of your team's product/service performance will elicit only head nods from customers as these issues decline in importance? Which performance features will emerge as hot buttons as they develop greater value for your customers?

3. Your team may feel that some of these factors (such as customers) will change relatively little in the new scenario, while other factors (such as resources) will be dramatically affected. One of the benefits of this tool is the ability to sift through aspects of an impending change to determine which ones will have the most influence on a team.

4. Use the information you have gathered to anticipate the types of trade-offs in staffing, resources, project priorities, etc., that will be required as a result of the impending change.

Tool Kit

FORECAST GUIDE

When we think about what we need to do to develop change-management skills, we tend to focus on accommodating large-scale changes that lie well beyond our control. At the same time, we frequently fail to consider how major change events initiated by our team might affect others in our organization. To explore this issue, ask your team to select one upcoming business initiative for review, and then have them answer the questions in the Forecast Guide in Exercise 20.

In addition, I strongly recommend that you invite several key stakeholders to participate in this exercise and also ask them to join your team discussion of the issue. By taking these steps, you will accomplish several things.

First of all, you will begin to identify potential obstacles that could derail your project. Next, while developing greater alignment among team members and stakeholders regarding your project implementation strategy, you will also be encouraging stakeholders to accept some degree of ownership for the success of your business initiative. Finally, by treating stakeholders as representatives of your overall organization, you will be able to identify issues and concerns that may need to be addressed when you present the initiative to other groups in your organization.

EXERCISE 20 • FORECAST GUIDE

Briefly describe a significant, future business initiative for your team:

Implications for Your Business Initiative?	Decision Criteria
	Ripple effects? Could this business initiative produce a strong, negative ripple effect in other areas of your organization? Example: The revised hiring system your HR department is proposing requires additional time and paperwork in other departments.
	Uncertain, unpredictable changes? Does the success of this business initiative depend on unpredictable large-scale factors? Example: You discover that the electronic database your team is trying to create must be compatible with the PeopleSoft® system your company is currently installing. The timetable for your project might be contingent on the timetable for the PeopleSoft® system.

Permanent and difficult to modify? Once the initiative has been implemented, how difficult will it be to modify the changes you've made?

Example: The business initiative you are considering requires a substantial redesign of facilities and equipment. Once the wiring for the workstations is in place, any changes could be very expensive.

High level of resistance? Are your managers and associates likely to react to this change initiative with a high level of resistance?

Example: The initiative calls for specific functional responsibilities to be shifted from one department to another, and you're sure certain managers will oppose what could be interpreted as a loss of status and power.

Complicated and requires coordination? Does the change initiative require coordination with other departments and/or external suppliers, as opposed to being something your team can accomplish entirely on its own?

Example: Your revisions to the format of your company's annual conference require the cooperation of departments that handle events and travel, training, purchasing, and marketing.

Uncertain financial payoffs? Are the financial returns for this initiative relatively uncertain? Could the investment turn into a financial black hole?

Example: Your initiative involves your company's first entry into Internet sales. Has your team developed an adequate cost-and-revenue model that predicts your financial break-even point, or are there too many variables to assess the financial payoffs for this endeavor?

Affects internal or external customers? Will the implementation of the business initiative adversely affect your customers?

Example: Your IT team is recommending major changes to your company's intranet server. Does this mean internal customers will experience an extended server shutdown?

Stuck in a Rut

How to Foster Innovation

As paradoxical as it may sound, success sometimes poses a serious threat to team innovation. A team that experiences a long period of success uninterrupted by difficult challenges is likely to find that its members are firmly nestled within their collective comfort zone. Team members may grow complacent and make only marginal efforts toward improving their performance. After all, why mess with success? Should the team encounter new and demanding challenges, team members may respond with routine or safe solutions. In short, their capacity for innovative thinking will be blunted, leaving them less able to tackle difficult challenges or exploit new opportunities that may suddenly arise.

Complacency can be particularly damaging to teams that function within such areas as marketing, sales, and design—because creative thought powers exceptional performance. Its effects are subtle and insidious, for unlike many other team problems, the lack of innovation shows up not so much in errors, rework, or damage to interpersonal relationships but in ideas and action plans that are mediocre and unimaginative. If left unchecked, this problem will restrict the scope of a team's activities, and the team may never realize its full performance potential.

In contrast, teams that practice a high level of innovation naturally assume they must and can continually improve their performance. More important, they do this not just by working more diligently but by remaining open to a variety of options for increasing innovation. These work groups tend to be early adapters; that is, they are the first in their organizations to experiment with new work methods and processes. They constantly scan the horizon to track new opportunities in their fields. They look for ways to seed their teams with outsiders who can provide a fresh, creative perspective on their job functions. These are the groups that are so frequently called upon by their organizations to take the lead in exploring the potential of new markets or tackling extremely complicated assignments. Truly innovative teams don't see these situations as trying or threatening; they view them as opportunities to stretch their abilities and explore stimulating and novel work challenges.

Symptoms

The symptoms of complacency and lack of innovation are quite varied and may be rather subtle. As you review the following symptoms, give some thought to which of these behaviors you have observed in your team.

Lack of Confidence in Ability to Meet New Challenges

Quite often, a vicious cycle develops as a team's complacency leads to a lack of innovative thinking, which in turn leaves team members even less prepared to deal with new situations. Teams that have lost their ingenuity rely heavily on tried-and-true approaches when attempting to solve work problems and are easily thrown for a loop when confronted with a problem that can't be solved by their usual methods. Their automatic, by-the-numbers remedies may prove totally inadequate for unique and unusual challenges, such as entry into a totally new product or service area.

If this cycle continues for a prolonged period of time, team members may begin to doubt their ability to tackle difficult challenges. Each new task will be seen as a potential threat rather than an opportunity for strengthening overall performance. As a result, team members may hesitate to take on challenges or explore emerging possibilities.

Ignorance of Cutting-Edge Technology and Work Methods

Teams that lack innovation not only fail to continually refine and strengthen their technical skills but are often unaware of cutting-edge developments in their particular professions.

I recall a recent discussion with a senior-level HR executive on the subject of Internet-based recruiting and résumé-screening systems. The executive conceded that such systems might be appropriate for entry-level workers but asserted that seasoned managers and executives would never utilize the Internet as a serious job search avenue. I hastened to point out that during the past few years, several major international executive-recruiting firms had opened up Internet gateways with the intention of attracting such audiences. This news came as a shock to my colleague, which gave me a keener insight into how far behind he had fallen in terms of new developments in the field of executive recruiting.

Mundane Solutions and Redundant Actions

It's easy to spot teams that have lost their ability to innovate by looking at the minimal level of creativity they display in their problem-solving activities. Such a team, three years in the future, will be offering the same service features to its customers, applying the same solutions to problems, and performing its functions with the same work methods.

Missed Opportunities

Complacent teams often fail to anticipate and exploit new opportunities. I know of a conference planning group that lost a major contract when one of its competitors approached an important corporate client with an innovative idea for completely revamping the format and presentation style of the company's annual corporate convention. The meeting team that lost the contract proposed the same tired and hackneyed format they had been providing for the past several years.

Defections in the Ranks

Sharp, creative professionals are attracted to work environments that inspire innovation. If the best and brightest members of a team begin to jump ship, either through transfers or voluntary terminations, perhaps these individuals believe that their fellow team members and leader don't place a very high premium on innovative thinking.

Case in Point: The Marketing Team

A marketing team responsible for managing the campaigns of a large medical equipment manufacturer underestimated the potential impact of the Internet within its specialized field and actively resisted suggestions from members of the senior team that it explore this new arena. Satisfied with its established set of marketing skills, the team didn't bother to keep pace with new developments in this area.

When the company CEO realized how far behind his company had fallen in Internet-based sales and marketing, he replaced the vice president of marketing with an outside candidate who was capable of moving the marketing group in this new direction. At this point, team members finally woke up to the seriousness of their situation. They realized that, despite their proven skills in reaching out to customers through television, radio, and print advertising, they would soon be left far behind by their competitors unless they began making substantial progress in Internet-based advertising.

The Underlying Causes

Complacency isn't the only reason for a lack of innovation. Other conditions may give rise to the situation, such as those outlined below.

Insular Views

Exposure to cutting-edge ideas and best practices within their industries allow teams to explore their limits and test new work approaches. Unfortunately, some teams suffer from a type of organizational inbreeding that provides little access to ideas and individuals outside their organizations. The most isolated teams are usually the ones with the greatest deficits in creative thinking. Not only are they cut off from the flow of new ideas; they also don't have access to informational networks that can keep them apprised of evolving ideas within a given area. When such teams finally do try to innovate, they end up re-creating the wheel because they don't realize that their new ideas and solutions have already been applied, tested, and improved by peers in other organizations.

A related cause is what I call the "not invented here" syndrome. The team may be operating within a work culture that emphasizes applied experience over creative thinking. In this type of work culture, ideas are often killed before they receive a fair hearing, and team members may be criticized for suggesting solutions that represent departures from the status quo.

Consequences That Discourage Risk Taking

In some work environments, team members feel that innovation is seldom rewarded and failure is consistently punished. With consequences of this sort in place, team members quickly learn that they're likely to suffer criticism for proposing new and untested approaches to problems. On the other hand, if they adopt or support solutions proposed by senior-level team members or their team leader, they avoid the risk of failure. As a result, such teams tend to wait passively for direction from their leaders and managers.

Censorship

Newer and less experienced team members tend to be strongly influenced by the opinions of their experienced and senior counterparts. Within some teams, the team leader or selected team members exert subtle but powerful control over the team's innovative thinking process. There are many ways in which these dominant team members censor and restrict the innovative ideas of the others. These behaviors include

- Sarcastic or critical responses to the ideas of other team members

- Aggressive, inappropriately timed challenges to team members to come up with complete solutions when they are just beginning to formulate new ideas

- Arguing that since the team has already partially explored a given line of thinking, it doesn't merit additional effort

- Implying that the presenter of an idea lacks the experience or skills to be taken seriously by the team

- Taking a team problem-solving discussion off-line with a subsequent, clandestine discussion with selected team members.

Whatever form the censorship takes, the result is usually the same— new or junior-level team members are reluctant to express new ideas and have great difficulty obtaining a fair hearing for their ideas.

Lack of Challenge

Innovation requires a work climate that compels teams to leap beyond barriers to problem solving and explore totally new approaches to their work. There are many reasons why teams do not feel challenged. They may simply be underutilized. It could also be that the organization has very low expectations for the team, which discourages team members from testing and strengthening their abilities. Another reason may be that the team has never felt pressured to change because it's been insulated from the performance of its competitors. (Nothing is better at creating a burning platform for change than the knowledge that competitors have gained a strategic performance advantage.) Another common cause is overstaffing, which allows team members to focus their attention on a relatively restricted set of routine tasks and assignments.

Limited Interaction

Innovation is a synergistic process that thrives within work environments where team members learn from and build on one another's ideas. This type of symbiotic learning may take many forms—from team members who exchange ideas on a particular project, to the team leader who shares an exciting new Internet research site with her group. Whatever its form, innovation is severely handicapped when team members lack ready access to one another, or if team norms and practices discourage them from freely discussing their ideas.

The Treatment

Fortunately, there are a variety of steps you can take to foster a spirit of innovation within your team. Consider implementing some of the following solutions.

Set the Stage for Creative Thinking

If your team is stuck in a pattern of noninnovative thinking, perhaps team members don't feel that their ideas and suggestions are fully encouraged and supported. Sometimes, the only way through this impasse is to sit down with your team and describe a work function or project that requires their full creative efforts. Set the stage for creative thinking by letting your team members know that you encourage and welcome their ideas. Here are some actions you can take to communicate your receptiveness to your team:

- When team members voice tentative ideas, draw them out by telling them you would like to hear more.

- Show that you intend to give careful consideration to team members' suggestions by recording all ideas on a board for later review.

- Refrain from offering your own ideas until everyone else has had an opportunity to speak.

- Play the role of traffic director by gently reining in dominant team members and giving others an opportunity to voice their thoughts.

- If a team member has trouble expressing an idea, paraphrase his or her comments and then invite the rest of the team to build on these ideas, or invite the individual to come back after the team meeting to speak to you about any additional thoughts.

Conduct a Structured Brainstorming Session

While the phrase "structured brainstorming" may seem like an oxymoron, it's not. The problem with brainstorming as it's traditionally envisioned is that team members are asked to throw out for review any and all ideas, in any order, thus allowing verbally dominant individuals to monopolize the discussion.

As an alternative, conduct a "go-round" and ask your team to present only one idea at a time; team members may pass temporarily if they can't come up with an idea. Continue around the circle until you've gathered all ideas from your team. Next, ask your team if there's any way to combine or modify certain ideas to create new ideas. Take a few additional minutes to identify these consolidated ideas, and then make your final selection from this expanded list.

Encourage Creative Risk Taking

One way to get team members to shake off their inhibitions and come up with creative ideas is to ask them to begin the discussion by giving you their craziest or weirdest ideas. To initiate risk taking, offer one or two wacky ideas of your own. Once team members propose these unorthodox suggestions for review, they are much more likely to extend their thinking in creative ways.

Suspend Limitations

Ask team members to list the most limiting constraints—time, money, staff, lack of information—that stand in the way of solving a given problem. List these constraints on a flipchart and explain that you'll come back to them eventually, but for the next thirty minutes, you want your team to pretend they don't exist.

For example, if "lack of funds" was previously identified as a principal constraint, you might say to your team, "If money were *not* an issue, what would be the ideal solution to our problem?" After you've identified all potential ideal solutions, go back and ask how they might be modified to meet the constraints you listed earlier.

Develop Graphic Solutions

Encourage team members to use pictures or graphics to illustrate the problem in question. I frequently find that when team members are encouraged to model or represent problems through the use of cartoons or icons, it liberates their thinking and enables them to address subtleties they may otherwise have overlooked. A related option involves deconstructing a problem into its component parts and then reassembling those parts in new and creative ways. The microanalysis technique in your Tool Kit (page 236) provides a method for "mapping out" such creative solutions to problems.

Make Use of Creative Software

ThoughtPath and Imagination are but two of several software packages developed to encourage creative ideas. These programs can be used by a single person or a small work team. Each software package is somewhat unique, but they're both based on the general idea of forcing problem solvers to systematically walk through their problems with the generous application of key words, images, analogies, and metaphors as methods by which to identify novel ideas.

Import a Fresh Pair of Eyes

A sure way to charge your team's creative battery is to bring in an outsider, someone who has not been influenced by the team's thinking process. These visitors don't have to be technical experts. Their job is not to provide expert advice but to ask questions that nudge team members beyond their problem-solving assumptions. When using these outside observers, I recommend the following approach.

Begin by asking a team member to provide your observer with a basic overview of the problem or challenge facing your team. This explanation should be stripped to its essence, devoid of jargon or technical terminology. Sometimes this first step will help your team see the problem or challenge in a new light. Proceed by asking your visitor to observe your team as it explores the problem under review. The visitor should feel free to interrupt at any time to ask questions as needed for clarification. The observer should take notes throughout the discussion but make no comments until your team has spent at least thirty minutes in review. Your observer should then share his or her observations and ask any probing questions that might guide your team to uncover additional information.

Review Best Practices

A best-practices review compares the best work processes, methods, and procedures of world-class organizations in order to discover those that can be imported into your organization. It's an excellent technique for selecting good ideas from other companies. You may want to start by searching the Internet or using professional or trade organizations to identify companies that are consistently cited as excellent performers in the area under review.

Ask for More Than One Solution

One way to encourage creative thinking is to ask for multiple solutions at the start of your discussion. Tell team members that you would like them to come up with at least three good methods for addressing the problem. Normally, the first solution will be the most routine, while every subsequent one will be unique.

Reframe Problems

The reframing technique can give your team a fresh perspective on the problem. This technique is introduced in Tool #2, in the Tool Kit for Chapter 2.

Related Problems

Chapter 9 (Painted into a Corner: Developing Better Foresight)—An important source of innovation is the ability to scan ahead and keep abreast of new developments within the team's field. If your team is having difficulty coming up with innovative solutions, you might find it useful to review the suggestions and tools contained in this chapter.

Chapter 12 (The Brittle Team: Learning to Adapt to Change)—Teams that don't innovate are vulnerable to technological obsolescence and are often much less prepared to deal with disruptive change. Read this chapter if you would like to enhance your team's change management skills.

Chapter 17 (Our Own Worst Enemy: Strengthening Customer Relationships)—An important aspect of innovation is the ability to anticipate shifts in customer requirements and develop creative ways for keeping abreast of these changes. Innovative teams are continually upgrading the quality of their products and services and improving the effectiveness of their work processes. Teams that are unable to keep pace with customer requirements soon find that their customers are looking elsewhere to meet their needs. Eventually, senior managers will begin to question why their teams are unable to match the performance levels of outside competitors.

Tool Kit

PLUS/DELTA TECHNIQUE

During problem-solving sessions, team members sometimes become preoccupied with criticizing alternative solutions. This is due in part to human nature, which finds it easier to identify the weaknesses in an idea than to discover its salvageable aspects. Team members also tend to focus on the negative because they sometimes view team problem solving as a competitive process ("My idea is better than yours"), which results in wasted time as participants defend their own ideas while attacking those of their teammates. The Plus/Delta Technique is one way to overcome this tendency.

To complete this technique, follow these steps:

1. Provide team members with several index cards each and ask them to briefly summarize potential solutions, one solution to a card.

2. Collect the cards and shuffle them.

3. Write each solution at the top of a flipchart page. I recommend doing this anonymously, without noting members' names.

4. Go back to the first flipchart page and draw a line down the middle of the rest of the page, separating it into two columns.

5. Label the left-hand column "Pluses" and the right-hand column "Deltas."

6. Go back to the first flipchart page. Read the solution aloud, and then turn to one of your team members. Ask this individual to identify one positive thing about the solution—for example, that it's easy to implement. Record this comment under the Pluses column.

7. Next, ask the same individual to think of one concern regarding the idea, such as that it would be costly to implement. Write this comment under the Deltas column. It's important to remember that whenever a team member presents a concern or criticism, he or she must also add a comment to the Pluses side of the sheet.

8. Take only one plus and one delta from this person; then move on to the second team member and continue the process.

9. Conduct multiple circuits until team members have shared all of their pluses and deltas, which you are recording in the two columns of the flipchart.

10. Repeat this exercise for the solution at the top of your second flipchart page. Continue until your team has evaluated all the solutions.

Tool
#34

Tool Kit

11. Post the solutions for review. Ask for suggestions on refining or building upon any of them.

12. Ask your team if any one solution stands out as being the strongest, based on having the largest number of pluses and very few deltas.

13. Propose that the team act on this solution. Use any additional time to explore ways to address the concerns that were listed in the Deltas column for this solution.

GALLERY TECHNIQUE

This evaluation process resembles the structure of an art gallery. I find it useful whenever team members are entering into an extremely sensitive problem-solving situation and may have some difficulty remaining open to one another's points of view. The premise behind the gallery technique is to force team members to carefully articulate their solutions before posting them, to consider all solutions before commenting on any one, and to express their concerns in writing. This latter point is especially important, since people tend to provide a more balanced perspective in writing as opposed to saying the first thing that pops into their minds.

To initiate this technique, complete the following steps:

1. Provide team members with a sheet of flipchart paper each and ask them to write out a statement or two (in large print, so the flipcharts can be read easily) describing a tentative solution to the problem.

2. Ask team members not to sign their names—all solutions should be anonymous. As soon as team members finish describing their solutions, they should scroll up their flipchart pages and hand them in to you.

3. Next, dismiss the team and post all solutions on the wall.

4. Reconvene your team and ask them to walk around and *silently* review all of the posted solutions. They should refrain from making comments during this time.

5. Give your team fifteen minutes to read and review all the solutions, and then invite them to identify those on which they wish to comment.

6. Give your team an additional fifteen minutes to write at the bottom of the flipchart pages they've selected any clarifying questions (when they're having difficulty understanding a solution), any suggestions for strengthening the solution, or any concerns regarding the solution. Tell them they may select as many pages as they wish, as long as they stay within the time limit.

7. At the end of this thirty-minute period, start at one end of your "gallery" and read aloud both the posted solution and the subsequent commentary.

8. At this point, the owners of the solutions are free (if they choose) to identify themselves and respond to any questions or concerns.

Tool Kit

Tool #36

MICROANALYSIS TECHNIQUE

With this technique, your team can attack a problem creatively by breaking it down into its components and then brainstorming selectively around each part. The last section of the technique rearranges these components in unique combinations that generate unexpected solutions.

When you are directing a team through the microanalysis exercise, you may find it helpful to construct a review chart, such as that shown in Chart 33, which encourages a team to explore all possible aspects of problem solving and provides a quick visual reference for combining separate components into new and unique solutions. In the hypothetical example shown in Chart 33, a transportation team has found that some of its company's products are damaged when shipped by truck to customer sites. The chart shows the array of solutions developed by this team. The solutions that were finally chosen by the team are in bold print.

Complete the technique by taking the following steps:

1. Divide the problem into possible categories of exploration. If the problem involves a product or service, divide the product or service into its component attributes.

2. Separate your team into subgroups, and ask the subgroups to explore solutions based on the particular categories to which they've been assigned.

3. Post all lists of partial solutions and determine how they could be creatively combined to form an effective composite solution.

Tool Kit

CHART 33

Microanalysis Technique Applied to Problem of Product Damage During Transport				
Solution Category	**Alternative A**	**Alternative B**	**Alternative C**	**Alternative D**
Transportation method	Ship by air instead of truck	Establish distribution center to reduce transport distance	**Change route to reduce damage caused by bad roads**	
Transport vehicle	Upgrade to new insulated trucks	Add foam covering and flooring to trucks	**Add upgraded suspension system to trucks**	Reduce stack height in trucks
Container supporting product	Use plastic reusable transport molds for bulk shipments	**Add insulating buffer sheet between columns of products**	Change current cardboard product container to foam container	
Product design	**Add layer of rubber insulation to base of product**	Redesign product housing to make it more impact resistant		

Tool Kit

CREATIVE WHACK PACK®

The Creative Whack Pack® is a problem-solving tool developed by creativity consultant Roger von Oech, the author of two best-selling books on creativity, *A Whack on the Side of the Head* and *A Kick in the Seat of the Pants*. The pack is a deck of sixty-four cards divided into four different suits. Each suit contains sixteen cards that pose questions about a different phase of problem solving:

- Explorer cards pertain to alternative ways of extracting information that relates to the problem at hand.
- Artist cards address the process of merging available information into creative combinations.
- Judge cards relate to analyzing potential solutions and deciding on the best way to apply them.
- Warrior cards apply to thinking through the implementation of potential solutions.

There are many ways to apply the Creative Whack Pack®, some of which are described in a miniguide that comes with the card deck. I've outlined below one approach that has been useful for me.

Divide the cards into their four suits, and then use them to supplement brainstorming as your team moves through the four stages of problem solving. If your team has been engaged in creative brainstorming regarding potential solutions to a problem, take out the Artist cards and ask team members to draw one card each and read the question on the card aloud. The team could then discuss how each question could be applied to the problem at hand. For instance, Card 19 of the Artist suit, entitled "Challenge the Rules," offers the example of Alexander the Great, who solved the problem of untying the Gordian knot by cutting it in half with his sword. According to von Oech, the creator of the deck, Alexander made up his own rules to the game represented by this problem. Card 19 poses the question "What rules can you challenge?" After reading this card aloud, challenge your team to list all the rules or assumptions they have imposed on the problem at hand, and ask them to determine which ones might be subject to change.

The Creative Whack Pack® is not a problem-solving process; it is a tool that can be creatively embedded in a team's problem-solving discussion. It may help your team develop innovative thinking on difficult problems. For more information, contact Roger von Oech at Creative Think, Box 7354, Menlo Park, California 94026 (telephone 650-321-6775).

Tool Kit

"KILL THE CRITIC" EXERCISE

Team members sometimes communicate in ways that inhibit their coworkers' creativity. Unfortunately, many behaviors such as sarcasm or hostile criticism become so ingrained that people don't even realize what they're doing. The following exercise provides a humorous and nonthreatening method for changing team communication habits that may be discouraging the free flow of ideas.

Tool #38

To conduct this exercise, complete the following steps:

1. Before initiating this game, ask your team to select for review an existing problem or challenge that requires some creative thinking.

2. To start the game, write "Killer Behaviors" at the top of a piece of flipchart paper. Then ask your team the following question: "Without giving specific examples, what are some of the 'killer behaviors'—behaviors that tend to discourage or censor good ideas—that you've observed in our own meetings or at other meetings in which you have participated?"

3. To get things started, offer the following examples:

   • Poking fun at strange ideas

   • Attacking ideas before the speaker has the opportunity to fully develop them

   • Continually harping on the constraints under which you're working

   • Attacking new ideas because they've never been tried and therefore aren't valid

   • Reminding new or junior-level team members that their ideas reflect their inexperience

4. Record these killer behaviors on the flipchart for later reference.

5. Next, distribute soft foam balls to your team members.

6. Tell your team that you will all begin to brainstorm ideas for addressing the current problem or challenge. Suggest that whenever someone engages in any of the killer behaviors you've listed, the other team members should throw balls at that person.

7. After you've concluded your meeting, take a few minutes to conduct a debriefing session and ask team members to go back to the flipchart list and circle behaviors that may be causing problems in your own team.

Tool Kit

This technique may sound a bit bizarre, but team members never fail to respond with humor the first time someone lapses into the habit of making critical comments. More important, it also encourages them to relax their thinking and consider novel ideas and solutions. Finally, it serves as a direct prompt for controlling the behavior of dominant, negatively focused individuals who may not pick up on subtle corrective feedback.

FORECAST GRID

Sometimes, teams hesitate to undertake a major business initiative because they fear the potential difficulties and negative repercussions that might ensue from innovative actions. One way to keep these fears in check is to encourage your team to explore all the possible implications of tackling a major project or initiative. To explore this area, I recommend the use of the Forecast Grid in Exercise 21, which encourages your team to think through a variety of effects that could result from new business initiatives, ranging from ripple effects for other organizational functions to the cost implications of taking on a new initiative.

This tool has four useful applications. First, it can help your team determine whether the potential payoffs outweigh the potential problems associated with the new initiative. Second, it can guide your team in anticipating and eliminating obstacles that might be encountered in undertaking the new initiative. Third, it provides a means of obtaining alignment on project goals, outcomes, and roadblocks well before you undertake the project. Complete the grid's troubleshooting questions and then share the results with your manager or any other important stakeholders who will play a strong role in your proposed business initiative. (Refer to Chapter 15 for additional suggestions on reaching alignment with senior stakeholders.) Finally, you can use this chart to compare the likely payoffs and problems associated with implementing two or more alternative projects. Such an assessment is especially useful when your team has limited time and resources and must select just a few new areas for innovation. To complete the grid, take the following steps:

1. Review the troubleshooting questions that have been provided for each potential repercussion.

2. Use these questions to identify all potential positive and negative repercussions that could ensue from this project.

3. Record your team's conclusions to each question in the "Team Response" column.

4. Use a rating scale of −5 to +5 (−5 is high negative impact and +5 is high positive impact) to rate the impact each repercussion will have on your organization.

5. Use a rating scale of 1 to 5 (1 is unlikely and 5 is very likely) to rate the likelihood that a given area of repercussion could actually occur.

6. Multiply the two rating scales to arrive at a total score. (Note that a given score could be either negative or positive). Record this score in the "Total" column.

Tool Kit

7. Select, for further discussion and team monitoring, two areas of repercussion:
   a. That which has the highest positive total score
   b. That which has the highest negative total score

EXERCISE 21 • FORECAST GRID

Potential Repercussion	Troubleshooting Questions	Team Response	Impact	Odds	Total
Ripple Effects	• Will this project create additional problems for other work functions? • Will this project eliminate efficiency, quality, or staffing problems for other functions?				
Cost and Revenue	• Will the completion of this project require a heavy initial investment? • Once completed, will this project help you reduce costs or generate additional revenue?				
Team Relationships	• Will this project produce a strain in your team's relationships with other work groups? Does it involve an area of great political sensitivity? • Will this project provide opportunities for your team to work with and strengthen relationships with other functions?				
Work Efficiency	• Will this project involve temporary disruptions to work flow or customer service? • Once completed, will this project increase overall work efficiency or customer service?				

14

Reversals

Dealing with Setbacks

Eventually, every team runs into an obstacle it can't overcome. These roadblocks take a variety of forms, ranging from projects that are dismal failures, to changes that the team can't quite manage, to sharp, unanticipated declines in work performance. The great paradox is that teams with the greatest drive for success are also the most likely to encounter setbacks. After all, the laws of probability suggest that the more we attempt, the more opportunities we have to fail. The only way we can ever truly insulate ourselves against failure is to take no action at all, thereby removing ourselves completely from the game of life.

Although every team encounters setbacks, teams (like individuals) respond very differently to difficulties and disappointments. When faced with reversals, some team leaders can rally their troops, quickly reassess the situation, and regroup. With renewed effort, these teams overcome and learn from damaging setbacks and then move forward, often emerging from their trials even stronger than they were before.

Other teams respond to setbacks by lowering their performance expectations. They pull their collective energy inward, redirecting their efforts away from constructive activities and toward blaming one another or succumbing to self-recrimination. These ineffective behaviors may further weaken a team, making it less prepared to deal successfully with subsequent roadblocks. Without intervention, such a chain of events may turn into a self-fulfilling prophecy, with the team drawn down into a debilitating whirlpool of failure.

The Symptoms

A team that is struggling with disappointments or setbacks often provides clues to its state of mind. Ask yourself if you have observed any of the following behaviors exhibited by your own team.

Low Morale

Team members appear discouraged and defeated. They seem to lack confidence in their ability to tackle tough challenges. When presented with a new problem, their demeanor is apprehensive and uncertain, and they are often reluctant to set tough performance goals for themselves. After falling off the high wire, these team members prefer to stay at ground level and limit themselves to goals that are 100 percent attainable and risk free. They also tend to incorporate substantial buffers into their budgets and schedules.

Problematic Communication Processes

When team members hold one another (or people outside the team) responsible for their setback, assigning blame becomes more important than overcoming the reversal and moving forward. This kind of behavior, which often immediately follows a disappointment, can drive a large wedge between team members and result in a communication breakdown that compromises the team's ability to perform effectively.

Outside the group, some team members may begin to distance themselves from their team. In backroom gossip sessions and coffee-break chats, individuals who don't want to be associated with the team's setback will describe themselves to others as totally separated from "those losers."

Ineffective Work Processes

Some teams fall prey to rear-view mirror vision. By this, I mean that team members become preoccupied with the past. They waste a lot of time on "if only" discussions, for example, "If only we had obtained the marketing research *before* we brought out the new product, none of this would have happened!"

If a team focuses entirely on avoiding failure, it inevitably loses its ingenuity and flexibility and concentrates more on protecting itself from risks than on successfully performing its functions. As more signatures are required for approval of decisions, and more meetings are called to distribute accountability across a larger group of people, the team begins to grind to a standstill.

Case in Point: The Construction Team

Jason Jones, the sales team leader for Alpha Corporation, a large commercial construction firm, recently found himself in a quandary. On one hand, his team was doing extremely well with proposals, having won contracts on the last three bids. At first glance, this may have looked like cause for celebration, but a quick review of his team's cumulative revenue earnings revealed that they were far behind in gross revenue production compared to the year before.

A closer look revealed that the situation was due in part to the smaller number of proposals produced by his team. The last three winning proposals took six months to generate. In comparison, during the previous six-month period, his team had generated ten proposals. True, they only won seven, but on average, last year's efforts involved much larger construction projects and created almost twice the gross revenue for the company.

Jason called a team meeting to discuss this problem and invited team members to share their ideas. One team member, Betsey, referred to a setback experienced by the team about six months ago. "Jason, do you remember the Omega project?" she asked. "Well, when we failed to get that one, there was a lot of friction within the team about who was at fault. And then you and Dara [the team's senior manager] gave us that speech about the incredible cost drain these lost bids placed on our company. You reminded us, in no uncertain terms, that we needed to make sure we won every bid we made, and that's exactly what we've done. Three proposals generated—three projects won. What's not to understand?"

Underlying Causes

The fundamental issue is not what causes setbacks (there are innumerable causes), but, instead, what allows some teams to bounce back from setbacks while others become mired in disappointment and insecurity. Here are some of the more common reasons for a team's inability to cope with reversals:

Unrealistic Expectations

Ask yourself whether your team has set unattainable goals for itself. Stretch goals can be very motivational, but it's also important that a team not invite failure by demanding the impossible of itself. Unrealistic expectations lead to setbacks that leave teams demoralized and puncture their self-confidence. Rather than focusing on the progress they've made over time, teams that set unattainable goals begin to define themselves as failures—an identity that's reinforced with each new disappointment.

Short-Term Focus

Some teams have difficulty moving past setbacks because they develop a myopic, short-term view of their efforts. From this limited perspective, every obstacle or detour is blown out of proportion. A team in this situation is a bit like a marathon runner who, forgetting the progress she has made over the past twenty-two miles and unable to see the finish line, feels overwhelmed as she approaches the final uphill run.

Focus on Blame Instead of Solutions

As I mentioned before, it's not uncommon for teams that encounter setbacks to try to place the blame on others. This is easy to understand when we remember the punitive manner in which many organizations react to failure. When a team is focused on avoiding failure rather than on seeking solutions, team members miss a valuable opportunity to use the reversal as a learning experience, thereby increasing their vulnerability to future problems.

Inequitable System of Rewards and Penalties

In some cases, team leaders or senior-level managers may unintentionally undermine a team's ability to bounce back from a setback by failing to balance rewards for risk taking with penalties for failure. Teams that try to accomplish more are likely to experience more temporary setbacks because they're continually pushing themselves to the limit. A leader who minimizes victories ("They're just doing what they're getting paid for") but metes out strong penalties for the smallest setbacks will inevitably develop a team that concentrates on minimizing its chances of failure. In short, this team will simply withdraw from the playing field. The result is a work group that protects itself with easily achievable goals, excessive resources, and soft schedules.

The Treatment

If you recognize any of the preceding symptoms in your team, there are a number of steps you can take to help the team overcome difficult setbacks. Try to determine which of the following steps would be appropriate to your team.

Take Quick Action

A Japanese saying defines success as "fall down six times, get up seven," meaning that success is often just a matter of being willing and able to get back on your feet after a temporary defeat. The speed and effectiveness of a team's recovery depend on its response during the first few critical days and weeks following the reversal. For this reason, don't allow a setback to fester over time. Instead, set a goal of conducting a team meeting within forty-eight hours of the setback to quickly mobilize your team for action.

Encourage Open Discussion

Begin this meeting by inviting team members to talk openly about their concerns and frustrations regarding the setback. Open the door to frank discussion by acknowledging the natural human reaction of withdrawing when confronted with a nasty obstacle.

Don't feel that, as the team leader, you have to mask your own concerns. Share your thoughts honestly with your team but also explain why you feel the reversal is surmountable. At the same time, after your team members have had a chance to vent their worries and frustrations, redirect them toward the future. Challenge them with a statement such as, "We all agree that this situation has created some real difficulties for us. The important question is, what are we going to do about it? I'd like to hear your opinions."

Assess the Damage

If you've ever watched the television show *Star Trek: Voyager,* you've seen a great model of how a high-performing team deals with setbacks. Almost every week, the *Voyager* is attacked by alien craft or encounters some other galactic catastrophe. The crew's first reaction is to assess the damage: How badly were they hit? What weapons are still on-line? Can they continue to navigate? Are the life-support systems still functioning? *Voyager*'s Captain Janeway quickly synthesizes this information and determines the crew's options. A good team leader will assess the situation immediately in much the same way, taking into consideration such factors as cost variances, schedule delays, and public-relations damage, with the aim of forming an unemotional, balanced picture of the team's ability to execute its objectives. With this picture in mind, the team can formulate plans for surviving and moving past the current situation.

For example, several years ago, I was working as a training manager for a Fortune 100 company when it underwent a sudden downsizing. One day, I had a training staff of twelve, and the next day, all but two positions had been eliminated. I met immediately with my remaining team members to map out a survival plan we hoped would get us through the next six months. First, we compiled a damage report and created an inventory of training commitments that were outstanding for the next few months. We then recalibrated, identifying courses that could be eliminated, scaled back, offered less frequently, and delivered by outside trainers. In this way, we were able to maintain a high level of training activity despite the imposition of severe resource and staffing restrictions.

Recalibrate Your Goals

Based on the information in your damage report, help your team recalibrate its goals. As illustrated in our Case in Point, a team that fears the consequences of failure will tend to scale down its efforts and tackle only sure wins. Use the damage report to realistically assess the effect of the setback on your team's long-term performance. Armed with this information, you can work with team members to determine the necessary readjustments to your objectives and work processes. Tool #40 in your Tool Kit can aid your team in regaining its momentum after a setback.

Place the Setback in the Context of Success

Major setbacks often cause teams to focus primarily on their failures. While it's important not to gloss over failures, take the time to remind your team of past victories. Rather than engaging in a superficial cheerleading session, consider performing a split-sheet review. In this procedure, team members list their many small and large successes of the past year on one side of a flipchart, and on the other side, the setbacks and disappointments they have experienced. Using the lists as the basis of your discussion, pose these two questions:

- "In terms of our overall performance scorecard, how would we rank this setback? To what degree is it truly representative of our team's long-term performance?"

- "If we were to think in terms of a footrace, would you say we've been running downhill, on level ground, or uphill over the past few months? If we've been running uphill, isn't it natural to assume we'd experience more setbacks as we pursue our goals?"

Agree on How to Discuss the Setback Outside the Team

An important part of dealing with a setback is reaching consensus with team members on how to talk about the setback to those outside the team. This doesn't mean masking problems or minimizing difficulties, but it does mean accepting the fact that every member must assume the role of ambassador to some extent. For example, if you've just finished a project that didn't achieve the desired results, there's a big difference between saying, "We didn't accomplish everything we hoped for, but in the process we've learned a lot about the steps we can take to perform better in the future" and "We really blew it this time—I don't actually know how we're going to get back on our feet." Discuss openly with your team how you would like the group to be perceived by others, and seek agreement on the best way for members to respond to difficult questions about the recent setback.

Position the Setback as a Learning Experience

During your first discussion with team members, they probably won't be ready to view their setback as a learning experience. Only after they've had an opportunity to voice their concerns, assess the damage, recalibrate objectives, and refocus on past successes will they be able to look at the reversal with a dispassionate eye. You can set the stage for this phase of the discussion by suggesting to team members that they can garner valuable lessons from this experience that will enable all of you to perform more effectively in the future. Ask your team the following questions:

- "Moving ahead, what steps can we take to ensure that this kind of problem doesn't happen again?"

- "What have we learned from this situation that we could use to our advantage?"

- "What do we need to do differently?"

Gain Recommitment to the Team

Overcoming a difficult problem and getting team members to refocus on their successes is only half the battle. The other half involves convincing individuals who are probably somewhat demoralized and low on self-confidence to get back up on that horse and try again.

Act to Regain Momentum

Once you've renewed your team members' commitment, it's important to regain any lost momentum. As a rough analogy, picture your team competing in a race. Although all team members are temporarily out of action on the shoulder of the road, you've convinced them to get back in the race. Now you have to figure out how to close the gap, or make up for the lost time and distance. Here are four options for regaining momentum. (Tool #40 at the end of this chapter outlines a method for exploring these options.)

Deploy Additional Resources

This is the most frequently used catch-up strategy in a team's arsenal. Unfortunately, it's also the most misused. Many people automatically assume that the easiest way to overcome a problem is to throw more resources at it. Before requesting additional resources, confirm the validity of your improvement strategy and assure yourself that additional resources will make a real difference in your team's ability to overcome the setback.

If you decide you can justify your request for additional resources, don't limit yourself to thinking about additional team members. Consider every possible option for adding to your project resources, including the use of outside experts, part-time help, college interns, volunteers, and personnel loaned from other departments or company subsidiaries. In addition, find out whether it's possible to acquire more time from team members who are already assigned to your project.

Reframe the Problem

Another approach to regaining team momentum is to reframe, or redefine, the nature of your setback. Quite often, our perception of a problem determines the types of solutions we're able to identify.

For example, take a marketing team that's having difficulty finding the funds to evaluate customer interest in a new product, an innovative design for a wheelchair. Faced with budget cutbacks, the team first redefines its problem, changing the question from "How can we get additional resources or staff?" to "What other avenues are available for testing the receptiveness of potential customers to our product?" The answer to the second question involves Internet discussion groups frequented by wheelchair-bound individuals who are potential end users of the team's product. The team posts a series of queries to gauge the level of interest in proposed product features. Within forty-eight hours, the team receives hundreds of responses from prospective customers. The Tool Kit in Chapter 2 provides additional details on the reframing technique.

Redesign Your Implementation Strategy

If your setback involves significant schedule delays in key projects, revise your implementation strategy for managing the project. This could require such actions as finding out whether activities that are now organized sequentially can be performed simultaneously, determining if you can reduce the completion time for your project by dividing into subteams, or identifying steps that can be eliminated from your project.

Renegotiate Project Parameters

Your final option is to renegotiate with your project stakeholders and sponsor. I know, you're probably a little skeptical. Most of the team leaders with whom I've worked respond with something like, "But you don't know our executives! It's impossible to negotiate with them. It's like trying to negotiate with those *Star Trek* Borg: 'Resistance is futile'!" Take heart; it's not as hopeless as it seems. You *can* negotiate with your senior managers if you're willing to follow a few simple guidelines:

First, know your facts. When you walk into the room to renegotiate, come armed with all available information. If you expect a probable delay to slow down your project, be precise in explaining its extent and projected impact. If you've discovered a fatal flaw in your attack strategy, be ready to justify your conclusions on how this flaw will likely affect your performance.

Next, ask for an independent audit. If your stakeholders are reluctant to renegotiate, it may be that they don't fully understand the problems you're facing. Invite them to learn firsthand about these problems by performing an informal audit and review of your project. This could include sitting in on team problem-solving sessions, reviewing your project plan, or inspecting your budget.

Finally, realize what can and cannot be negotiated. Accept the fact that some aspects of your project are etched in stone, while others are negotiable.

Related Problems

The following chapters contain additional information that may be helpful in developing an effective response to team setbacks.

Chapter 6 (The Team Divided: The Problem of Intra-Team Conflict)—Assigning blame after a reversal can generate additional team conflicts. If you've found that your setback has led to friction between team members, you may find it helpful to review this chapter.

Chapter 9 (Painted into a Corner: Developing Better Foresight)—A team's inability to anticipate and plan for disruptive obstacles is a key factor in team setbacks. This chapter provides a variety of guidelines and tools that can help your team spot potential difficulties before they spiral out of control.

Chapter 12 (The Brittle Team: Learning to Adapt to Change)—The ability to manage setbacks is only part of overall change management. This chapter provides additional tools and techniques for increasing your team's adaptability and agility.

"CLOSING THE GAP" CHART

The last method of treatment in this chapter outlined a number of options for helping your team regain lost momentum, in other words, to close the gap on temporary performance shortfalls. The chart shown in Exercise 22 provides a tool for helping your team explore each option.

Tool #40

Apply this technique by completing the following steps:

1. In the space provided for each option, briefly describe the setback your team is experiencing.

2. Next, describe how each of the four options outlined in this chart could be applied to your team's current setback.

3. Invite an objective third party from outside your team to play the role of troubleshooter as your team selects the most applicable options for regaining momentum.

EXERCISE 22 • "CLOSING THE GAP" CHART

Solution Options	Applicable to Your Team?
Deploy additional resources: Obtain additional staff or resources to raise your level of work activity.	
Reframe the problem: Redefine your setback in a way that makes it easier to overcome.	
Redesign your implementation strategy: Revise your project plan through such actions as dividing into subteams or looking for ways to eliminate nonessential steps from your project.	
Renegotiate project parameters: Determine the possibility of renegotiating elements such as scope of the project, final delivery schedule, or deadlines for completion of key milestones.	

Mending External Relationships

15

Cast Adrift

Securing Senior-Management Sponsorship

You can't overestimate the importance of executive sponsorship as a factor in a team's success. Senior managers supply essential coaching and guidance for projects. They often have an in-depth understanding of the inner workings of your organization and can provide a big-picture view that would otherwise be difficult to obtain. Senior sponsors are also in a position to help you anticipate business and organizational changes that can significantly affect your team's future performance. Furthermore, they play the vital role of running interference for your team. Your sponsors can plead your case to executive staff and make certain your team's objectives receive a fair hearing in your organization. They can assist in procuring resources and ensure that your team's objectives are strategically linked to any other change efforts that may be under way within your company.

Without a firm base of executive support, all your team's efforts may go unrecognized as your work group finds itself cut off from needed direction, information, and guidance. Quite often, a team that lacks senior-level support will find itself groping blindly toward the future, without a clear sense of its organization's overall goals and business strategy.

In tough times, senior sponsorship can be an especially important survival issue. The backing of senior executives may determine whether teams succeed in the competition for scarce resources and talent. Once the budget ax falls, or difficult downsizing decisions are made, it's fairly clear which teams have succeeded in winning support from their senior executives. Unfortunately, by then, it is usually far too late to begin the intricate process of building senior-level sponsorship.

Apart from these reasons, you will find it absolutely essential to secure firm senior sponsorship if your team is attempting to implement major projects with the following characteristics:

- Require resources from other corporate units or direct interfacing with your company's customers or suppliers

- Could be blocked by other senior-level managers

- Are viewed as volatile political footballs

- Address very sensitive work issues

- Involve large-scale organizational changes, such as restructuring, reengineering efforts, or significant changes in company policy

- Require complex, time-consuming, and costly implementation processes

Winning Senior-Level Sponsorship

Senior-management sponsorship is difficult to get and even harder to sustain. When you stop to consider the political realities of today's workplace, it's not hard to understand why. Today's executives are under incredible pressure to perform under perhaps the most competitive business conditions they've ever known. Within this turbulent work environment, today's so-called top priorities quickly fall by the wayside to be replaced by the next emerging crisis.

The higher the priorities attached to your team's objectives and responsibilities, the higher the degree of change and risk they represent to senior sponsors. Executives who are averse to risk may be reluctant to sign on as team sponsors, even if they want a particular team to succeed in achieving its objectives. Instead, they may find it more comfortable to wait in the wings until they can determine the likely outcome of a given initiative before they commit their support. Sometimes, senior executives may agree to provide support but underestimate the level of sponsorship a team needs in order to succeed. They may think they can fulfill their responsibilities by attending a project kick-off meeting or speaking on your behalf during a senior staff session.

Finally, you have to accept the fact that some executives (individuals whom I call "blockers") may view your team's objectives as detrimental to their own personal agendas. Keep in mind that any business change, no matter how innocuous it seems, may appear threatening to others. This might be especially true if your team is undertaking projects that could lead to changes in company policies, work methods, staffing or budget allocations, or the scope of responsibilities for different work functions. In such cases, some executives may mistakenly view the success of your project as a threat to their own power base.

The Symptoms

If your team is attempting to operate inside your organization without an adequate level of support from senior-level management, you may observe some of the following symptoms. As you read through these symptoms, try to determine which of these behaviors are most prevalent within your team.

Lack of Access to Information

When teams lack senior sponsors, they're usually the last to hear of impending organizational or business changes; in fact, they may be told merely as an afterthought. Working in isolation, a team may attempt to take action or set objectives without understanding the larger organizational context for these changes. For example, not too long ago, a colleague of mine made the unfortunate discovery that the performance-appraisal training program she had been designing for three months was being shelved due to a complete revamping of the company's appraisal process. Had she known of these changes earlier, she could have saved herself and her training team a significant amount of time and effort. Being out of touch is likely to affect many other aspects of team performance.

Difficulty Procuring Resources

Teams that lack senior sponsorship are at the end of the line when it comes to allocations of needed staff and resources. They have a much more difficult time convincing their organizations that they really require such resources. Sometimes the teams themselves are regarded as unnecessary overhead expenses, not important corporate investments.

Threats to Team Functions from Outside Suppliers

Senior executives who lack faith in their teams' abilities occasionally seek external suppliers for comparable resources and services. For example, an executive might hire outside strategic consultants instead of using the organization's resident strategic planning group, or obtain IT consulting assistance and bypass the internal IT department. Once senior managers begin to import outside experts to provide internally available functions, a kind of self-fulfilling prophecy begins to take hold, as the very fact that senior managers prefer an external supplier to comparable internal teams further reduces those teams' credibility in the minds of other managers.

Lack of Recognition

Teams that are unable to secure the sponsorship and support of their senior leaders are most frequently found squirreled away behind the boiler rooms of their organizations. The old adage "out of sight, out of mind" aptly describes this situation. The lack of sponsorship shows up in a lack of recognition, and team members and their leaders are bypassed for promotions and receive only meager pay increases or bonuses.

Inability to Attract Talent

High-performing players have an innate compass that allows them to home in on the power centers of an organization. Associates who want to make solid contributions to their company tend to seek out managers who are able to advance their agendas with senior management. A team that lacks senior support and access to these levels of influence will simply not be able to attract exceptional performers.

Vulnerability of Team Leaders

Teams that are out of touch with their senior managers generally find their leaders excluded from organizational decision-making discussions. These leaders are seldom consulted for advice and may even be expected to implement initiatives that directly affect their own work areas without being given the opportunity to provide input.

In the worst-case scenario, teams that are cut off from executive support may eventually find that they have completely lost the faith and confidence of their executives. As a result, team leaders may be replaced with other individuals who can inspire confidence within the senior team.

Case in Point: The Sales Support Team

Even though she had prepared carefully for the meeting, Sara Griffin was having a hard time keeping her nervousness under control. Sara was the manager of her company's sales support team, and her group was primarily responsible for developing the sales collateral and support systems for the company's sales team.

A few months earlier, Sara had attended a professional conference where she discovered a very innovative software package—a contact-management tool that could drastically improve the efficiency of her company's sales operation by enabling the sales force to create a networked database of all client profiles and sales contacts. With this tool, sales representatives would have immediate access to a wide range of client-related information, which would allow them to track the effectiveness of their activities. Although the program required some initial IT support for installation, once in operation, it would run effectively on the company's intranet system.

For the past few months, Sara had been on a personal campaign to convince her manager and her team of the advantages to be gained from this software system. Finally, after several weeks of deliberation, Sara and her team had the opportunity to make their pitch before the company's executive team. As she stood there, looking out over the noncommittal faces of her audience, Sara wondered if she was getting her point across. She was particularly worried about the skeptical reactions she was getting from John Halsbury, the vice president of sales and marketing. Surely, if anyone was going to appreciate the value of this software program, it would be him.

After the meeting, Sara asked for a debriefing session with her director, Carla Valerlos. Carla began the meeting by thanking Sara for all the effort she had put into the presentation but then followed up by revealing the bad news that the senior team had decided to delay the introduction of the software program.

Sara: "I don't get it. The program offers so many advantages. Why didn't they want it?"

Carla: "Don't take it the wrong way. Bill and Linda were both somewhat concerned about costs, but I get the feeling John was really the blocker on this one. From some of the follow-up comments he made, my guess is that he's worried the program might be used somehow to micromanage his group."

Sara: "That's ridiculous! How could he possibly think that?"

Carla: "Sara, I think the underlying problem here is that John felt a little left out of the loop with this entire thing. Did you take the time to meet with him on this subject prior to the presentation?"

Sara: "Well, no, not exactly. We wanted to wow everyone at the presentation. I thought he'd be excited about this project."

Carla: "I think that's where you made your mistake. I watched John closely in the meeting and talked with him immediately afterward. I think he felt this idea was being imposed on him. I don't think you gave him the opportunity to position himself as a stakeholder in the process. Next time around, be sure you take the time to work with him and the other members of the senior team up front. That type of individual commitment is essential if you want the support and endorsement of our senior team."

The Treatment

If you have observed any of the preceding symptoms, you need to act quickly to secure the support and endorsement of your senior team. The following approaches may prove useful in building that support.

Identify Key Senior-Level Stakeholders

Senior stakeholders are those who are directly responsible for supervising or approving your team's work efforts, budget, etc.; manage work functions that are (or soon will be) affected by your team's work performance; or direct work functions that supply your team with necessary support and assistance.

Stakeholders can be divided into three categories. At one end of the spectrum are supporters who are willing to take action to move your team's efforts forward. Somewhere in the middle are the passives who don't care one way or the other about the outcome of your project. At the other end of the support spectrum are the blockers who, because of their particular interests and concerns, will actively resist your project. The first step in gathering stakeholder support is determining which of these three descriptions fits the individuals and functional groups within your organization. Exercise 22 in your Tool Kit can aid your team in identifying and categorizing the relevant stakeholders as either supporters or blockers.

Determine Potential Sources of Resistance

For various reasons, it's often quite difficult to identify resistance. Some people are reluctant to express criticism, while others assume that their concerns are self-evident and don't need to be formally communicated. Still others, operating with hidden agendas, mask their resistance with pseudoconcerns that they feel will be more acceptable to their organizations than outright opposition. Regardless of the cause, the result is the same: unless you're able to detect pockets of resistance, you could be facing a few nasty surprises when it's time for your team carry out its responsibilities and implement its objectives.

Identify Appropriate Senior Sponsors

By definition, a senior sponsor is any executive who can provide your team with needed information, guidance, direction, troubleshooting, and resource support. Tools #41–43 in your Tool Kit outline techniques for identifying potential sponsors and determining the most useful roles these individuals could play in supporting your team's project objectives.

In seeking out senior sponsors, don't limit yourself to those executives who are positioned directly above you within the chain of command. For many reasons, described briefly below, some of the most effective senior sponsors are those who don't have a reporting responsibility to your team.

Fresh and Objective Viewpoints

For one thing, these individuals are not part of your department or function, which means they can often provide objective feedback on your team's performance. From their vantage points in other departments, they may also be able to spot changes that could seriously affect your team's performance. For example, the executive who directs your company's IT strategy may be able to warn you of impending changes in your company's network system.

Expertise and Experience

Certain executives may have specialized expertise and experience that's lacking in your own line management. Perhaps you could enlist the CFO of your company to provide feedback to you and your team members on the feasibility of a cost and revenue model you've developed to support your project. In the same way, a senior manager of your company's organization development function may be the best person to advise your team on how to manage the implementation of a complicated and sensitive change to your organizational structure.

Coaching and Feedback

Some senior managers play a very valuable role by offering coaching and feedback on your effectiveness as a team leader. These senior managers not only have sound business judgment but are also intimately connected with the underlying corporate culture that permeates your company. As such, they'll know how a proposed project, presentation, or change initiative is likely to be viewed by employees and managers. This kind of feedback could save you from stepping into some potentially nasty situations.

Influential Positions

Senior-level stakeholders may also be in a unique position of influence within your organization. Some are wired closely to your company's board of directors, while others have access to suppliers, customers, or your executive team. The support of these individuals may be the deciding factor when you're seeking approval for a new proposal.

Finally, keep in mind that career decisions can be affected by a favorable or unfavorable word delivered at the right time by a senior executive. For example, consider the annual corporate leadership talent review, which attempts to identify managers and leaders of high potential for rapid profitability within an organization. During the review, a managerial candidate is introduced by his or her reporting manager, and other executives are invited to share their views on the candidate's competencies and leadership potential. These discussions can exert a major influence on a team leader's future career progression. It's at this point that having the support and sponsorship of your senior managers can have a crucial, positive effect on your own career goals.

Keep Your Sponsors Informed

Senior sponsors are of no use to you unless you work to keep them informed of the issues and challenges facing your team. Here are some suggestions for keeping your sponsors alerted to your team's activities.

Meet Regularly with Sponsors

Schedule time on your calendar for regular meetings with your sponsors. Make sure you let them know you're willing to accommodate their schedules, even if this means an occasional breakfast or after-hours meeting.

Share Important Correspondence

Supply your sponsors with copies of important correspondence and e-mail. The key word here is "important." The fastest way to lose credibility with executives is to waste their time by flooding them with all the details of your team's regular work activities.

When forwarding correspondence, provide a cover note that briefly sums up not only what you're sending but why you're sending it and what action (if any) you would like the sponsor to take based on this information.

Provide Briefings on Key Projects

For key projects, prepare a briefing that highlights some of the most important factors that are likely to influence the success or failure of your project, as well as any potential pitfalls and obstacles you've tentatively identified. This briefing should be a high-level summary; therefore, omit all the minutiae and detail that fill your project folder. In addition, be prepared to translate into user-friendly terms some of the more technical aspects of your project.

Ensure Adequate Lead Time

Bring sponsors in as early as possible. It doesn't do a lot of good to inform your sponsor on Friday afternoon that a major work issue is going to be under consideration by your company's executive team on Monday morning. In general, sponsors find it easier to take action when they're given sufficient notice regarding impending issues and the type of support that would be helpful in furthering team objectives.

Encourage Frankness from Your Sponsor

The best sponsors are willing to provide tough troubleshooting and hard, critical feedback. As illustrated in this chapter's Case in Point, it's better to receive this type of information in private from someone you trust than to find out about a situation when you're in the middle of a presentation with a group of managers. In short, the best sponsors don't tell you what you want to hear—they tell you what you need to know.

Don't Get Caught in the Cross Fire

Take care to manage the relationship between your managers and your sponsors with tact and sensitivity. Keep in mind that you don't report to your sponsors, nor are they responsible for authorizing your projects, setting your budget, or running interference for your team. Use your best judgment in determining how to inform your managers that key sponsors will be involved in selected projects and activities. You might want to introduce the idea with comments such as the following:

- "Before we launch the new customer survey, I'd like to run it by Jim Hardwell. He's had a lot of experience with this type of thing, and I think he really has a good grasp of our customers' needs."

- "If you're comfortable with the idea, I'd like to bring in Silvia Rodregas to help us troubleshoot our plans. I think she might be willing to sit in on our review session."

Respect Your Sponsors

Senior-level sponsors are not only of crucial importance in terms of providing guidance and support for your team; they're also at high levels of influence and achievement within your organization. Give them the respect they deserve by adhering to the following guidelines.

Be Honest

Sponsors should be people you can trust. It's essential that you provide them with an accurate and unembellished view of the issues and challenges facing your team. If things aren't going well, be frank about it. If you're requesting support for an initiative that you believe will meet with a lot of resistance within your organization, provide an accurate assessment of the level of difficulty involved.

Ration Your Requests for Support

Your project sponsor isn't your uncle, counselor, or father confessor. Recognize that this individual's time is at a premium and respect it. Ask for support only when you absolutely need it. Before making requests for support, try to determine if the project challenge you are facing can be managed effectively by yourself and your team.

Cut to the Chase

A typical project briefing with your sponsor should take no more than twenty minutes. Prepare for the meeting by identifying the essential points of your discussion and determining the specific action you'll be requesting from your sponsor. Walk into the meeting armed with an agenda of items arranged in order of priority. In this way, you'll be able to keep the discussion on track and cover the most important issues in a small amount of time.

Related Problems

Chapter 9 (Painted into a Corner: Developing Better Foresight)—The lack of senior sponsorship may also affect a team's ability to anticipate and respond to potential threats and opportunities. Senior managers not only enjoy a clearer view of potential large-scale changes but may also advise team leaders on the best means of exploiting opportunities and neutralizing potential threats.

Chapter 10 (The Broken Compass: Finding a Sense of Direction)—Senior managers play a guiding role in helping teams interpret the broader changes that may be under way in their companies. Without senior sponsorship, teams won't have a sufficiently broad and balanced view of their organizations and consequently will have difficulty setting a direction that is well aligned with overall departmental and corporate goals.

Chapter 17 (Our Own Worst Enemy: Strengthening Customer Relationships)—Senior executives are among a team's most important customers. Teams that are not responsive to these internal customers will certainly lose out on senior support, while teams that fail to stay connected to their senior managers will have greater difficulty interpreting their changing needs and requirements.

Tool Kit

STAKEHOLDER ANALYSIS CHART

This tool can be used to map out key stakeholders within your organization. Before you attempt to apply this tool, let's take a quick look at a stakeholder analysis performed by a hypothetical cross-functional team that's been asked to design changes to its company's performance appraisal process. Chart 34 shows the completed analysis.

CHART 34

Stakeholder Analysis Chart for Performance Appraisal Project				
Type of Stakeholder	Who are these stakeholders?	When during our project are we most likely to first encounter them?	Why would they support or resist our project?	What action can we take to secure support or reduce resistance?
Supporters	Vice president of HR	Will provide sponsorship from the beginning if asked	Believes it would create a more equitable pay system	Use as sounding board and troubleshooter to ensure our recommendations are well considered
	Company president, U.S.	Will officially launch project and personally support team's recommendations	Believes it will match rewards to performance and better identify high-potentials	Provide interim reviews; create better vehicle for tracking high-potentials
	Engineering staff	Will probably respond favorably to planned changes in system. Believes it would create a more equitable pay system	Last employee survey indicated high voluntary termination rate due in part to frustration with performance appraisal system	Conduct focus groups to confirm employee support for changes; use groups to fine-tune process

Tool Kit

Blockers	Vice president of sales	May attempt to discredit team's recommendations	New system forces her to give up some control over dispensing merit increases	Perform bench-marking study of other sales groups that use similar system to boost their performance
	President, Mexico	Has already made his concerns known to CEO	Is concerned that the team's proposed uniform performance standards won't be applicable to his employees	Check research for types of performance standards used in Mexico
				Conduct personal review of performance standards; consider creating a separate set of competencies for performance within this country

In this example, the company's performance appraisal process currently operates in the following way:

- Managers obtain appraisal sign-offs only from immediate senior-level managers, resulting in unreliable ratings based on varying personal standards.

- In the last performance review, more than 50 percent of employees received "exceeds" and "greatly exceeds" ratings, producing a skewed evaluation system.

- There is little direct relationship between performance ratings and merit increases. Allocation of merit increases varies across functions.

The team will be proposing the following changes to the appraisal process:

- Prior to approval, all appraisals must be reviewed by the corporate HR director to ensure more equitable and consistent performance ratings.

- The company will utilize a "forced distribution" appraisal process in which no more than 20 percent of employees can be given ratings of "exceeds" or "greatly exceeds."

- Merit increase ranges will be established for each performance category. Managers will not be able to award increases outside these ranges.

Tool Kit

With these project specifications in mind, the team leader has used the chart to identify those stakeholders who can be expected to support or block the proposed changes. Team members have also determined those points in the project schedule at which they are likely to encounter support or resistance. In addition, they have tried to identify the reasons why a given executive would support or attempt to block their project. Using this information, the team can develop proactive strategies to secure support or reduce resistance. The team has listed these actions in the last column of the chart.

When applying the Stakeholder Analysis Chart to your own team, I recommend completing the following steps:

1. Select a team objective or major project to review. This objective or project should be one that will directly affect other functions in your organization.

2. Ask your team to list on a flipchart all the potential stakeholders for your objective or project. Before doing this, you might find it useful to review the section of this chapter that provides guidelines for identifying potential stakeholders. Don't attempt to categorize stakeholders at this point—simply list them on the flipchart.

3. Now, review your list and identify stakeholders who are expected to be key supporters or blockers. List these names in the appropriate rows of the blank Stakeholders Analysis Chart shown in Exercise 23. If your team has identified a large number of stakeholders, you may find it easier to focus on the top five from your list for the remainder of this exercise.

4. Determine when, in the course of pursuing your objective or project, your team is likely to encounter initial signs of support or resistance from these stakeholders.

5. Discuss the reasons for their support or resistance. Although it may be a challenge, try to put yourselves in the shoes of the people you're reviewing.

6. Identify the actions your team can take to gain support or neutralize resistance.

7. Once your team has completed the chart, step back and highlight the most important elements of your analysis.

8. Consider reviewing your analysis at a later point with your most trusted sponsor. Make certain that this person is politically savvy and understands the power network within your organization.

Tool Kit

EXERCISE 23 • STAKEHOLDER ANALYSIS CHART

Name of Project or Business Initiative: _____

Type of Stakeholder	Who are these stakeholders?	When during our project are we most likely to first encounter them?	Why would they support or resist our project?	What actions can we take to secure support or reduce resistance?
Supporters				
Blockers				

Tool Kit

Tool
#42

TEAM SPONSOR IDENTIFICATION FORM

Exercise 24, the Team Sponsor ID Form, can be used to select appropriate team sponsors. As you glance over the list of desirable characteristics for an executive sponsor, you'll develop a better understanding of the challenge involved in locating such an adviser and guide. What makes your search mission even more difficult is the fact that good sponsors are in high demand. While you're searching for sponsorship, your peers are also trying to locate reliable supporters for their goals. As you'll soon discover, the reputations of the best team sponsors precede them, meaning that the person you're seeking may very well already be committed to other projects and objectives.

To complete this form, take the following steps:

1. Identify a current major project or business initiative for your team.

2. Ask your team to suggest managers who would be good candidates for sponsors of this project or initiative and list their names at the top of the form.

3. Review with your team the list of selection criteria shown on the chart.

4. Using a 1–5 scale (with 5 being the highest), evaluate each managerial candidate in terms of the selection criteria.

5. Your team should use this process to select the ideal sponsor, as well as several back-up sponsors in case your first choice is not available.

6. This evaluation can also be used to identify problems you might encounter in working with your selected sponsor.

EXERCISE 24 • TEAM SPONSOR ID FORM

Selection Criteria	Managers Who Might Make Good Sponsors			
Knowledgeable about designated project area or objective under review				
Aggressive change advocate				
Strongly committed to success of your project				
Flexible; open to alternative ideas and opinions				
Willing and able to invest time in coaching and advising your team				
Tenacious; willing to push an agenda and maintain commitment over time				
Sufficient persuasive and negotiating skills to weather a long debating process with peers				
Trustworthy; can keep a confidence				
Sound business judgment				
In touch with the "heartbeat" of your company				
Good communication skills				
Has a solid, positive relationship with you				

Tool Kit

Tool #43

TEAM SPONSOR EVALUATION SHEET

The Team Sponsor Evaluation Sheet (Exercise 25) can be completed before you meet with your potential sponsor to help you think through the types of support you are seeking. The sheet summarizes five key roles typically filled by project sponsors: coach, troubleshooter, seer, political adviser, and guard.

Use the blank column of this chart to record the names of team sponsors who could assume each of these roles.

EXERCISE 25 • TEAM SPONSOR EVALUATION SHEET

Sponsorship Role	Description	Appropriate Sponsors
Coach	Provides suggestions and coaching on how to move more effectively through a given phase of your project	
Troubleshooter	Reviews your project plan to uncover weaknesses and provides recommendations for improvement	
Seer	Helps you scan the horizon to identify emerging changes that could affect the outcome of your project	
Political adviser	Provides advice regarding others in your company who are likely to support or block your efforts	
Guard	Runs interference to remove obstacles to project success (resource constraints, lack of support, etc.)	

The Raised Drawbridge

Resolving Inter-Group Conflict

We sometimes visualize teams as self-contained entities that are largely independent of their surrounding organizations. In reality, all work teams are permeable. In other words, their very existence depends upon the efficient flow of information, resources, products, and services between themselves and the other work groups within their organizations. It's not uncommon, however, for teams to feel that they're operating without a lot of support, assistance, or understanding from other work groups. Team members may see their requests for assistance ignored by other departments, hear their work functions criticized in business meetings, or feel they waste an excessive amount of time trying to resolve petty conflicts between themselves and other work teams.

When we stop to look at some of the changes that have occurred in our business climate and organizational cultures over the past twenty years, we can see a number of factors that contribute to increased inter-team conflicts; among these are the complexity of most work functions and the high degree of change that occurs within most organizations. How frequently have your company's budgeting process, performance-appraisal review process, marketing functions, and IT systems been revised in the past three years? Many organizations undergo such changes on an annual basis, leaving departmental users confused and frustrated about what they perceive as arbitrary alterations to familiar work methods or processes.

Another source of inter-group conflict is the wholesale importation of new work teams into many organizations through corporate mergers and acquisitions. Overnight, hundreds, or even thousands, of professionals who have developed within very different corporate work cultures can be combined in a single organization. Consider a work team accustomed to freewheeling brainstorming sessions with other work groups. This team may suddenly find it has been acquired by a company whose culture does not encourage the open sharing of information among different work functions. The resulting clash of talent and beliefs can tax the skills of even the most competent team. In addition, reorganizations often lead to rapid reassignments of team leaders and executives, who may have their own, very different ideas of how their newly acquired teams are supposed to interface with other organizational groups.

Still another factor that sets the stage for inter-group conflict is the increased interdependency experienced within many work functions. Examples include the wide variety of cross-functional process improvement teams, problem-solving teams, project development teams, and customer action teams that have sprung up over the past ten years. In many cases, these cross-functional teams include representatives from a wide range of work functions. Although such teams are set up to improve work processes throughout the organization, address business problems, and strengthen customer and supplier relationships, their leaders are seldom given formal reporting authority over their members. Instead, they're challenged to work through difficult issues using only their interpersonal skills and technical abilities.

Together, these changes present teams with an interesting array of challenges when it comes to preventing and managing inter-team conflicts.

Unique Characteristics of Inter-Team Conflict

At this point you might be wondering how inter-team (group-to-group) conflict differs appreciably from intra-team (within team) conflict, which was introduced earlier, in Chapter 6. After all, aren't the issues and solutions that pertain to conflicts within teams equally applicable to conflicts that exist across teams? In reality, while there are some areas of overlap between these two types of organizational conflict, inter-team disputes have several unique characteristics.

First, consider that most of the conflicts occurring within teams are largely relationship based—for example, "Mary and Tom don't get along well." In contrast, inter-team conflicts span team boundaries and center predominantly on task-related issues that occur along the interface between different work functions. As an analogy, think of two associated work groups as neighboring geographical entities with the battle zone occupying the shared border between the two.

Another difference is that inter-group conflicts disrupt work processes that flow across a company; consequently, they produce much broader ripple effects throughout the organization than do intra-team conflicts. As a result, inter-team conflicts are often much more noticeable to senior managers and outside customers.

Consider also that when the members of a single team are engaged in a dispute, they can always call upon their team leader to serve as final arbiter and judge. In contrast, because inter-team conflicts frequently involve teams that report back to different departments or business units, they lack a single arbiter for resolution. In most cases, the leaders of these teams are left to their own devices to resolve the conflict and improve the situation.

Unlike the members of a single team, the participants in inter-team conflicts are less likely to share the same location and may have fewer opportunities for personal, face-to-face communication. As a result, they have fewer opportunities to engage in joint problem solving and conflict resolution.

Finally, despite differences in personal agendas or interpersonal styles, the members of a given team are bound by the team goals and vision that define their group, whereas separate work groups often support very different (and perhaps contradictory) sets of objectives. These differences may be exacerbated by personal conflicts between their respective executives.

For all these reasons, it's important to look at conflicts across teams as distinctly different from intra-team conflicts. Although they may test many of the same interpersonal skills, they revolve around very different work issues and demand their own solutions and problem-solving techniques.

The Symptoms

Teams that are struggling with other work groups within their organizations display several types of behaviors characterized by difficult communications and nonproductive use of time and resources.

The "Us Versus Them" Phenomenon

I've titled this chapter "The Raised Drawbridge" because a team at odds with its neighbors is very much like a town under siege. It's not uncommon to see teams respond to inter-team conflicts by intentionally shutting themselves off from other groups and going into self-imposed exile. When team members speak in terms of "us versus them" or stop talking whenever someone from the supposed enemy camp approaches their work area—or when teams sever the lines of communication altogether—you can assume the groups are embroiled in an inter-team conflict.

Restricted or Antagonistic Forms of Communications

Increasingly stilted and formalized communications between teams is another tell-tale sign of inter-team conflict. Team leaders may caution their members to limit communications with the other team or may even insist on controlling all communications with the "opposition." Work groups separated by no more than fifty feet of office space begin to communicate only via formal e-mails and memos. Instead of getting to the point, such correspondences frequently include a host of supportive, self-justifying documentation. Each sender reminds the other of the history behind the current problem. Accusations are made and criticisms are leveled, and copies of these e-mails and memos are distributed to everyone in the organization.

"Dropping Rocks" on the Other Team

I use the term "dropping rocks" to refer to actions taken by team members or leaders to escalate their disputes to higher organizational levels. This may involve appealing to management for support against the other parties in the conflict, supplying senior-level executives with copies of hostile e-mails, or criticizing other work groups in departmental meetings or at senior staff forums. In worst-case scenarios, teams may also make critical comments about other work groups to external customers or suppliers ("Sorry we don't have the design changes ready for you, but you know those slackers in our engineering department!").

Hostile Payback Cycles

I'm sure you've observed the following scene many times in your own company. A sales team makes commitments to its customers without first consulting the software design team to confirm the feasibility of the commitments.

Members of the software design team respond by remarking that if they're pressured into meeting the delivery schedule, they can't guarantee the program's beta version will be bug free. The sales team leader counters by attacking the software team's proposed budget during the annual budget review. The leader of the software team responds by suggesting to senior management that the sales team lacks the technical competence needed to successfully interface with corporate customers. And so it goes, with each new turn of events adding more fuel to the fire. If two teams appear to be locked in an escalating war, you can be sure their conflict has reached dangerous proportions.

Duplication of Services

One final symptom you should watch for is when warring departments begin to duplicate each other's services, either because they don't trust the service performance of their counterparts or because they don't want to lose control over important service functions.

For example, I know a marketing team that has repeatedly acquired outside training services because of a long-standing war with the in-house training department. By circumventing the company's own training department, this team sends a not-so-subtle signal that it doesn't respect the quality and effectiveness of the department's training services.

Case in Point: Acquisition Versus Maintenance

A few years ago, I was asked to provide team-building assistance to two departments in a public service agency. One department was responsible for acquiring public land bordering on state-regulated bodies of water, and the other was charged with managing the acquired land by performing day-to-day tasks such as clearing away underbrush and constructing dirt levies. For some time, the two departments had been arguing about complaints from the public regarding the agency's failure to properly maintain certain pieces of acquired land.

When I sat down with teams from the two departments to learn more about the steps involved in the purchase of a given piece of land, we quickly located the source of the conflict. Sometimes the maintenance department couldn't perform upkeep on a piece of property because the acquisitions department had failed to purchase adjacent tracts of land. As the team leader for the maintenance group put it, "How can we be expected to clear a piece of land if it's totally surrounded by private property and we have no way of getting our trucks onto the land?" The maintenance team's proposed solution was that the acquisitions department consult with them before making land purchases.

For its part, the acquisitions team informed the maintenance team that private land had to be purchased according to a set timetable. Up to this point, the maintenance department's three different subgroups had been providing the acquisitions department with separate reports. Unfortunately, the information wasn't always complete, consistent, or delivered in a timely manner. We developed a new procedure in which the three subteams provided the acquisitions department with a single, consolidated report that worked with the timetable. Once these guidelines were ironed out, the long-standing problem was eliminated.

Underlying Causes

The reasons behind inter-team conflict are varied, ranging from the personal to more general, process-related conditions. An important aspect of pinpointing the underlying causes of such conflict lies in determining the scope of the conflict, the organizational context in which it is embedded, and the personalities of the participating team leaders. As you review the following causes, determine which are relevant to your team.

Interpersonal Conflict

Sometimes, inter-team conflict begins with intense personal grudge matches between the leaders of the respective teams or their senior managers. Executives or team leaders who are involved in disputes may very well make disparaging comments about their counterparts, criticize one another in public forums, or demonstrate clearly that they're withdrawing support from the other parties. Team members watch their leaders very closely. If a leader defines another team as the "enemy camp," the whole team will often follow suit out of loyalty. Even when problematic personal relationships between team leaders isn't contributing to inter-team conflict, their antagonistic attitudes may set the tone for their teams.

Conflicting Goals

Organizations may unintentionally establish conflicting goals for different departments. For instance, take a sales team that wants to sign on the greatest number of customers. At the same time, because bonuses for the credit department are based on the total dollar value of late and failed collections, this group may establish a stringent screening process for new customers.

Likewise, to compete effectively in a tight job market, an IT team may want to offer very high salaries to job candidates. In doing so, the team may encounter resistance from the HR recruiting team, which, in an effort to keep the lid on staffing costs, has adopted a more conservative salary level for those same job candidates.

The point is that organizations often set potentially conflicting and demanding goals for different work groups. One of the real challenges for team leaders is finding common ground in what might first appear to be a highly competitive, win-lose situation.

Defective or Inefficient Work Processes

Previously I mentioned that team conflicts sometimes lead to breakdowns in work processes. The opposite can also be true. A poorly designed work process will result in errors, wasted time, deteriorating customer service, and redundant work efforts. (See this chapter's Case in Point for an example.)

In addition, when teams lack effective methods for achieving alignment on important issues, decision-making sessions may degenerate into winner-take-all battles. The conflict-management guidelines introduced in Chapter 6 can be helpful in resolving this problem.

In a way, work groups and processes are a bit like the proverbial blind men and the elephant; because each group performs a discrete function, the separate teams are rarely aware of the entire process. Hence, when the process breaks down, a team may tend to blame other groups for its problems.

Boundary Confusion

Occasionally, I find that teams have entered into conflict because they're operating within highly ambiguous and confusing organizational boundaries. In such cases, regardless of the interpersonal skills exhibited by the respective team members and leaders, some degree of inter-team conflict is inevitable, simply because the teams are performing within overlapping areas of responsibility. For example, a company's IT function and its corporate training function might both believe they're responsible for delivering generic software training to their organization's associates.

In other cases, teams face the great challenge of trying to work within the evolving definitions of their respective charters and accountabilities, which fluctuate continually in response to changing business conditions and organizational pressures. As a result, for many teams, managing team boundaries is an ongoing responsibility.

The Treatment

If you believe your team is caught up in inter-team conflict, some of the following suggestions may be of value in resolving the situation.

Educate Others About Your Team's Operations

One of the reasons behind inter-team conflict is that teams often simply don't understand the challenges or pressures faced by others in their organization. In addition, they may not have a clear conception of how those other work groups contribute to overall organizational goals and objectives. One way to overcome this problem is to invite leaders from other work groups to sit in on your team discussions or ask if your team members may visit the work areas of other groups.

A great example comes from an international sales and marketing team that decided to educate other work groups in its company on its newly expanded role. To do this, the team produced a type of traveling road show and visited different corporate facilities to share information on its goals, objectives, and work challenges. The team then went further by inviting key executives to travel with team members to selected international sites to meet major international corporate customers. These actions greatly improved the team's relationships with its fellow work groups, who developed a greater appreciation of the international team's value to the organization.

Improve Underlying Work Processes

If part of your inter-team conflict stems from problems caused by ineffective work processes, consider creating a cross-functional team to improve those processes. An approach like this can shift the focus of attention from faultfinding to joint problem solving.

A process improvement team should be composed of representative team members from all teams directly involved in implementing and managing the work process in question. It's beyond the scope of this book to outline a systematic approach to process improvement, but a good way to start is by reviewing *Business Process Improvement: The Breakthrough Strategy for Total Quality, Productivity, and Competitiveness,* by H. James Harrington (McGraw-Hill, 1991).

Focus on Superordinate Goals

In the crunch of day-to-day fire fighting, it's very easy to focus exclusively on the different perspectives that separate your team from other work groups. To build strong bonds with other work groups, it's useful to occasionally reference shared goals and objectives. In the case of teams whose functions are so disparate as to make this impossible, try to focus the other group's attention on superordinate (overriding) goals or performance issues on which you are both strongly aligned, such as

- Strong desire to improve customer service

- Recognition of the need to reduce costs within your organization

- Belief that your organization can score a substantial victory by entering a new market area

- The imminent threat posed by an outside competitor

Separate Behavior from Intentions

One of the most effective ways to prevent issues from blowing up into inter-team conflicts is to separate behavior from intentions. You can easily see another team's behavior and determine whether or not its actions are adversely affecting your team's performance. It's quite a different matter to make assumptions about the motives behind this behavior. Many times, what we view as another party's intent to commit harm is nothing more than ignorance of how that behavior is affecting us. Instead of jumping to conclusions when someone from another work group acts in a way that upsets you, try taking another approach.

First, describe the incident in objective terms. For example, you might say something like this: "Judy, I don't know if you remember, but a few days ago when we were sitting together in the project meeting, I asked if there was some way your department could free up some graphic support personnel to help us with the proposal we're working on. What upset me was that your immediate response was to cut me off halfway through my request and tell me, 'No way—we just can't do that.'"

Next, explain how the other party's actions are affecting your team: "As I'm sure you know, we're really under a time crunch and could use some help from your support team. I'm upset, in part, because you weren't willing to offer that support. But what really upsets me is the way you shut me down without even hearing me out."

Communicate to the other party the underlying message in her behavior: "When you did that, it was like you were saying our team isn't worth your time and attention."

Finally, confirm your assumption: "Is that what you were trying to communicate?"

Stay Out of the Line of Fire

Occasionally, teams may find themselves sucked into conflicts stemming from personal clashes between higher-level executives. If you feel your team has been caught up in an executive quarrel, try to keep team members out of the line of fire. In other words, let the other team know that regardless of the personal conflicts taking place at a higher level in your organization, there's no reason why your two teams can't work together effectively. If a member of another team attacks you for something that was allegedly said or done by your manager, offer a response such as: "Before you go on, I need to say that I'm not sure what Jerry said or did. I don't really have all the facts. I'm not going to waste time bashing my manager, but what I want you to keep in mind is that you and I have always had a good relationship and I want to keep it that way. Now, tell me the whole story, but remember, you're not talking to the enemy here."

Develop a Process for Managing Team Boundaries

A consistent theme of history is that wars are often the result of border disputes between neighboring tribes, states, or nations. Likewise, inter-team conflicts frequently center on disagreements over which teams should play what roles in managing certain organizational responsibilities. Such conflicts may result in overlapping work responsibilities, projects that fall between the cracks, or mixed messages to customers or suppliers. If your team appears to be caught up in a conflict of this sort, I recommend you set aside some time and meet with the other team to establish a process for managing team boundaries. See page 286 for instructions on how to conduct a boundary management review.

Break Down the Walls

If your team interacts with certain work groups only when conflicts break out, you're setting up a very negative Pavlovian reflex—team members will always associate inter-group encounters with stress and frustration. As an alternative, consider proposing social activities involving other teams.

The occasion could be as simple as ordering pizzas for a joint team luncheon or arranging an informal after-hours get-together. Some companies conduct annual conferences or meetings, which provide perfect opportunities for preconference activities. The only ground rule for these meetings is that there should be no shoptalk; ideally, the purpose is to build relationships and mutual respect.

Another twist on this option is for both teams to work together on a community project, such as a walkathon for a worthy charity. I know of one team that invites internal customers to volunteer with team members once a year at a soup kitchen for the homeless. There's a lot to be said for having the members of opposing teams walk away from a common experience feeling that they've worked together to make a valuable contribution to their communities.

Utilize Your Best Negotiators

Every team has certain members who somehow manage to rub other people the wrong way, just as it usually has at least one or two people who are very skilled in negotiation, consensus building, and conflict resolution. Whenever possible, identify your team's best negotiators and allow them a high level of responsibility for conducting inter-team meetings or representing your team on cross-functional projects. On the other hand, give serious thought to identifying those whom you may wish to remove from the front lines. Do you really want a rude and abrupt team member responding to questions from other departments or fielding complaints from outside customers? Other work groups and customers may form negative opinions about your entire team based on the damage caused by isolated individuals.

Conduct a Diplomatic Exchange

If inter-team conflict stems partly from a lack of mutual respect and understanding of respective functions, consider a diplomatic exchange that permits team members to trade places and spend a set period of time in their counterparts' work groups.

Years ago, I was employed at an aerospace manufacturing firm that sponsored an annual program in which U.S. Air Force officers served a year on-site at our facility to gain a better sense of our work challenges and business procedures. This was an excellent program for tearing down walls between our company and our counterparts in government. Not all exchanges have to be this lengthy. In many companies, sales representatives are required to make periodic service calls with selected customer support representatives, so that both departments gain a better understanding of how their companies' products and services operate in the field. There are a number of options available in this area, limited only by your imagination.

Conduct a Boundary Management Review

As I mentioned earlier in this chapter, a common cause of inter-team conflict is the ambiguous or overlapping areas of responsibility between two affiliated work groups. The boundary management review is an excellent means of resolving boundary issues with other work groups. Be sure to let the other team leader know that you're not preparing a hostile win-lose confrontation and would like to set the stage for a productive discussion by taking the following premeeting steps.

Explain to the other team leader that you believe many of the problems between your teams are caused, not by deliberate attempts to attack or hinder each other, but by the organizational pressures affecting both teams. Go on to explain that you hope both teams can use this meeting to look ahead and determine if you can (1) agree on which work processes or responsibilities are currently being affected by the actions of both teams and (2) seek out joint solutions to these problems. Finally, assure the other team leader that you and your team members are walking into the meeting with open minds; that is, you're not going to start off the meeting by trying to impose your solutions on them. Ask the other team leader to extend the same courtesy and be willing to consider alternative solutions. The Group Interaction Matrix in your Tool Kit can prove helpful in resolving team boundary issues.

Related Problems

Chapter 6 (The Team Divided: The Problem of Intra-Team Conflict)—Before teams can work together in harmony, they must operate in a somewhat consistent fashion. If the members of a team are experiencing a lot of internal conflict, they may supply other teams with contradictory or inaccurate directions and information. In this way, one team's internal problems can set off conflict between associated teams.

Chapter 10 (The Broken Compass: Finding a Sense of Direction)— Occasionally, teams collide with one another because they have not clearly defined their relative roles and accountabilities or communicated their charters to other work groups in their organizations. If your team has not yet defined its long-term direction, you may find it useful to carefully review this chapter.

Chapter 17 (Our Own Worst Enemy: Strengthening Customer Relationships)—When different work groups are involved in serious conflict, their work processes begin to erode, resulting in poor customer service. In addition, when team members make disparaging comments to their customers about other work groups, they may damage the reputation of the entire organization.

GROUP INTERACTION MATRIX

One way to resolve team boundary disputes is by using the Group Interaction Matrix, which is shown in Figure 5. The matrix can help you establish the relative importance of work issues by assigning team responsibilities to four different quadrants, labeled A–D. Each quadrant represents a different aspect of team performance, as outlined below:

- **Quadrant A:** Work processes, ongoing responsibilities, and objectives that require a high degree of interdependent activity between your team and associated work groups and significantly affect the performance of other groups. These are important issues that warrant joint review.

- **Quadrant B:** Processes and objectives that require the support of other work groups but affect only your own team's performance. Conflicts in these areas usually have an impact on other, third-party, work groups, which means it's imperative to address them, particularly if the affected third parties are external customers or suppliers.

- **Quadrant C:** Activities, work processes, etc., that do not require much interdependent action (i.e., can be performed almost exclusively by your work group without information, feedback, or assistance from the other team) but do affect the performance of other work groups. These actions usually involve services supplied directly by your team to other teams.

- **Quadrant D:** Items that call for a low degree of interdependent action and do not affect the other team's performance. These processes and objectives aren't relevant for discussion with other work groups, since they are completely self-managed by your team and do not affect the performance of other work groups.

Follow these directions to apply the Group Interaction Matrix to inter-team conflicts:

1. Ask the members of your team to help you identify their most important team-based work processes, ongoing responsibilities, and objectives.

2. Write each item down on a separate index card.

3. Introduce the Group Interaction Matrix to your team. Explain that the four quadrants of the matrix represent four ways of classifying team responsibilities in terms of their impact on other work groups in your company and the degree of cooperative effort required from those groups to complete these activities. Describe the criteria for

Tool Kit

FIGURE 5

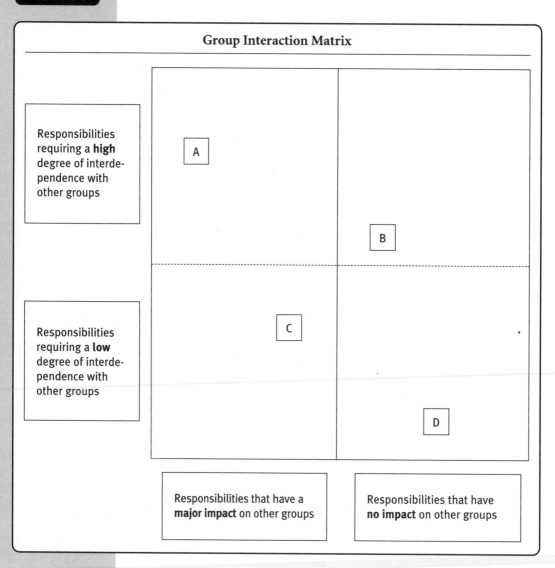

Group Interaction Matrix

Responsibilities requiring a **high** degree of interdependence with other groups

A

B

Responsibilities requiring a **low** degree of interdependence with other groups

C

D

Responsibilities that have a **major impact** on other groups

Responsibilities that have **no impact** on other groups

Tool Kit

each quadrant as given above. It's important to note that the solutions to items placed in quadrants A and B often demand extensive negotiations on modifying jointly managed work processes and activities. Also explain that solutions to issues in quadrant C may require learning more about the other team's operations so you can adapt your activities to support its requirements; it may also be necessary to educate the other team on the rationale behind your own work operations.

4. Draw a copy of the matrix on a flipchart.

5. Have team members place each of their cards in one of the four quadrants shown on the flipchart.

6. Based on the results of the previous step, select the work activities, processes, or objectives that are most important for review and have the greatest overall impact on both teams' performance.

7. Meet with the other team to review the topics you've selected for discussion. Sometimes, it's useful to ask the other team to complete a Group Interaction Matrix before your meeting so that you can both bring in matrixes for review. This gives both teams the opportunity to provide feedback on how they view the relative interdependence and impact of different work functions.

8. During the joint meeting, explain to the other team how its performance may unintentionally be problematic for your own team. In the Case in Point presented earlier in this chapter, the acquisition team didn't realize the impact of its actions on the maintenance team. In the same way, teams are often ignorant of how they may affect work groups that are downstream within a work process.

9. Encourage the other team to give concrete, detailed examples of how its performance or other work functions are being adversely affected by your team's performance.

10. Explore options for resolving team boundary issues as well as for jointly or individually resolving critical work issues. Such solutions might include the following:

   • Set up a subteam composed of representatives from both teams and authorize this subteam to make decisions affecting the work area in question.

   • Have your teams agree on mutually acceptable decisions on a case-by-case basis. This allows both teams to assume direct ownership and accountability for their decisions.

Tool Kit

- Establish definitive borders between your two teams by creating uniform boundary guidelines. This requires explicit and precise definitions of the functions and areas of responsibility of both teams.

- Select solutions that are acceptable to both teams and create a plan for testing these solutions. A test period assures the teams that they will not be prematurely locked into a solution and provides a method for jointly monitoring the success of the solutions.

11. Finally, be sure to follow up on the results. Conduct a joint team review approximately three to six months after the initial meeting. During this review, both teams should evaluate the success of the solutions they have tested and decide whether to establish them on a permanent basis.

RELATIONSHIP MAP

Sometimes, a simple graphic depicting a team's relationships with other internal work groups makes it easier to understand the factors that are driving inter-team conflicts. This is the idea behind relationship mapping. Figure 6 shows a relationship map drawn by a hypothetical team that manages all training activities for one division of a large corporation.

Tool #45

FIGURE 6

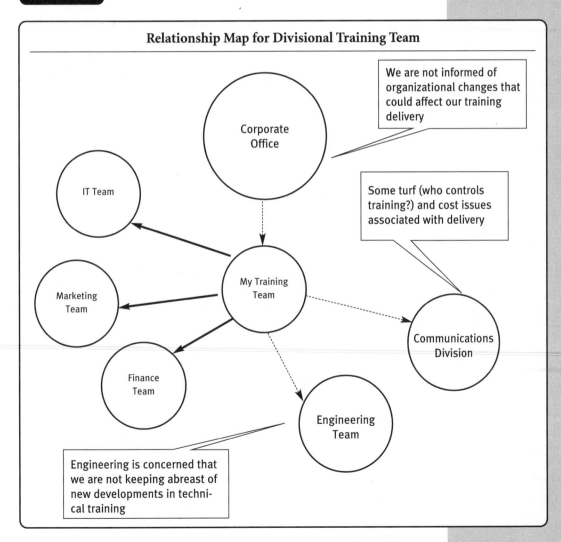

Relationship Map for Divisional Training Team

- Corporate Office — We are not informed of organizational changes that could affect our training delivery
- IT Team
- Marketing Team
- My Training Team
- Finance Team
- Communications Division — Some turf (who controls training?) and cost issues associated with delivery
- Engineering Team — Engineering is concerned that we are not keeping abreast of new developments in technical training

Tool Kit

The training team in our example is having problems with the services and/or information it receives from the corporate office, while its two largest internal customers—the engineering department and the communications division—seem to be dissatisfied with the services they're getting. These three work groups, which the training team has indicated as especially important to its survival, are represented by large circles on the relationship map. On the other hand, the IT, marketing, and finance departments—less crucial to the functions of the training team, as shown by the smaller size of their circles—are relatively satisfied with the training team's services.

Follow these steps to create a relationship map for your team:

1. Draw a circle in the middle of a flipchart to represent your team.

2. Now draw other circles around your team to represent internal suppliers, customers, support groups, or any other stakeholder groups that influence your team's performance. Use bigger circles to represent groups that are especially important to the survival of your team, as shown in the example in Figure 6.

3. Draw the other circles close to your circle if your team interacts frequently with the stakeholder groups they represent.

4. Use arrows pointing outward to indicate services or products you provide to these other work groups, and arrows pointing inward to indicate services or products you obtain from these work groups.

5. Use solid, thick arrows to indicate strong positive relationships, medium arrows to indicate satisfactory relationships, and dotted arrows to indicate areas in which concerns have arisen with the other teams.

6. Use dialogue boxes to summarize some of the inter-team issues that may be creating conflict between your team and affiliated work groups.

7. Invite selected individuals to review your team's relationship chart and offer their own commentary and feedback. Third-party representatives are often able to provide your team with completely different perspectives on inter-team conflicts. They may, for example, point out key stakeholders whom you've omitted from your chart or challenge the relative importance of different stakeholders or the types of conflict issues identified by your team. They may also be in a position to share insights regarding factors that could exacerbate inter-team conflicts.

RELATIONSHIP AUDIT

There are many ways to obtain input from other work groups on your team's performance. You can conduct meetings involving both teams, or representative members from each team; you can selectively interview members of the other team, or talk informally with the other team's leader. Unfortunately, because none of these approaches utilizes anonymous feedback, the other team may not be completely candid about its concerns. In addition, in groups settings, you'll often find that a few dominant and extremely vocal team members end up speaking for everybody. Finally, such face-to-face methods don't provide a means of assessing changes in team relationships that are occurring over time.

One way to overcome these limitations is by using a simple questionnaire that invites other work groups to provide feedback on their relationship with your team. Chart 35 provides a sample relationship audit, which is closely related to the Customer Relationship Audit in Chapter 17 (see page 318).

To apply this technique, I suggest the following guidelines:

1. If you feel it's advisable to audit several work groups, I strongly recommend that you start by focusing on a single work group and avoid taking on too many improvement actions at one time. Start with the one work group that you feel would benefit most from improved inter-team relationships.

2. Before conducting the relationship audit, clear it with the leader of the team you'd like to survey. Explain your purpose in conducting the audit, the steps you will use to collect and apply the feedback you obtain, and how you intend to report the results of the survey to the other team. I also recommend that you draft a cover letter to accompany the audit and review this letter with the other team leader before you distribute it.

3. Identify an innocuous third party such as an office coordinator or college intern to distribute and collect the audit forms. These individuals should average the scores for each question and then transfer the averaged scores and all answers to open-ended questions onto a second sheet.

4. Discard the original audit forms to assure the other team that you're addressing concerns regarding the anonymity of responses.

5. Caution your team that the audit is designed to obtain feedback on your team as a whole, not on the performance of individual team members.

Tool Kit

CHART 35

Team Relationship Audit

Relationship Factors	Team Ratings Low...Moderate...High
Accessibility	
You can reach us easily by phone or e-mail.	1...2...3...4...5...6...7
We are readily available for face-to-face meetings.	1...2...3...4...5...6...7
We take the initiative to arrange meetings with you.	1...2...3...4...5...6...7
Relationship Building	
We make an effort to understand your operation, work processes, and performance issues.	1...2...3...4...5...6...7
We enlist your feedback before we take actions that could affect the performance of your work team.	1...2...3...4...5...6...7
We have effective one-on-one relationships with your team members.	1...2...3...4...5...6...7
Listening Skills	
We give you our full attention during discussions.	1...2...3...4...5...6...7
When you leave a discussion with us, you feel we clearly understand and have not misinterpreted what you've said.	1...2...3...4...5...6...7
We present ourselves as open-minded and willing to listen to different points of view.	1...2...3...4...5...6...7
Information Sharing	
We freely share important information with you (we're not reluctant to disclose information you need to perform your job).	1...2...3...4...5...6...7
We provide timely information about changes that could affect your department.	1...2...3...4...5...6...7
When sharing information, we communicate clearly and succinctly.	1...2...3...4...5...6...7
Conflict Resolution	
We make an effort to work harmoniously with you.	1...2...3...4...5...6...7
We look for win-win solutions to problems.	1...2...3...4...5...6...7
When involved in a conflict, we conduct ourselves professionally (no yelling, personal criticisms, etc.).	1...2...3...4...5...6...7

What one behavior should we continue, or improve upon, to strengthen relationships between our teams?

What one behavior do we need to change to strengthen relationships between our teams?

What is the most important work issue our teams need to resolve together?

What steps do you suggest we take to resolve this work issue?

6. Don't conduct the audit during periods of intense organizational change, when broader concerns and issues may influence the survey responses you receive.

7. Give some consideration to your methods for reviewing the findings from your audit with those who completed it. My general recommendation is to conduct a very candid and informal review session with these individuals. Here are some additional suggestions:

- Instead of presenting the audit as a team report card, it's more effective to discuss the major benefits you've extracted from it. One way to do this is to summarize the areas that have been identified in the survey as your team's two greatest strengths as well as those that represent your team's two greatest performance improvement opportunities.

- Share any suggestions from your team on how to strengthen team relationships. At the same time, solicit suggestions from the other team regarding additional improvement actions that can be undertaken by your team.

- Toward the end of the discussion, don't hesitate to indicate actions the other team can take to help strengthen the relationship and resolve critical problems between the teams.

Our Own Worst Enemy

Strengthening Customer Relationships

It never fails to surprise me that teams so frequently end up antagonizing the one group that validates their credibility and confirms their value to their organizations—their customers. In making this mistake, teams become their own worst enemies. Think about it for a moment. Your team exists for only one reason: to serve an internal or external customer. This is true regardless of whether you work in your company's legal, HR, contract, procurement, or IT department or on the front lines of your organization's sales force. If you visualize your team as a living entity, connected to your organization via a series of lifelines, then perhaps the most important lines are those that link a team to its customers. At the end of the day, the only way you can honestly assess the value you bring to the table is by determining whether your team is meeting the needs of your customers.

When a team is unable to respond effectively to its customers' needs, its value to its employer is dramatically decreased. From the customers' point of view, it doesn't matter whether this problem is exemplified in the deliberate disregard of an arrogant supplier or is due to unintentional factors such as the absence of an effective customer feedback process. In either case, the results are much the same; the team cuts itself off from its most important organizational lifeline.

The Symptoms

A team that has lost its customer focus displays four symptoms. It is important to recognize and address these symptoms before they grow out of control, affecting both customer satisfaction and your team's reputation as a service provider. Which of the following symptoms have you observed in your own team?

Repeated or Unresolved Complaints

The most common symptom is repeated complaints from customers that the team is not meeting their needs. These complaints may center around performance areas such as schedule delays, cost overruns, excessive charges, or shoddy practices, or they may involve more subtle factors, such as a team's unwillingness to be flexible in response to changing needs. Both types of problems represent a serious gap between a customer's requirements and a team's ability to deliver needed products and services.

In a related symptom, repeated complaints are not addressed in a timely and adequate manner, and customers are compelled to escalate the complaint process to higher levels. One way to learn the severity of the situation is to determine how many repeated requests for resolution go unanswered and end up on the desk of a department vice president or member of the executive team.

Unexpected Changes or Developments Among Customers

If you suddenly discover that a client has been moving in an unanticipated direction for some time, you may be losing touch with your customers. Examples include finding out late in the game that a key customer is defecting to a competitor, has launched into a completely new market, or has made significant work changes that will affect your team's ability to deliver quality service.

Loss of Customer Trust

When your customers repeatedly second-guess you by challenging your cost estimates, questioning your ability to meet delivery dates, double-checking your work, or attempting to micromanage your activities, they're sending you strong signals that they've lost trust in your team.

Customers who trust their suppliers bring these groups into their confidence, while those who lack this trust keep their suppliers at arm's length. If you notice that customers are reluctant to reveal information about impending organizational changes or the underlying business challenges that are driving their requirements, they probably don't think of you as an intimate partner in their work efforts.

Customers Become Competitors

Potentially, your customers could be your competitors. If customers don't feel they can count on a team for support, they'll often respond by duplicating the services of that team for themselves. A department that creates its own finance, training, or IT team is probably not satisfied with the quality of its in-house support functions. The same phenomenon can occur with external customers. For example, a corporate client became so disgruntled with the poor service it was receiving from a large quality-consulting firm that it decided to design and deliver its own quality improvement training. The corporation's training courses were so well received within the industry that the company went on to market these programs to other organizations, taking a sizable amount of business away from the consulting firm.

Case in Point: The Shipping Team

The team responsible for shipping its company's products to external customers made the mistake of defining its performance standard of "on-time delivery" as transferring merchandise from the dock to delivery trucks by a specified date. However, this definition masked any problems that may have occurred afterward, during transportation. In fact, the shipping team was so intent on demonstrating improvements to its delivery function that it ended up creating more problems than it solved. To expedite what it saw as the timely shipment of products, the team made certain changes that created a bottleneck of delivery trucks at the shipping bay.

The team certainly met its improvement objective—after all, the time required to get the company's packages onto the waiting trucks was reduced.

Unfortunately, the team failed to realize that to its customers, "delivery" meant when they *received* the shipments, not when the products were shipped. In the end, the delays the team created in the shipping bay led to even later deliveries to customers.

Underlying Causes

Weak relationships between teams and their customers, both internal and external, develop from problematic work processes and attitudes. Ask yourself if you've ever observed some of the following behaviors in your team.

Unavailability of Team to Customers

A common cause of poor customer relationships is inaccessibility on the part of team members. Obvious examples range from not answering phones or responding to e-mail to waiting for customers to bring forward their questions and concerns before making an effort to address them.

Lack of access also reveals itself in more subtle ways. One company I know hosts yearly "customer appreciation" meetings, yet members of the company's senior staff inevitably isolate themselves from customers who attend. The meeting theme may be "customer appreciation," but the underlying message is "we don't really want anything to do with you." Segregated seating also means the company misses out on a terrific opportunity to build strong ties with its customers.

In a related problem, teams fail to bring their customers into the decision-making process when they're setting objectives or taking actions that directly affect their customer base.

Value Migration

Customers' needs change over time. What is valuable today in a product or service may not be valuable tomorrow. Successful companies become adept at anticipating these migrations in customer values and plan changes to their products and services to meet these evolving needs.

A great example is the creation of the "line-free" bifocal lens. Optical manufacturers should have seen this trend coming by noting that aging baby boomers want to view themselves as perpetually youthful. Anything that smacks of the traditional stereotypes of advancing age, including old-fashioned bifocal lenses, will be actively rejected by this group in favor of new products that meet their changing needs.

Teams may also fail to keep pace with the changing expectations of internal customers. Consider the case of HR functions. Many HR teams are beginning to realize that their internal customers don't want to take the time to contact an HR specialist for simple questions on their 401K retirement programs or benefits packages. Quite often, when these customers need answers, they need them right away. Savvy HR departments provide this information on the company's intranet, thus allowing employees direct access to retirement and benefit information. Those HR departments that can't adapt to these changing needs will find themselves increasingly out of favor with their internal customers.

Failure to Benchmark the Competition

Occasionally, teams run into trouble because they concentrate solely on historical performance when evaluating current performance. This approach may not match the perceptions of customers, who tend to consider not only how a supplier's performance has changed over time but how it compares to other options available for meeting their needs. Thus teams that fail to keep track of their competition run the risk of being viewed by customers as a poor second choice. This phenomenon also occurs in relationships with internal customers, who may bypass the functions of their own companies if they believe these internal work groups don't compare favorably to their external competitors.

Arrogance

Arrogance in customer relationships can best be described by the phrase "we know what's best for you." Arrogance manifests itself in many ways, as shown in the following examples:

- A technical provider treats an unsophisticated customer in a condescending way: "What do you mean, you don't know how to access the server? Anyone should know how to do that!"

- A team refuses to listen to the concerns voiced by its customers on the grounds that the customers "don't know what they're talking about."

- A team makes disparaging remarks about its internal customers.

- Customers who ask for special assistance are given a blanket "no" and told that their requests are not covered by the company's policy.

- A team member cuts off a customer in the middle of discussion, telling the customer, "I already know what the problem is."

All of these examples reflect situations in which customer relationships are damaged through lack of caring and inadequate communication skills.

Failure to Understand the Effect of Work Processes on Customers

Sometimes, teams make erroneous assumptions about their work performance. One airline discovered the truth behind this statement during an innovative market research study aimed at determining how to better serve its customers.

As the first step in the study, the company created a simple graphic time line depicting the full sequence of events experienced by customers during their flights, from making initial queries about potential flights to concluding their flights and picking up their baggage at the baggage claim area. Customers were asked to indicate their assessment of typical service experiences encountered at each stage of the flight process and were given an assortment of color pens to color code their responses on the time line. The airline was surprised to learn that its customers were relatively satisfied with their flight experiences after they boarded their planes. The area that caused them the greatest frustration (shown in red on the time lines) was the poor communication and extended delays they underwent while waiting at the gate. Armed with this information, the airline redirected its improvement efforts.

Absence of a Formal Customer Feedback Mechanism

Even if your team is making a sincere effort to respond to your customers' needs, if you don't have a reliable process for measuring customer satisfaction, you'll be able to perform only a rough guesstimate of your capability. In addition, without such a feedback mechanism in place, your team will only hear about customer service problems after they've resulted in complaints.

Failure to Build Customer-Focused Performance Metrics

How well is your team performing? How do you know? Teams maintain their customer focus by basing a major share of their performance standards on their ability to fully meet customer requirements, and they place a high degree of importance on the performance feedback they receive from their customers. In contrast, teams that are disconnected from their customers rely almost exclusively on *internal* measures to evaluate their effectiveness. Take a look at the top three performance measures you track on a weekly basis. If at least one of these measures doesn't relate to customer satisfaction, you're not paying enough attention to your customers.

The Treatment

There are a variety of approaches for improving customer relationships, ranging from simple attitudinal adjustments to large-scale systems changes. As you review the following changes, determine which are appropriate to your team.

Identify Your Best Customers

It's not always possible to meet the needs of all customers. If your team has limited amounts of time and resources, you'll have to establish priorities. It may be useful to focus on meeting the needs of your "gold" customers, or those that are most crucial to your organization's success. In almost every business setting, there are a few customers that account for the lion's share of value obtained from a team's products and services.

Consultant Sheila Kessler, in her book *Measuring and Managing Customer Satisfaction* (ASQC Quality Press, 1996, p. 45), claims that 60 percent of Delta Airline's revenues are derived from only 6 percent of its customer base. These gold customers provide a disproportionately large share of revenue obtained from Delta's total investment in seeking that revenue. Obviously, Delta is going to focus a lot of attention on trying to please these customers.

For a team that supports an organization's internal customers, such as the company's engineering or marketing and sales groups, gold customers might be the largest or most influential organizational function. Gold customers may also include senior managers who can have a major effect on a team's success. Tool #47 in the Tool Kit at the end of this chapter provides step-by-step instructions for identifying your gold customers.

Create Opportunities for Customer Feedback

Invite customers to attend your meetings. You may want to set a goal for maintaining customer contact, such as having each member of your team meet a different customer for lunch every week. Ask for permission to attend your customers' meeting sessions, or create social events that bring together people from your work team with members of your customers' work teams. Create focus group sessions where representative customers are encouraged to provide your team with honest performance feedback and share suggestions for improving its performance. Tool #48 in your Tool Kit describes how to create a variety of customer listening posts.

Put Yourself in Your Customers' Shoes

This approach encompasses any actions your team undertakes to achieve a customer's-eye view of your products and services. Here are a few examples:

- Retail stores regularly employ "mystery shoppers" to evaluate such factors as responsiveness to customer inquiries or effectiveness in dealing with customer complaints.

- Many hotel owners and general managers periodically spend a night in one of their own hotels to evaluate service from the guest's point of view. These visits can uncover details such as electronic door locks that aren't working properly or noisy ice machines that keep them up all night.

- Some manufacturing companies create mock test areas where customers are invited to use their products. One Japanese manufacturer changed its microwave ovens from top-loading to front-loading after watching U.S. customers struggling to use the top-loading models in U.S.-style test kitchens. (Japanese kitchens don't have overhanging cabinets that get in the way of top-loading microwaves.)

- An IT team for a computer company observed nontechnical employees as they attempted to read, interpret, and apply instructions for connecting and installing hardware components. Only then could team members make sense out of the recent customer complaints about the difficulty of assembling and installing the company's products. By watching fellow employees struggle through this process, team members became aware of significant improvements they could make to their "no hassle" assembly instruction booklet.

Keep Track of Your Customers' Customers

Your customers' needs are determined by the requirements of their own customers. Staying informed about changing needs or markets for these groups will enable you to anticipate new developments in your own customers' expectations and needs. For example, if your customers' clients implement an ISO 9000 quality improvement program, this will increase your customers' quality requirements, and they will in turn need improved performance from you. There are several steps you can take to track your customers' customers:

- Accompany your customers when they make field visits to their customer sites.

- Ask your customers if they're willing to share feedback from their customer base that pertains to your team's performance.

- Read trade and business journals to gain a better sense of the changing demands your customers are experiencing.

- For internal customers, get to know the associates that work in these customer departments. Ask them to keep you informed of any impending changes that could signal the need for adjustments to your team's service delivery process.

Periodically Audit Your Team's Performance

There are critical performance requirements for every work function, such as delivery time, quality, or cost. Don't assume that you automatically know your customers' performance requirements. Instead, identify their most important needs and devise a method for measuring your team's performance against those needs. Tool #49 in your Tool Kit introduces a useful method for auditing team performance.

Perform a Periodic Customer Relationship Audit

Sometimes, complaints are not caused by your team's performance but by its lack of skill in forming positive relationships with customers. One way to evaluate your relationships is to ask customers for performance feedback on such factors as the friendliness and accessibility of team members. Tool #51 in your Tool Kit outlines a technique for performing a customer relationship audit.

Related Problems

Chapter 16 (The Raised Drawbridge: Resolving Inter-Group Conflict)—Difficulties with customer groups can be viewed as a specialized form of inter-departmental conflict. This chapter provides several tools and guidelines for improving relationships with other work groups.

Chapter 11 (The Missing Scorecard: Strengthening Accountability)—It's important that your team develop and implement evaluation measures that are relevant to your customers' requirements. This chapter introduces a variety of tools for establishing effective team scorecards.

Tool Kit

Tool #47

CUSTOMER ASSESSMENT MATRIX

Not all customers are equally important to the success of your team. Some have more impact on the success of your organization and your team. Assuming that your team has limited staff, time, and resources, it makes sense to focus most of your attention on meeting the needs of these crucial customer groups. To do this, you must determine which of your customers are truly "gold customers." Use the Customer Assessment Matrix to help your team identify these customers.

Chart 36 shows a Customer Assessment Matrix completed by a hypothetical sales team. The team has listed four of its most valuable customers in the first column; the factors used to rate these customers head the next five columns to the right. These factors are

- The current total sales volume for each account

- The total *potential* sales volume for each account over the next three years

- The account's strategic importance to the company's long-term business plan

- The investment requirement, or amount of resources that will be required to service the account

- The gateway potential, or likelihood that the account will lead to additional business

CHART 36

Customer Assessment Matrix

Customer	Current Sales Volume (8)	Projected Volume (10)	Strategic Importance (7)	Investment Requirement (5)	Gateway Potential (7)	Total Score
Alpha Co.	2/16	3/30	3/21	5/25	4/28	120
Beta Co.	3/24	2/20	3/21	2/10	5/35	110
Delta Co.	4/32	5/50	5/35	4/20	3/21	**158**
Theta Co.	4/32	4/40	2/14	3/15	3/21	122

Tool Kit

To create your matrix, follow these steps:

1. List all customer groups served by your team.

2. Agree on the distinguishing factors that characterize gold customers. Refer to the matrix shown in Chart 36 for examples of the kinds of factors you might want to consider.

3. Use a 1–10 scale (with 10 as the highest score) to determine the relative importance of each factor. Write these scores next to the corresponding factors in the top row (refer to Chart 36).

4. Evaluate your customers in terms of each factor on a 1–5 rating scale. Write these scores to the *left* of a slash, as shown in Chart 36.

5. Multiply the relative importance of each factor by the rating score for each customer. Place this number to the *right* of the slash.

6. Add up the scores for each factor and record the totals in the last column.

7. Customers who receive the highest scores are your team's gold customers. In Chart 36, we can see that Delta Company is the most important customer, with an overall score of 158. If your assessment doesn't reveal any definitive differences in scores, it probably means that your team either hasn't identified the factors that truly distinguish gold customers or hasn't given sufficient thought to its comparative review of these customers.

Tool Kit

LISTENING POST CHART

Listening posts enable your team to stay in touch with your customers' changing needs. However, it's important to develop more than one kind of approach to keeping track of your variety of customers. This simple exercise will guide your team as you brainstorm options that will best suit the needs of each customer.

Chart 37 shows a sample Listening Post Chart for an HR team that has identified four departmental customers: marketing, field support, IT, and finance. Actions representing potential listening posts are listed across the top of the six columns to the right.

To apply this technique with your team, complete the following steps:

1. Create a Listening Post Chart similar to the one in Chart 37.

2. In the left column of your chart, list customers currently served by your work team.

3. Identify five to seven options that might be used as listening posts for your team and write them at the tops of the columns to the right. Just provide a general idea of the actions or events; don't concern yourself with specifically defining them at this time.

4. Once you and your team have identified the options, fill in the columns next to each customer with specific descriptions of actions or events.

5. If your team identifies an idea that could be applied to several customers, or to your entire customer base, indicate that in your chart. The HR team in our example has determined that inviting customers to attend its meetings and creating an intranet newsletter are solutions that will work for all their customer groups.

6. If you identify too many options for immediate implementation, go back and highlight the ones you feel are particularly valuable. These should be the first actions your team takes to create your customer listening posts.

Tool Kit

CHART 37

Listening Post Chart: Human Resources Team						
Your Customers	POTENTIAL LISTENING POSTS					
	Attend Their Meetings	**Have Them Attend Our Meetings**	**E-Mail & Company Intranet**	**Customer Social Events**	**Focus Groups**	**Meetings with Senior Managers**
Marketing				Volunteer to facilitate the yearly sales & marketing meeting		Meet with the SVP of marketing to discuss staffing impact of impending reorganization
Field Support	Attend quarterly market area meetings	Invite them to attend our meetings on a rotational basis	Create an HR newsletter on the company Intranet alerting customers to upcoming changes and inviting questions & responses through e-mail			
IT	Attend monthly staff meetings					Call a meeting with the IT directors to identify their concerns regarding our benefits program
Finance					Conduct a finance focus group centering around problems they have been encountering with our recruiting process	

Tool Kit

CUSTOMER REQUIREMENTS RATING TABLE

So far, we've provided tools to help you identify your gold customers and create listening posts for enhancing access to these customers. This tool, the Customer Requirements Rating Table, will help you pinpoint your customers' key requirements and evaluate your effectiveness in relation to those requirements. The word "requirements" refers to the features of your team's products and services that are especially important to your customers. Requirements come in all shapes and sizes. Some of the most common are shown below in Chart 38.

Some requirements are more important than others. For example, your customer may care less about the attractiveness (four-color layout, fancy graphics) of a financial report than about its timely delivery. It's important for a team to know the relative importance of different requirements in order to make the best trade-offs, when necessary, between competing requirements. Going back to our example, your customer may be willing to work from a rough spreadsheet, minus graphics, if it means getting this report a few days earlier each month. In fact, the ideal solution may be to offer your customer the ability to pull financial data as needed, by placing the report on the company's intranet.

To complete the Customer Requirements Rating Table for your team, follow these steps:

1. Review the list of gold customers you identified with the Customer Assessment Matrix in Tool #47.

2. If you could improve your team's performance for just one customer on this list, which one would it be? Write this customer's name in the space provided in the Customer Requirements Rating Table in Exercise 25.

3. Select one of the most important outputs your team provides to this customer. An output is a specific product or service outcome. For instance, the following teams might identify these vital outputs:

   - Help desk: a service call
   - Design team: a software program
   - Training team: a training program
   - Finance team: a financial report
   - HR team: phone responses to inquiries regarding company policies

   Briefly summarize this output in the space provided in Exercise 25.

4. Compile a list of requirements—performance factors you feel are especially important to your customer. These are the expectations

Tool Kit

CHART 38

Representative Customer Requirements

Timeliness	The degree to which your team provides products and services in a timely manner. A computer manufacturer that requires the completion of an elaborate purchase order before shipping the product via snail-mail would be rated as poor in this area, while a competitor that offers direct ordering through the Internet and guaranteed overnight delivery would be rated extremely high.
Responsiveness	The degree to which a team responds quickly and with enthusiasm to customers' needs. The team that makes it a point to answer all phone calls on the first ring and immediately take action on customers' concerns would score high in this area. In contrast, a team that lets phones ring off the hook and fails to follow up on voice-mail messages would score very low in its ability to meet this requirement.
Cost	"Cost" doesn't mean the actual price of a product or service but the degree to which customers perceive value obtained for their investments. Consider a video production department that bills its marketing department $20,000 to create a ten-minute infomercial. If the marketing department believes a well-known external production house is prepared to provide the same service for half this price, the video team will receive a low rating on this requirement.
Friendliness	The degree to which your team is viewed as friendly and helpful. A team that responds to a request with "No, we can't help you" would score low on this requirement. A highly rated team might respond with a statement such as "We can't provide that service, but I can put you in touch with a department that can help you. If you'll stay on the line, I'll see if I can connect you."
Quality	The degree to which a requirement is error free and meets all necessary specifications. A software design team that produces a program with few glitches would be rated high in this area, while a team that has to go through several versions of a program to keep debugging it would receive a poor rating.
User-friendliness	The degree to which a product or service is easy for the customer to use and apply. A tax guide that's only a few pages long and clear enough to eliminate alternative interpretations would be rated high on this requirement. In contrast, the guidelines provided by the IRS are generally rated low in this area.
Reliability	The degree to which a product or service can be used repeatedly without flaws, errors, or deviations in a consistent fashion. A cleaning team that is assigned to service an office at 8 P.M. and only keeps the appointment sometimes would be rated poor on this requirement, but a team that shows up promptly and consistently would be scored high.

Tool Kit

your team must meet when generating its outputs. List these requirements in the left-hand column of Exercise 26.

5. Using a scale of 1–7 (with 7 as the highest value), ask your team to rate the relative importance of each requirement. This is your team's best guess as to how your customer would rate the relative importance of each requirement for the selected output. Record these scores in the second column, labeled "Importance to Customer."

6. Again, using a scale of 1–7 (with 7 as the highest value), ask your team to rate its current effectiveness in performing each requirement. Record these scores in the last column, labeled "Importance to Team."

7. You are now ready for the moment of truth—asking your customer for feedback. You may obtain this feedback from discussions with your entire customer team, team leader, or representative members of the team. Without sharing your own ratings (to avoid influencing the results), ask your customer to use a scale of 1–7 to indicate the relative importance of each performance requirement. Place these ratings in the Importance to Customer column of the Customer Requirements Rating Table.

8. Ask your customers to use a 1–7 scale to rate your team's performance with regard to each requirement.

EXERCISE 26 • CUSTOMER REQUIREMENTS RATING TABLE

Customer:			
Output:			
Customer Requirements		**Importance to Customer**	**Importance to Team**
1.			
2.			
3.			
4.			
5.			
6.			
7.			
8.			

Tool Kit

Tool #50

CUSTOMER SATISFACTION/IMPORTANCE MATRIX

The easiest way to interpret the customer feedback you've obtained with Tool #49 is by creating a Customer Satisfaction/Importance Matrix, such as the one shown in Figure 7.

FIGURE 7

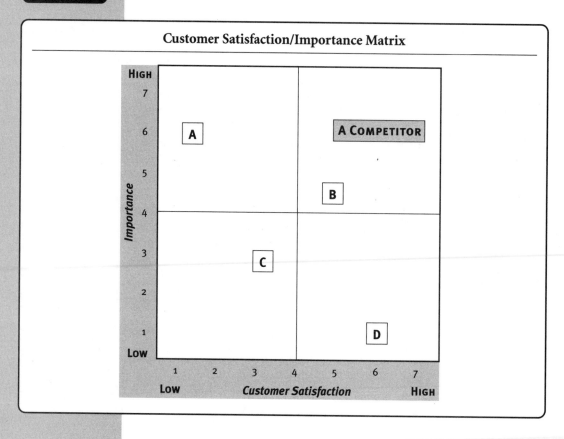

Customer Satisfaction/Importance Matrix

Tool Kit

Note that the matrix in Figure 8 displays all requirements for a selected team output along the two continua of Importance and Customer Satisfaction. This example involves a team responsible for installing cable television. The output in question is the service installation call. The team has asked a sampling of its customers for feedback on four service requirements, which are represented on the chart by the letters A–D:

- **A—Dependability:** Will the team show up at the customer's house as scheduled?

- **B—Quality:** Is the installation completed effectively without the need for a second service call?

FIGURE 8

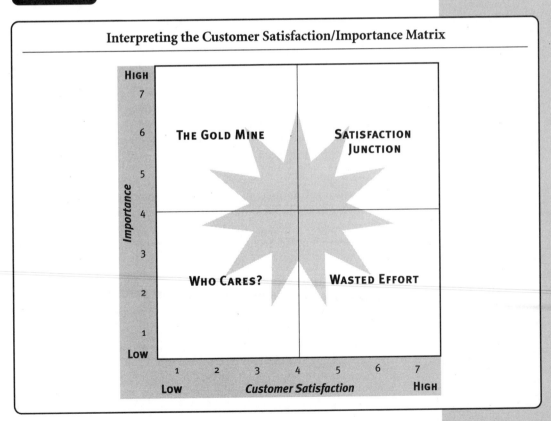

Tool Kit

- **C—Friendliness:** Is the installation technician courteous and professional?

- **D—Timeliness:** How long does it take to complete the installation?

After studying Figure 7, we can draw the following conclusions:

- Customers are very dissatisfied with the team's performance in the area of dependability (A), a requirement that is very important to these customers. In Figure 8, I label this quadrant the "Gold Mine." In other words, requirements in this quadrant represent areas for improvement, which can be mined to yield increased customer satisfaction.

- In contrast, customers rate the team fairly high on quality (B). In Figure 8, I refer to this quadrant as "Satisfaction Junction" because these requirements represent important service features on which the team is performing well.

- The team's service technicians may not be perceived as the world's friendliest (C), but this requirement is not very important to the cable customers. In Figure 8, I've labeled this quadrant "Who Cares?" to remind you that these items represent relatively insignificant service problems.

- Customers say that while the team is performing very well on timeliness (D), this requirement is not very important to them. I refer to this quadrant as "Wasted Effort" to indicate that, considering their comparative unimportance, it's not really worth the team's effort to make improvements in this area.

Given all this information, we can say that if the team had to target one aspect of its installation process for improvement, it should be the area of dependability. In other words, the team needs to determine how to change its work process to enable technicians to arrive at customers' houses as scheduled.

The Customer Satisfaction/Importance Matrix helps your team identify perception gaps, or the difference between your team's view of its performance and your customers' views of the services you provide. For example, the installation team may overestimate the quality of its performance on dependability, while customer feedback shows otherwise. Or the team may rate friendliness above dependability, while customer ratings place a greater value on dependability.

The matrix can also be used to evaluate how your customers view your performance and the performance of your competitors. For example, the installation team could ask former customers to compare the team's performance on these four requirements with the service they receive from their current cable suppliers. Such a comparison might show that the team scores poorly on the requirement of dependability (one competitor's scores are shown in the shaded block in Figure 7). This information would be extremely valuable in helping the team determine what steps they could take to surpass their competitors.

Tool Kit

Tool #51

CUSTOMER RELATIONSHIP AUDIT

Your customers might feel you do an excellent job when it comes to your work output yet still express concerns about the interpersonal relationships between your respective groups. One way to evaluate the quality of your customer relationships is to perform a customer relationship audit. This involves sitting down with your customers and identifying improvements in five key areas:

- **Accessibility:** How available is your team to your customers?

- **Responsiveness:** How quickly, and with how much enthusiasm, does your team respond to customers' requests and inquiries?

- **Listening skills:** How much attention does your team pay to customers' inquiries and concerns?

- **Information sharing:** How open is your team about sharing information with customers?

- **Conflict resolution:** How effective is your team at problem solving and conflict resolution?

You may use the Customer Relationship Audit in Exercise 27 to obtain performance feedback on these five factors.

The questionnaire contains fifteen questions that address behaviors related to these five factors, plus two additional open-ended questions to help your team identify which behaviors work for your team and which ones need to be changed.

To complete this questionnaire, I recommend the following guidelines:

1. Because the questionnaire pertains to somewhat sensitive performance factors, you might consider giving multiple questionnaires to one of your customer groups and then having one member of that group provide you with the team's averaged scores and collected comments. By offering respondents this type of anonymity, you increase the amount of feedback you can obtain from the questionnaire.

2. Once you've received your customers' feedback, you'll want to ask for their help in interpreting it. If your customers are unwilling to describe specific incidents of problem behaviors, suggest that they provide your team with hypothetical examples. For instance, a customer might say, "We don't feel your team listens completely to us. For example, if we were to ask for an exemption to company policy, we feel you'd refuse our request on the spot without even considering it at all."

Tool Kit

Relationship Factors	Customer Ratings Low...Moderate...High
Accessibility	
1. You can reach us easily by phone or e-mail.	1...2...3...4...5...6...7
2. We are readily available for face-to-face meetings.	1...2...3...4...5...6...7
3. We take the initiative to arrange meetings with you.	1...2...3...4...5...6...7
Responsiveness	
4. We make an effort to respond quickly to your requests for assistance.	1...2...3...4...5...6...7
5. If we are not able to respond to your requests, we try to direct you to others who can help.	1...2...3...4...5...6...7
6. We convey a high level of enthusiasm when responding to your requests.	1...2...3...4...5...6...7
Listening Skills	
7. We give you our full attention during discussions.	1...2...3...4...5...6...7
8. When you leave a discussion with us, you feel that we clearly understand and have not misinterpreted what you've said.	1...2...3...4...5...6...7
9. We present ourselves as open-minded and willing to listen to different points of view.	1...2...3...4...5...6...7
Information Sharing	
10. We freely share important information with you (we're not reluctant to disclose information you need to perform your job).	1...2...3...4...5...6...7
11. We provide timely information about changes that could affect your department.	1...2...3...4...5...6...7
12. When sharing information, we communicate clearly and succinctly.	1...2...3...4...5...6...7
Conflict Resolution	
13. We make an effort to work harmoniously with you.	1...2...3...4...5...6...7
14. We look for win-win solutions to problems.	1...2...3...4...5...6...7
15. When involved in a conflict, we conduct ourselves professionally (no yelling, personal criticisms, etc.).	1...2...3...4...5...6...7

16. What one behavior should we continue, or improve upon, to strengthen relationships between our teams?

17. What one behavior do we need to change to strengthen relationships between our teams?

Tool Kit

3. Next, convert the feedback into suggestions for improving your team's relationship with your customer. Let your customer know that your team is open to suggestions for improving its performance.

4. The Customer Relationship Audit is useful for periodically assessing team performance, but you might want to consider other, informal, methods of obtaining follow-up feedback on a regular basis, such as luncheon meetings with customers, regular informal phone surveys, or meeting with the team leader of your selected customer group.

Index